S0-EYP-765

CATALOGING HERESY:
CHALLENGING THE STANDARD BIBLIOGRAPHIC PRODUCT

CATALOGING HERESY:
CHALLENGING THE STANDARD
BIBLIOGRAPHIC PRODUCT

Proceedings of the
Congress for Librarians
February 18, 1991

St. John's University
Jamaica, New York

with additional contributed papers

Edited by
Bella Hass Weinberg

Learned Information, Inc.
Medford, NJ
1992

025.3
C74d

Copyright © 1992 by   Learned Information, Inc.
143 Old Marlton Pike
Medford, NJ 08055

All rights reserved. No part of this book may be reproduced in any
form without the written permission of the publisher.

Printed in the United States of America

Book Editor: James H. Shelton
Proofreader: Amy Lynn Rosen

Cover Design: Sandy L. Brock
Book Design: Shirley Corsey

MB

Library of Congress Cataloging-in-Publication Data

Congress for Librarians (1991 : St. John's University)
    Cataloging heresy : challenging the standard bibliographic product :
proceedings of the Congress for Librarians, February 18, 1991, St.
John's University, Jamaica, New York, with additional contributed
papers / edited by Bella Hass Weinberg.
    p. cm.
    Includes bibliographical references and index.
    ISBN 0-938734-60-1 : $35.00
    1. Cataloging—Congresses. I. Weinberg, Bella Hass. II. Title.
Z693.A15C66 1991
025.3—dc20   92-9374
                                                CIP

Dedicated to the memory of

Dr. Mildred Lowe

*former Director of the Division of Library
and Information Science, St. John's
University, and a driving force behind its
annual Congress for Librarians;
beloved colleague, friend, mentor, and
a Jewish grandmother to us all.*

זכרונה לברכה

May her memory be a blessing.

Bella Hass Weinberg
and the
Faculty of the
Division of Library and Information Science

UNIVERSITY LIBRARIES
CARNEGIE-MELLON UNIVERSITY
PITTSBURGH, PENNSYLVANIA 15213

CATALOGING HERESY: CHALLENGING THE STANDARD BIBLIOGRAPHIC PRODUCT

Congress for Librarians

Presidents' Day

Monday
February 18, 1991

Marillac Hall
St. John's University
Jamaica, New York

Sponsored by

St. John's University
Division of Library and Information Science

and

The School of Continuing Education

PROGRAM

Speakers at the Congress on Cataloging Heresy.

From left to right:

Sanford Berman, Glenn Patton, Cathy Whitehead, Sheila Intner,
Ed Glazier, Norman Anderson, Bella Hass Weinberg, John Byrum,
Sally Sinn, Mary Parr, Emmett Corry.

Photo credit: Robert Floyd.

TABLE OF CONTENTS

PART II - CONTRIBUTED PAPERS

ACKNOWLEDGMENTS

A cataloger's mind is necessary for conference planning: a sense of organization, attention to detail, and the ability to store a great deal of information and retrieve it on demand. Just as a cataloger is part of a team of professionals and paraprofessionals, so the conference organizer relies on numerous specialists and support staff to put a program together.

Many of the people who contributed time and talent to the 1991 Congress for Librarians were listed in the printed program, but that document is ephemeral. The publication of the proceedings affords me the opportunity to thank those who helped make the Congress possible in a book that I hope will make a lasting contribution to the library science literature.

The invitation of prominent speakers from many different states was made possible by a grant from the H.W. Wilson Foundation. It was a pleasure to work with the speakers both before the Congress was held and during the editing of the proceedings. I am grateful to all of them for preparing stimulating presentations and then reworking them for publication.

Many people at St. John's University assisted with the multifaceted preparations for the Congress. In a volume on cataloging, it is perhaps best to arrange their names alphabetically:

Mr. Tom Arens, Director, Food Services

Ms. Nan Foley, Director, Reproduction and Printing

Dr. Dorothy Habben, Director, Grants and Research

Ms. MaryRose Kenny, Director, Special Events

Ms. Denise Paulson, Assistant to the Vice President,
    Public Relations

Mr. Herbert Schwartzman, University Counsel

Mr. Peter Taras, Director, University Mail Services

Ms. Charlotte F. Tomic, Assistant Vice President,
    Public Relations

We also acknowledge the assistance of the University's travel agent, Milt Rosenbaum, and of Ace Audio Visual Co., which produced audiotapes of the program. Ebsco Industries, the Highsmith Co., and the H.W. Wilson Co. contributed useful materials for the conference packets.

Without a doubt, the office staff of the Division of Library and Information Science put the most time and effort into the Congress. I worked closely with

Patricia Tansky on all stages of the project, but Mary Egan and Adrienne Van Brackle also handled numerous inquiries and assisted with many logistic aspects of the Congress.

The graduate assistants of the Division of Library and Information Science were incredibly helpful with both pre-conference preparations and on-site registration. My own graduate assistants, Patricia-Ann Tuohy and Elaine Galligan, carried out a myriad of tasks cheerfully, and Andrew Hamilton performed miracles with the database of registrants.

I am grateful to the entire faculty of the Division of Library and Information Science for sharing their graduate assistants as well as their own expertise with me. The Director of the Division, Br. Emmett Corry, was helpful in ways too numerous to mention, given his extensive contacts within the University, his expertise in audiovisual production, and his experience in the management of Congresses at St. John's.

Instead of celebrating his birthday on February 18, 1991, my husband Gerard drove me to St. John's at the crack of dawn so that I might greet the 350-odd registrants. Even the heavenly powers cooperated on the day of the Congress by withholding the predicted snowstorm until the program was well underway.

It is a pleasure to be working again with the nicest of publishers, Mr. Tom Hogan, President, Learned Information, Inc. I am grateful for his prompt acceptance of my proposal that his company publish the proceedings of the Congress on "Cataloging Heresy" and I hope that the response of the library community to this book will confirm the wisdom of his decision.

Finally, I am grateful to my daughter, Kira, for tolerating the many late nights that I spent at the office while planning the Congress and editing these proceedings.

Bella Hass Weinberg

INTRODUCTION OF
THE CONGRESS CHAIR

Emmett Corry, O.S.F.
Director
Division of Library and Information Science
St. John's University
Jamaica, NY 11439

It is my pleasure to welcome you to St. John's University and to our annual Congress for Librarians. I believe that the title of our Congress has more than provoked your interest. This is one of the largest groups of registrants that we have had in the past few years, and again I offer you a hearty welcome. It is also my pleasure to introduce the Chair of today's Congress.

Bella Hass Weinberg was first introduced to technical services as a work-study student at the Library of the City College of New York in the late 1960s. From ironing Se-Lin labels for the reclassification from Bliss to LC, she was soon promoted to filing in the mammoth card catalog of the Library. In college she majored in languages and linguistics, and wrote a term paper on bias in LC subject headings for a course in General Semantics. (Even then, she was criticizing the standard bibliographic product!)

After graduating Magna Cum Laude and Phi Beta Kappa, Bella went straight to library school. She received her master's degree from Columbia in 1971 and the doctorate in 1981. She joined the faculty of the Division of Library and Information Science at St. John's in 1982, after having acquired professional experience in a variety of types of libraries, working primarily in the management of technical services.

Dr. Weinberg has published extensively in the areas of non-Roman cataloging, indexing theory, and thesaurus design. She has held grants from the National Endowment for the Humanities and the National Science Foundation for both applied and theoretical research on the organization of catalogs and indexes. Prof. Weinberg recently served as President of the American Society of Indexers, and currently chairs the committee of the National Information Standards Organization which is developing the revised standard on thesaurus construction. She is the Editor-in-Chief of the highly regarded journal, *Judaica Librarianship*, and co-editor of the recently published five-volume *Yiddish Catalog and Authority File of the YIVO Library* (G.K. Hall, 1990). I shall not begin to try to tell you what Bella does in her spare time, because she has none!

Dr. Weinberg will introduce the theme of the Congress.

Introduction to the Congress Theme

Bella Hass Weinberg, Chair

It is a pleasure to welcome so many heretics to St. John's University. Many of you have traveled great distances to come to this Congress, and all of you have given up a national holiday in order to examine some of the assumptions behind standard methods of providing access to information in libraries. I hope that you will find the program stimulating.

Library Heresy

Before discussing cataloging heresy, I would like to note that we are living in a heretical period in librarianship in general. In recent months, challenges to many sacred cows of the field have appeared in the literature. For example, the extent of resource sharing has been shown to be low despite the widespread use of bibliographic networks, possibly because one cannot judge the relevance of a document from a catalog record. [1] The value of bibliographic instruction has recently been questioned in view of the fact that it does not significantly lower the number of questions posed to reference librarians. [2] These are thought-provoking observations that are sure to lead to debate and perhaps a rethinking of these facets of the library field. I believe that this questioning is a healthy phenomenon, a sign of the vitality of our profession, and of the intelligence of its practitioners.

Participants in the debate regarding many topics in librarianship are not limited to the professionals. Our patrons are frequently affected by changes in library practices, including cataloging, and may voice their opinions. Publishers monitor our acquisitions, photocopying, and resource sharing policies, and perhaps our Cataloging-in-Publication data as well.

Those of you who come from the public library world are surely aware of the "give 'em what they want" approach to library collection building, challenging the traditional view that the librarian should steer the reader to quality literature. [3] I recently encountered a bookdealer's statement on the deaccessioning of so-called quality literature by libraries: "Timeless classics are discarded by barbarians who pretend to be librarians, in order to make room for bright new novels and best-sellers". [4]

So much for library heresy in general. Now on to cataloging heresy.

Cataloging Heresy

The critique of centrally supplied cataloging data is not a new phenomenon in American librarianship. I am willing to bet that when the first Library of Congress printed cards became available in 1901, recipients started complaining about the subject headings. Much of the cataloging literature of the past decades consists of critiques of LC descriptive and subject headings for specific genres or domains.

We are not here today to ask the Library of Congress for more or different headings in specific areas. Instead, we are examining a more basic, theoretical question. Is the idea of standard cataloging data valid? Can a single set of centrally supplied descriptive access points, subject headings, and classification numbers serve the needs of all types of library users?

Several types of standards for catalogers must be distinguished. The first type is standard *formats* for cataloging such as the International Standard Bibliographic Description, which is incorporated into AACR2 (Anglo-American Cataloguing Rules, 2nd ed.), and the MARC (machine-readable cataloging) format. The latter certainly has its critics, but I think that there is general agreement that a prescribed sequence of bibliographic elements and a standard format for machine-readable cataloging data are desirable.

The second type of standard is a list of authorized headings or an established classification scheme. The LC Name Authority File, Library of Congress Subject Headings, and LC Classification are all examples of this type. Walt Crawford has pointed out that these are "codified forms of common practice," but not true standards. [5] There is something about an LC main entry in boldface type, however, that gives many librarians the impression that it is engraved in stone.

The third type of standard—and the primary type we shall consider today—is the data in a centrally supplied bibliographic record, generally from a national library. This record is based on the two types of standards mentioned previously: it features a standard format as well as headings selected from standard lists. A library may subscribe to the standard format and even accept the standard lists, but the cataloger may question the headings or class numbers selected by the central agency for a given work, or recognize the need for additional access points.

Questioning the standard bibliographic product is cataloging heresy, and altering the central bibliographic record flies in the face of all the arguments for copy cataloging, i.e., that it is economical, and that it is advantageous to users to find a book cataloged and classified identically in all libraries. These arguments will be examined from a variety of perspectives today, but I shall begin by presenting a case for rejection of the very notion of standard bibliographic data.

NOTES

1. Ballard, Thomas H. "The unfulfilled promise of resource sharing." *American Libraries* Vol. 21, No. 10 (Nov. 1990), pp. 990-993.

2. Eadie, Tom. "Immodest proposals: user instruction for students does not work." *Library Journal* Vol. 115, No. 17 (Oct. 15, 1990), pp. 42-45.

3. Robinson, Charles. "Can we save the public's library?" *Library Journal* Vol. 115, No. 14 (Sept. 1, 1989), pp. 147-152.

4. Ashkenazy, Daniella. "A reader's delight." *Jerusalem Post International Edition* Dec. 8, 1990, p. 16A.

5. Crawford, Walt. "Technical standards: a common ground." *The Bookmark* Vol. 47, No. 3 (Spring 1989), p. 166.

PART I
INVITED PAPERS

EDITOR'S NOTE

The first person has been retained in the published papers, but they are not exact transcripts of the oral presentations. Some stylistic editing has been done to enhance readability of the papers. Furthermore, many of the published papers are far more detailed than the versions presented at the Congress.

Because it is anticipated that this volume may be read by library science students in addition to practitioners and educators, acronyms and abbreviations that are part of the professional jargon of the field have been explained, and complete formal references have been provided for well-known cataloging tools.

The presentation of ten papers in a one-day conference, each preceded by an introduction to the theme and biographical data on the speaker, did not leave much time for comments or questions from the audience. These have therefore not been included in the proceedings, but audience feedback stimulated postscripts and addenda to several papers.

Audiocassettes of the entire Congress program (or of selected papers) may be ordered from the Division of Library and Information Science, St. John's University, Jamaica, New York 11439.

B.H.W.

A THEORY OF RELATIVITY
FOR CATALOGERS

Bella Hass Weinberg

Associate Professor
Division of Library and Information Science
St. John's University
Jamaica, NY 11439

The theme of the Congress includes the phrase "standard bibliographic product." The word *standard* suggests permanence and immutability. It is my purpose in this paper to challenge the notion of standard cataloging data and to demonstrate that every major component of a bibliographic record is relativistic, i.e., that it is created to differentiate works in a given catalog or collection.

Bibliographic Description

The structure of AACR2 emphasizes the fact that we describe a work before providing access points to a bibliographic record: Part I of the code is entitled "Description," while Part II offers guidance on "Headings, Uniform Titles, and References." [1] As Cutter pointed out in his *Rules for a Dictionary Catalog*, one of the purposes of a catalog is to assist in the choice of edition. [2] Works produced in a great many editions, such as the Bible, require numerous bibliographic details to identify particular editions, e.g., name of editor or translator, city of publication, and date. Works published in only a few editions may be distinguished simply by title proper and edition number, e.g., *Encyclopaedia Britannica,*14th ed., although our cataloging code requires additional bibliographic details.

AACR2's allowance of multiple levels of description is in recognition of the fact that for smaller libraries, the lowest (or first) level provides sufficient detail to identify a particular work in the collection and to distinguish it from all others. [3]

Individual elements of bibliographic description may require modification in light of real-world phenomena. We generally record city only in the place of publication subfield, but if there are two cities with the same name, we add state, province, or country qualifiers to both or the lesser-known city, e.g., London [Ont.]. [4]

Descriptive Access Points

It is probably most widely recognized that descriptive headings are established with respect to a given file, in keeping with the principle of *no conflict*. If two authors have the same name, their headings are distinguished through the addition of a date or qualifier to the name of the one established later. [5] Some national libraries have decided to anticipate conflict by adding full names and dates to all author headings, but our cataloging code only specifies this as an option. [6]

The Library of Congress establishes name headings with respect to its own authority file, and libraries participating in NACO, the Name Authority Cooperative, submit the headings they establish to the Library of Congress for validation. Since most catalogers use LC's Name Authority File, all the headings they establish are created relative to LC's authority file, not to an individual library's.

Bibliographic records are most often changed because of changes in cataloging rules, but sometimes another work comes along that creates a need to modify a prior related record. *Cataloging Service Bulletin* illustrates the establishment of a uniform title, qualified by place of publication, for a French monograph entitled *France,* as a result of the subsequent appearance of an English edition of the book. [7]

Most title access points do not require the establishment of headings, but when multiple editions of a single work appear under different titles, e.g., *Martin Chuzzlewit* and *The Life and Adventures of Martin Chuzzlewit,* it is necessary to establish a uniform title. The heading is established relative to the bibliographic universe, not to the holdings of a given library. For example, if your library owns only one edition of *Guide for the Perplexed* by Moses Maimonides, if you follow AACR2 and LC practice, the uniform title will be the Romanized name of the Arabic original, *Dalalat al-ha'irin,* even if your library has no Arabic readers.

When two *different* works have the same name, uniform titles with qualifiers are required to distinguish them. AACR2 (1988) rule 25.5B1 provides the examples:

Genesis *(Anglo-Saxon poem)*
Genesis *(Book of the Bible)*
    (Use only as a reference)
Genesis *(Middle High German poem).*

City of publication is the qualifier often used in *key-titles* (the unique name assigned to a serial by the International Serials Data System) to distinguish identical names of serials, e.g., *Volunteer* (New York); *Volunteer* (Washington), but initial date of publication may be required as well to differentiate common titles, e.g.,

Science bulletin (Akron, Ohio: 1921)
Science bulletin (Akron, Ohio: 1980).

Subject Access

In American cataloging practice, we provide two types of topical access: classification and subject headings. In the systems employed by the Library of Congress, the principle of *literary warrant* applies both to classification and subject headings. New class numbers and subject headings are developed by LC only when the Library acquires literature to warrant them. It is therefore inappropriate for a special library to criticize LC subject headings or classification as not being specific enough. Specificity is a relative term, and as James Anderson has explained in an indexing context, it means "goodness of fit." [8] We may, on occasion, find that LC has assigned a general heading to a work on a specific topic, which violates its principle of specificity. For example, the sole subject heading assigned by LC to Theodore C. Hines' *Computer filing of index, bibliographic and catalog entries* is "Indexing" (LCCN 66-23484). We must keep in mind, however, that LC is not indexing articles or cataloging technical reports, so it should not be expected to develop a vocabulary for these purposes.

Perusal of the outline of the LC classification serves to illustrate the fact that larger blocks of notation are allocated to the subjects on which the Library is expected to acquire numerous books than to subjects of lesser interest. For example, "History: General and Old World" is allocated one letter (D), while "History: America" gets two; the notational base of the LC classification of "Law of the United States" is KF, while "Law of France" has a longer base notation: KJV-KJW. The Library of Congress now collects comprehensively in many areas, and has had to resort to decimal subdivision of class numbers, subject cutters, or revision of schedules to accommodate the large number of works being published in certain fields. In the schedule for Computer Science, for example, the topic of "Firm-ware" features a three-digit decimal subdivision of the integer: QA76.765. [9]

One of my favorite examples of the impermanence of centrally supplied bibliographic data is the revision of the schedule on cataloging in LC class Z (Bibliography and Library Science), first to create a distinction between descriptive and subject cataloging, both of which used to be classed in Z 695, [10] and then to further break each of these topics down. When this change was implemented, the classification number printed in the Cataloging in Publication (CIP) Data for AACR2 (1978)—Z 694—became invalid: the class number assigned to AACR2R (1988) is Z 694.15.

The inclusion of CIP in books suggests that the data are permanent and immutable; but all of the elements included in CIP are subject to change.

The Dewey Decimal Classification has more of a philosophical basis than LC classification, but in it as well, subjects considered to be of major interest to American libraries are allocated larger blocks of notation than "minor" subjects. [11] There are, for example, 60 main numbers for Christianity in Dewey—230-289—and one apiece for Judaism (296) and Islam (297). Specialized classification schemes for the latter two religions invert this relationship. For example, Sardar's classification scheme for Islam assigns one letter apiece to Judaism (C) and Christianity (D), and the range of letters E-V to Islam. [12]

One of the main reasons that libraries select LC classification over Dewey is that Library of Congress records feature complete class marks, saving the time required for shelflisting. LC Cuttering is clearly done relative to its own collection. Unlike the Cutter tables [13] which enumerate three digits per name, LC uses only one digit, unless there is a conflict. To avoid conflict with LC, it has been suggested that libraries add an *x* to every locally assigned Cutter number. [14]

There is less room for local variation in LC classification (LCC) than in LC subject headings (LCSH). Pattern headings and free-floating subdivisions allow us to create combinations that may not exist in the Library of Congress catalog. For example, based on the pattern heading *Shakespeare, William* for literary authors, a library may assign the subdivisions Allusions, Autographs, Biography, and Characters to works about a lesser-known author on which the library has an extensive collection. On the other hand, the limited number of subject headings that may be subdivided geographically reflect LC's needs and perhaps its assumptions regarding the amount of literature that is likely to be published on a subject. Enumerated period subdivisions for the history of individual countries reflect LC's holdings as opposed to the literature that could, in theory, be published regarding a particular country's history. "Iceland—History—To 1262" and "—1918-1945" are the sole two period subdivisions enumerated for that country in LCSH (1989). [15] A special collection on Iceland would certainly require a finer breakdown.

Conclusions

It has been demonstrated that cataloging data are neither permanent nor absolute. Bibliographic description has the purpose of distinguishing and identifying units in the bibliographic universe. Descriptive headings, classification notation, and subject headings are established relative to a given collection and are subject to frequent modification as new works are published.

In light of the relativity of bibliographic data, we may question the validity of the concept of standard cataloging data. Centrally supplied bibliographic data must be evaluated by the local library, which may own works not held in the national library. This may create the need for modification of descriptive headings to prevent internal conflict, for subdivision of standard subject headings to increase specificity, and for refinement of classification schemes to reflect the literary warrant of the local collection. All this assumes mastery of cataloging and classification theory by the local cataloger and the wisdom to modify the central bibliographic record when this is in the best interests of the library's user community.

NOTES

1. *Anglo-American Cataloguing Rules.* 2nd ed. Chicago: American Library Association, 1978, rev. 1988.

2. Cutter, C.A. *Rules for a Dictionary Catalog.* 4th ed. Washington: Government Printing Office, 1904, p. 12, object 3G.

3. *Anglo-American Cataloguing Rules,* 2nd edition, 1988 revision. Chicago: American Library Association, 1988, p. 15.

4. ibid, p. 35.

5. ibid, rules 22.17-22.19.

6. ibid, p. 415, 416.

7. [LCRI] "25.5B. Conflict resolution." [Rev.]. *Cataloging Service Bulletin* No. 50 (Fall 1990), p. 46.

8. Anderson, James D. "Indexing and Classification." In: *Indexing: The State of Our Knowledge and the State of Our Ignorance: Proceedings of the 20th Annual Meeting of the American Society of Indexers.* Edited by Bella Hass Weinberg. Medford, NJ: Learned Information, 1989, p. 73.

9. Library of Congress. Subject Cataloging Division. *Classification. Class Q, Science.* 7th ed. Washington: Library of Congress, 1989, p. 15.

10. *Anglo-American Cataloging Rules.* North American Text. Chicago: American Library Association, 1967. LCCN 68-81060.

11. Dewey, Melvil. *Dewey Decimal Classification and Relative Index.* Ed. 20, ed. by John P. Comaromi. Albany, NY: Forest Press, 1989. 4 v.

12. Sardar, Ziauddin. *Islam, Outline of a Classification Scheme.* London: C. Bingley, 1979.

13. Cutter, C.A. *C.A. Cutter's Three-Figure Author Table.* Swanson-Swift Revision. Chicopee, Mass.: Distributed by H.R. Huntting Co., 1969.

14. Gore, Daniel. "Further Observations on the Use of LC Classification." *Library Resources & Technical Services* vol. 10, no. 4 (Fall 1966), p. 522.

15. Library of Congress. Subject Cataloging Division. *Library of Congress Subject Headings.* 12th ed. Washington, DC: Cataloging Distribution Service, Library of Congress, 1989. 3 v.

THE DESCRIPTIVE
CATALOGER'S PERSPECTIVE:
INTRODUCTION

The need for different sets of subject headings for the layperson and the scholar, for adults and for children, for the generalist and the specialist is widely recognized. It is frequently assumed, in contrast, that descriptive cataloging is acceptable to all user communities. Upon closer inspection, however, descriptive cataloging is not all that neutral. Many AACR2 rules for the establishment of headings call for the best-known English form rather than a vernacular form, which is indicative of a linguistic preference. Transliteration in bibliographic description reflects a bias in favor of the Roman alphabet. Some honorifics are retained in headings, while others are omitted, which reflects a cultural bias.

Several years ago, in teaching a course on information sources in religion, I encountered a paper by Norman Anderson which demonstrated that the headings for Apocrypha and Pseudepigrapha will vary depending on whether one takes a Catholic, Protestant, or Jewish view of the Biblical canon. I therefore invited Mr. Anderson to address the theme of "The Non-Neutrality of Descriptive Cataloging."

Norman Elliott Anderson received the Master of Divinity degree from Gordon-Conwell Theological Seminary in 1976 and the Master of Science degree from Simmons College's School of Library Science in 1978. In September of 1976 he was appointed to the position of Reference Librarian and Cataloger in Goddard Library at Gordon-Conwell Theological Seminary. Four years later, he was promoted to the position of Associate Librarian for Reference and Technical Services. He served as Interim Librarian of Gordon-Conwell a couple of times, then as Interim Director of Learning Resources in 1989/90 (overseeing the libraries, media, academic computing, and other learning-resource modules). In October, 1990, he was appointed to the position of Head Librarian.

Norman Anderson has been active in the American Theological Library Association, and currently serves as Chair of its Public Services Committee. Of his publications, by far the most consulted is his *Tools for Bibliographical and Backgrounds Research on the New Testament*, the 2nd edition of which was published in 1987.

Mr. Anderson will provide a theological perspective on Cataloging Heresy.

B.H.W.

THE NON-NEUTRALITY OF DESCRIPTIVE CATALOGING

Norman Elliott Anderson
Head Librarian
Gordon-Conwell Theological Seminary
130 Essex St.
South Hamilton, MA 01982

"Description is revelation. It is not
The thing described, nor false facsimile."

Wallace Stevens in "Description without Place"[1]

Rote versus Compositional Cataloging

Among non-catalogers, a common attitude is that cataloging is mechanical. Any two libraries cataloging the same book should, of course, come out with identical catalog records down to the last digit in the call number. Even if the libraries' classification systems are different, certainly the descriptive part of the catalog records should be identical. What's to be different? And the vision is entertained of computers, in the not-too-distant future, taking over the cataloging process. [2]

Catalogers generally know better. We know about the errors in cataloging copy to be corrected, and about the frequent difference between CIP (Cataloging in Publication) data and finished Library of Congress catalog records, and about series cataloging versus individual-item cataloging versus analytics, and about the impact of such things as additional volumes, and about differences in judgment, sometimes vast, and about how challenging can be the application of rules to an endless stream of variations in the particulars. [3] Nevertheless, I would venture to guess, most of us work with a more-or-less standard model in mind of what cataloging should look like, perhaps a composite of a long stream of Library of Congress cataloging.

My intention here is not to bash the Library of Congress—let us be kind to an agency that has done us great service—and, in fact, the model just described is helpful in making sure that we are systematically asking the right questions and seeing what is not yet in the catalog record that should be. The trouble comes when we regard descriptive cataloging as a rote process with objective rules that need only be objectively and mechanically applied in order to come out with a universal product.

It is my contention that descriptive cataloging is an interpretive and compositional process; that the records we create should be regarded as living, not static; that many of the elements of descriptive cataloging are non-neutral in several different ways, some good and some not good; and that we ought to take a new look at how we handle the mix of universality and non-neutrality in our descriptive cataloging.

Factors in Non-Neutrality

Allow me to unravel some of the strands of non-neutrality in descriptive cataloging, and please understand from the outset that I am discussing non-neutrality in the broadest terms, and not just in the ways that our cataloging might offend one group or another.

1. Rules Reflect their Time

First, the descriptive records we create reflect our time. They reflect the rules of our time and, perhaps more than we usually realize, the traditions of our past—this despite the revolution brought about by the 2nd edition of *Anglo-American Cataloguing Rules*. [4] Our cataloging will not be adequate in the distant future, perhaps not even in the near future. Not only will the rules continue to evolve, but the demands will change, or certain demands that we tend to hear only dimly today will become much louder.

For example, in my opinion, one of the most egregious oversights in much of present-day cataloging is the failure to provide access to supplementary information that is part of an item being cataloged, a failure that starts in descriptive cataloging. I think the lack of access is going to be increasingly felt.

Further computerization is likely to change the way that cataloging functions. One possible strategy for the future is to nest series and individual-item cataloging and analytics together, with the appropriate level being nested into reviews and evaluative comment, which are nested into a citation index, which is nested into a detailed index to the text, which is nested into the text itself. If such a scenario developed, the emphasis with regard to the function of cataloging would then shift more to sorting and away from the reporting of holdings, or the indication of location, or even the provision of access. Whatever course we find ourselves taking, the point is that the cataloging we compose today is simply a stage in a process.

2. The Bias of "Objective" Data

Second, the descriptive records we create reflect what may be called a bias of expectation laid upon the user, a bias some might call typical of Western civilization. It is only the highly trained eye that can pick out from the "objective" data provided by the cataloger the clues needed to zero in on the sorts of titles a person may be looking for. Who is the author? Where does that author fit in the scheme of things? What sort of title is the publisher known for? Is this a title of quality, whether juvenile, general, or scholarly?

To illustrate this point, I cite J. Gresham Machen's book entitled *The Origin of Paul's Religion*, reprinted by Eerdmans in 1947. [5] The bibliographic data is lackluster. An experienced eye will recognize Eerdmans as a Christian publisher of books that are usually Protestant, often conservative, frequently of good quality, and sometimes oriented to scholars. Other details in the descriptive component of the catalog record suggest that this is indeed a scholarly book. It is 329 pages long. It represents "The James Sprunt lectures delivered at Union Theological Seminary in Virginia." And it has bibliographical references and indexes. The standard subject cataloging provides two headings: "Paul, the Apostle, Saint" and "Bible. N.T. Epistles—Theology." So we find that this is one more in the endless spate of books on Paul the Apostle. Knowing this much, why should anyone except perhaps—and only *perhaps*—the specialist care about this book?

The answer is that the catalog record has provided no information at all that would appeal to the natural constituencies of the book. Who was Machen? He was a New Testament scholar who taught at Princeton until he withdrew along with several other conservative professors to found Westminster Theological Seminary in Philadelphia. He was a major figure in the Modernist-Fundamentalist controversy, and he played a central role in the founding of the Orthodox Presbyterian Church. His book argued a thoroughgoing continuity between Jesus and Paul in answer to critics who asserted otherwise. Many in the Reformed tradition of Christian theology consider his book to be the definitive treatment of the subject, a treatment that stands to this day, despite the enormous activity in the current scholarly examination of the question.

When the catalog user possesses this information, the book suddenly assumes dimension and character. It looms as a must-read title for anyone studying the Modernist-Fundamentalist controversy or the history of New Testament criticism (especially in such a way as to embrace conservative approaches) or the classics of biblical scholarship in America. Furthermore, many intelligent adults in Reformed circles will have a special interest in the book because of the role it played in helping to defend and mold their tradition. Some catalog users will know to shy away from the book, because its dimension and character do not match what they seek. Shouldn't the business of the catalog be to help users just so, matching them efficiently with the right titles?

Patrons approach library catalogs as a realm of absolute mystery, because catalogs fail to decipher the "objective" code, which is perceived as hostile and, therefore, definitely and ironically non-neutral. I am afraid that AACR2 has exacerbated this feeling because of its departure from the notion of the library catalog as a reference tool. The catalog is now understood almost exclusively as a mechanism of access.

I suggest a return to the catalog as reference tool, in fact treating it so more deliberately than we have ever done before. The idea is not to create a file of catalogers' opinions, but to be more assiduous in providing information for sorting and evaluation by users of the catalog. While ever mindful of diminishing returns, we should be helping users of the catalog to find their way through the information explosion, not piling it upon them.

3. Language

Third, the descriptive records we create are oriented to people who speak our language. A cataloging agency oriented to English-speaking users casts the "flexible" parts of its cataloging in English. AACR2 (and here I am citing the 1988 revision) frequently prefers English, for example, in headings for classical and Byzantine Greek works (rule 25.4B), even though in this case a standard Latin or Greek title that has been used in citations for centuries may serve as a better identifier, both for users of the catalog holding those citations in their hands and for bibliographic systems that are multilingually oriented.

When it comes to titles, the original is the closest we can come to a fixed and universally findable point. So language is one area where I would be inclined to change the mix of universality and non-neutrality in favor of universality, at least with regard to the most formal parts of our catalog records, i.e., the headings. Later in this paper, I present one possible solution to many of the language problems we face in cataloging.

4. Romanization

Fourth, and closely related to the issue of language, is the matter of romanization, i.e., romanization to the exclusion of the original script. Now I was as happy as anyone to receive the recent compilation of *LC Romanization Tables and Cataloging Policies*, by Sally C. Tseng. [6] I and my staff work with a number of scripts; AACR2 calls for romanization in some fields, for example, in certain headings for corporate bodies (24.1B1) and some uniform titles (25.2D); and OCLC requires full romanization; so Tseng's compilation was immediately recognized as a time-saver. But I am also aware that, for people who know the original scripts, working with romanization is more difficult. In fact, for many it is impossible. I ask, Shouldn't it be relevant that these are the people who are likely to make use of the materials in non-Roman scripts?

5. Religion

Fifth, the descriptive records we create are sometimes oblivious to the information needs of different traditions, and here I am referring principally to religious traditions. Take the Bible, for example. Our cataloging rarely takes account of the different canons of the different religious traditions.

Consider the person trying to find First Esdras and Fourth Maccabees, both of which, by the way, happily appear in the "Apocryphal/Deuterocanonical Books" of the recently published *Holy Bible . . . New Revised Standard Version.* [7] Of course, few people know that, and so we must put ourselves in the position of those who seek. Fourth Maccabees generally appears in Eastern Orthodox Bibles; but Jewish traditions, Roman Catholics, and Protestants generally place it among the Old Testament pseudepigrapha. First Esdras does not generally appear in Roman Catholic Bibles; but it will appear in Protestant Bibles, if they contain the Apocrypha or the Deuterocanonical Books as defined by Protestants. A person using the Doubleday edition of the *New Jerusalem Bible*, [8] which contains the Deuterocanonicals as defined by Catholics, and the Doubleday edition of the *Old Testament Pseudepigrapha*, [9] which should contain everything else on Old Testament themes composed before A.D. 200, except for Christian writings, will not find First Esdras!

If you think that you are already confused, believe me, this is only the beginning—not least because the Old Testament Ezra is sometimes called First Esdras, and First Esdras itself is sometimes called Second Esdras or Third Esdras or the Greek Ezra.

The point is that generally our cataloging does nothing to help. It does not even provide notes indicating the presence or absence of the Deuterocanonical books or which canon is being cataloged. Instead, it glosses over the differences and adopts terminology that fits no tradition in any consistent way. (An example would be the simultaneous use of "Apocrypha" and "Apocryphal books." See AACR2 25.18A5 and A14 and, more significantly, earlier cataloging policy, e.g., *Cataloging Service* 80, [10] which superimposed, in large part, *A.L.A. Cataloging Rules for Author and Title Entries*, [11] rule 34.) Our cataloging should respect, reflect, and describe the differences between canons; and it should do so in a context of avoiding cause for offence while speaking to the access needs of catalog users from different traditions. [See the author's postscript for an elaboration of this point.–Ed.]

6. *Type of Library*

Sixth, the descriptive records we create are relative to our individual libraries. AACR2 is good enough to recognize, for instance, that different cataloging levels may be appropriate for different libraries (1.0D), or that "the need to use uniform titles varies from one catalogue to another," and that the rules for uniform titles should be applied "according to the policy of the cataloging agency" (25.1A). I would go further and insist that the cataloging for our libraries ought frequently to be customized in order to bring out the reason the item was acquired for the collection in the first place, and to highlight material that may be of special interest to our particular clientele.

For example, a year or two ago I cataloged Weil's edition of the *Masorah Gedolah* [12] for a theological library. The Masorah is a compilation of ancient textual notes on the Hebrew Bible. Weil's edition is intimately related to what is currently the best critical edition of the Hebrew Bible, *Biblia Hebraica Stuttgartensia* or BHS, which serves as a textbook in many seminary classes. [13] I made sure in my cataloging that I spelled out the precise connection between the two works, and that I also pointed out the misleading description of Weil's work that appeared in BHS, which spoke of volumes that have to this day never been published. Without those notes, our students would have been left in a quandary.

You may observe that the customization in this example may be useful well beyond the walls of my own institution. In fact, that is true of most of the customization of which I speak. The trouble is that the standard bibliographic product tends to be too skeletal to be truly helpful to many of our catalog users. We ought not only to customize, but also to be able to consult and share each other's customization.

7. Descriptive versus Subject Cataloging

Seventh, the descriptive records we create are often perceived to be free-standing, discrete, and separable from subject cataloging. Therefore, we think we may change rules and generally operate with impunity in the descriptive cataloging world vis-a-vis the subject cataloging world. I suggest that the line of demarcation is not quite so clear. For one example, I return to the Old Testament pseudepigrapha.

The heading for collections of pseudepigrapha was once "Bible. O.T. Apocryphal books." AACR2 did away with that heading and provided no substitute for drawing collections of the pseudepigrapha together in the catalog. (See rule 25.18A14. As a result of the policy of superimposition [continuation of the use of formerly established headings], AACR1 114 was largely circumvented, and so the problem did not arise.) Library of Congress Subject Headings supplied us with "Apocryphal books (Old Testament)," but for works ABOUT the pseudepigrapha, not collections of the ancient writings themselves. (See the scope note in the 9th ed., 1980 [14]). The library user who wanted to find recent collections of the pseudepigrapha was suddenly bereft of access points. [15, 16]

Liturgies, manuscripts, and Festschriften are examples of other types of materials that sometimes fall in the cracks between descriptive and subject cataloging—either that, or they are overdone, with descriptive and subject cataloging providing entries that function redundantly.

Consistency over time in either rule interpretation or cataloging practice is nearly impossible to find. We might consider turning all subject headings that represent form of material over to descriptive catalogers. (I wonder if that would mean adding another chapter to AACR2.) Yet I suspect that, rather than solving the problem, such a course would only further reveal how interrelated are description, form, and topic. The increasing use of key word access to online library catalogs (in which there is no necessary distinction between descriptive and subject entries and in which annotations, abstracts, and contents notes may often be more useful for topical searches than subject headings) only underscores this observation.

8. *Form of Heading*

Eighth, the descriptive records we create often fail in universality with respect to the form that headings take. Consider these two rules from AACR2:

> Rule 22.1B: "Determine the name by which a person is commonly known from the chief sources of information . . . of works by that person issued in his or her language."

> Rule 22.3A: "If the forms of a name vary in fullness, choose the form most commonly found."

These rules as written, it seems to me, call for a universal approach, especially in the context of databases being built by multiple cataloging agencies. The cataloger may reasonably expect to take upon him or herself the task of looking at the set of all appearances of an author's name in a way that the same conclusions will be drawn whether the work of establishing a heading is done at the Boston Public Library or at my school, Gordon-Conwell Theological Seminary. Theoretically, this would allow for an internationally developed authority file which would be subject to critical evaluation and quality control.

When the Library of Congress threw away the universal approach in favor of exclusive use of the limited sets that could be drawn from its automated system (the acronym, you may remember, was TOSCA = Total Online Searching and Cataloging Activities), it at the same time precluded certain cooperative approaches to cataloging, and therefore to the control of information. What is wrong here? That AACR2, perhaps, did not mean what it said or was confusing? That LC's interpretation of the rules turned the rules on their head? Or that, because of fiscal exigencies, the other libraries of this nation depend heavily enough on Library of Congress cataloging that its interpretation (some may say subversion) of the rules leaves the rest of us wondering how to cope, i.e., how to integrate its parochial practices with what we are doing?

As matters stand now, the chances are good that the Library of Congress's authority work will conflict with perfectly executed authority work done by a different library. Of course, if we allow the Library of Congress to play the role that it does in cataloging because of our own fiscal concerns, how can we be strongly critical when it bows to its own? Universality in descriptive cataloging, then, remains elusive and will remain so until realistic criteria are set for establishing the form of catalog headings or until we take advantage of some of the alternatives that technology can provide.

9. *Fiscal Concerns*

Ninth, speaking of fiscal concerns, the records we create are anything but fiscally neutral. The implementation of AACR2 in 1981 is the preeminent example of the fiscal havoc that rule changes can create. Libraries at that time had the difficult choice to make of (a) allowing innumerable split files within a single catalog, (b) changing old forms of headings in a catalog over to AACR2 forms in order to avoid split files, (c) closing old catalogs and starting new ones, or (d) trying to buck AACR2 and the rest of the library world by conducting all new cataloging in isolation. Every choice was costly in terms of staff time and service to users, if not also equipment.

I can testify that, in my library, one of the impacts of AACR2 was to substantially increase the cataloging backlog each year over a period of several years. I have yet to hear a kind word from a library administrator of the early '80s regarding the impact of AACR2. Mostly I hear, "If only AACR2 could have left the forms of headings alone . . . ," the implication being that the library world could have swallowed AACR2 much more easily, fiscally speaking, and with much less time lost on other important library functions, such as preservation.

I am not suggesting that we should pursue the cheapest cataloging possible. No, I think that, in most libraries, quality cataloging is worth paying for. What I am pointing out, however, is that decisions about what we do with description, including changes we decide to make in how to do description, affect that comparatively small pool of money we have available to us, which in turn affects everything else we would like to do in libraries. Decisions regarding descriptive cataloging are not fiscally neutral and should never be regarded as such.

Summary of the Factors and Additional Factors

I have mentioned nine ways in which our descriptive cataloging is non-neutral. (1) Our cataloging reflects our time, for instance, in the way we intend cataloging to function. (2) It lays expectations upon catalog users in a way that may be perceived as unfair and unrealistic. (3) It bears a language slant, sometimes actually to the detriment of research. (4) It puts a veil between the records and those who most need to use them when romanization is used to the exclusion of the original scripts. (5) It glosses over differences between traditions in a way that sometimes conceals rather than reveals information. (6) It is specific to the policies and, one would hope, the needs of the cataloging agency. (7) It is affected by and affects subject cataloging. (8) The headings it creates are non-universal in a way that undermines cooperative cataloging. And (9) every adjustment in rules, policies, and practices has fiscal implications.

The list could go on to include, for example, non-neutrality with respect to forms of information, i.e., how well the rules work with regard to materials libraries handle infrequently, such as artifacts; or what is neglected for cataloging, such as pamphlets or, in some prominent public institutions, religious works; or the cursory treatment given in some libraries to many religious works such as biblical commentaries and ancient religious writings by means of set rather than individual cataloging; or the use of cryptic abbreviations and culturally biased designations, such as A.D. (anno domini = the year of our Lord) instead of C.E. (common era); or the bumping of locally developed records on

OCLC by Library of Congress MARC (machine-readable cataloging) records. Or we could jump into philosophical hermeneutics, which analyzes in minute detail the inseparable relationship between author and audience, and between text and interpreter. But I had better turn to re-weaving the strands.

A Vision for the Future

The cataloger is an interpreter, and the range of interpretation runs from the smallest details of transcription to the much larger issues of what we are trying to make our cataloging do and where we are going to build bridges between the materials and those who seek them. As such the interpreter is very much a part of his or her work. I suggest that there can be good interpretation and bad interpretation. One measure is how much of ourselves we allow to get in the way as opposed to how much we make our work translucent windows into the mass of information that we handle. Mine is not a call for idiosyncratic cataloging, but for thoughtful flexibility and (I would hope) a flexibility exercised in a way that will enrich us all. It is a call for reevaluating the way that universality and non-neutrality mix and for taking the possibilities fully into account, relative to how we intend our cataloging to function.

Allow me to suggest a vision for the future. I suggest that we finally and definitively view cataloging as a cooperative enterprise, not just in terms of adding to the numbers of catalog records, but also in terms of building individual catalog records and authority files. Any library would be able to add descriptive detail that may be regarded as optional by any other library. Translation into various languages and romanization would be among the options. In other words, each record would be a smorgasbord. The concept of main entry heading (AACR2 21.0A1) would be abandoned because it pushes certain elements of cataloging into non-neutral territory in a way that puts many catalog users at a disadvantage.

For example, AACR2 tells us that if a corporate body uses "more than one official language and one of these is English, use the English form" (24.3A1). Why select only one form? Because only one form can serve as a main entry heading. Break that bondage, particularly in the context of computerization, and suddenly we have available to us virtually all of the cross-references that we put in our authority records. In this day and age, why shouldn't any form of a name lead a catalog user directly to a useful set of titles?

Most importantly, the purpose of cataloging would be seen as revelation. It would not inundate, but rather would elucidate the path for the user.

Wallace Stevens in the same poem cited above speaks of:

> "A point in the fire of music where
> Dazzle yields to a clarity and we observe,
> And observing is completing and we are content." [Section III, p. 341.]

POSTSCRIPT: UNIFORM TITLES FOR THE "TANAKH" AND THE "OLD TESTAMENT"

Christian Terminology

Following the above address, the question of cataloging terminology for the "Old Testament" was repeatedly discussed. One minor problem that was raised was the cryptic abbreviation "O.T.," which confuses some people. More seriously, the term "Old Testament" is a Christian designation, which some claim entails a denigration of Jewish scriptures. The charge is that the term "Old Testament" implies simultaneously a Christian appropriation of Jewish scriptures and a displacement of the message of those scriptures by the *New* Testament; also that the cataloging world, by incorporating Christian terminology in its uniform titles for the Bible, is complicitous in a form of cultural bias.

The question could be engaged at the level of Jewish-Christian debate. One side could say that every effort should be made to eliminate anything that might give offence, including ambiguous or complicitous terminology. Another side could say that "Old" means older, not displaced, and that there is no bias inherent in the terminology or necessary in the Christian theology of the "Old Testament."

Current scholarship may be brought to bear on this question. Some scholars are painting a picture of Christianity and Rabbinic Judaism as siblings, both arising out of a vast welter in the Classical (Second Temple) Judaism of the first century of the common era. In Classical Judaism, according to this picture, the place and interpretation of the scriptures was an *internecine* affair (in the sense of family conflict) in which Christianity played a part, even as it was moving beyond the ethnic bounds of Judaism. In other words, many of the assumptions giving rise to the issue are subject to debate, not only between traditions but also vis-à-vis an important contingent of current scholarship. (Among the most significant publications are those by Sanders and by Charlesworth [17-19]. Anderson provides research guidance and an heuristic model. [20])

The Cataloger's Role

What is the role of the cataloging world and of the individual cataloger with regard to this debate? I suggest that the issue of what to call the "Old Testament" is a matter to be settled in Jewish-Christian dialogue or by each of the traditions on its own. Our job as catalogers is to reflect the literature as it presents itself or as it is presented in reference sources, with appropriate qualifiers, additions, and notes. Even if a title is deliberately inflammatory, that should not affect our decision about how to cast it into uniform title form.

The Different Canons

The question still remains: Is there a better way, a less discriminatory way than we find in AACR2 25.18A1-5, for catalogers to reflect the different canons of the Bible? Here is a suggestion: When handling the Jewish canon, which is frequently called the Tanakh because it is arranged according to the Law (Torah), the Prophets (Nevi'im), and the Writings (U-Khetuvim), use the uniform title "Bible (Jewish canon)" or, alternatively, "Bible (Tanakh)." When handling the Roman Catholic canon of the Old Testament, use "Bible (Roman Catholic canon). Old Testament" or "Old Testament (Roman Catholic canon)." When handling the Eastern Orthodox canon of the Old Testament, use "Bible (Eastern Orthodox canon). Old Testament" or "Old Testament (Eastern Orthodox canon)." When handling the Protestant canon of the Old Testament, use "Bible (Protestant canon). Old Testament" or "Old Testament (Protestant canon)," a heading that would not cover the Apocrypha.

The latter collection would be covered by adding a note indicating its presence and a heading such as "Bible (Protestant canon). Apocrypha" or simply "Apocrypha," the term implying "as defined or set apart by Protestants." Alternatively, an approach more in the direction of neutrality could be taken by using the heading "Apocrypha/Deuterocanonical Books," but this may lead to confusion: As defined by which tradition? Does it or does it not include First Esdras and Fourth Maccabees? Which tradition's nomenclature will one find for the individual books in the collection? The confusion could be resolved in one of two ways. The first is to employ a simple principle, which should in any case apply to all the above: Make notes regarding any variations from what is expected (or, in this case, from what is common to all the canons), basing expectations on master lists provided, one would hope, in both future cataloging codes and library catalogs. The second is again to use qualifiers, e.g., "Deuterocanonical Books (Roman Catholic)" and "Deuterocanonical Books (Eastern Orthodox)."

Obviously, the cataloger will face situations that do not neatly conform to traditional categories. For example, what does one do with abridged and ecumenical and chronologically arranged Bibles or with harmonies? Should we continue old practices—which would mean employing the term "Old Testament" in a non-traditional context—or should we invent a heading like "Bible (Non-traditional)"? I suggest multiple approaches, which are elaborated, using a variety of examples, below. In any case, the problems created are outweighed by the effort to reduce bias in cataloging terminology and to help improve access.

Allow me to forge ahead and to develop three points that can amplify the approach I am suggesting, all of which further challenge current cataloging practices.

1. Direct Access

First, direct access to each one of the books and sections of the Bible would not only reflect the fact that each one of the canons of the Bible is a collection of individual titles written over a span of centuries, but it would also help extricate the cataloging world from having to select biased terminology, such as "Bible. O.T. Esther." Could this be a Jewish version, upon which Christian terminology has been imposed? Which Esther is it? The one without the Additions as the Jews and Protestants would have it? Or the one with the deuterocanonical Additions as the Roman Catholics and Eastern Orthodox would have it? Why not elude the problem by creating two simple headings: "Esther (Biblical book, without Additions)" and "Esther (Biblical book, with Additions)." Two other examples of direct access would be "Judith (Apocrypha/Deuterocanonical book)" and "Fourth Maccabees (Pseudepigrapha/Deuterocanonical book)." Perhaps direct access will raise new issues regarding bias in terminology, but we are at least working at a level where everyone will understand that the issue is far more one of simple communication than of avoidable bias.

2. Redundancy

Second, catalogers generally avoid redundancy or partial redundancy when providing uniform titles for a work. The references and scope notes, which comprise part of the infrastructure of a catalog, are supposed to make the appropriate links for catalog users. Thus the addition of the tracing "Deuterocanonical Books (Roman Catholic)" when the heading "Bible (Roman Catholic canon)" is present would be thought unnecessary. I suggest that since the Protestant collection of the Apocrypha/Deuterocanonical Books should always be traced when included in editions of the Bible (see above), the Deuterocanonicals should be traced whenever they appear in any canon—this for the sake of the catalog user who might well appreciate a consistency of access that transcends the differences between traditions.

I would go a step further and suggest that since Jewish Bibles do not include the New Testament ("Christian Testament"?) the New Testament should be traced whenever it appears in an edition of the Bible. Failure to provide such redundancy can discriminate against catalog users belonging to one tradition who may be seeking or who may be glad to light upon materials in another tradition, e.g., someone looking for a variety of translations of some of the Deuterocanonicals.

3. Multiple Headings

Third, so far much of this discussion presupposes the establishment of one fixed form of heading for a work—in the case of the Old Testament of the Protestants without Apocrypha, a single uniform title. So long as this is the approach, issues of access will continue to conflict with issues of bias.

Consider, for example, First Kings and First Chronicles, which in the Douay-Rheims (Roman Catholic) tradition are called Third Kings and First Paralipomenon, respectively. The only differences are of translation and nomenclature, not of text. Under current principles, access means choice of one title with a cross-reference from the other. But whichever is chosen, both traditions are slighted. Why? Because members of those traditions are sometimes looking for the familiar titles, such as a Roman Catholic looking for editions of First Paralipomenon, and sometimes they are looking for the unfamiliar titles, such as a Protestant (whose terminology AACR2 uses most) looking for First Paralipomenon.

The simple solution is not to choose one heading, but all of the above—making sure that mechanisms, notes, and references are in place to prevent confusion, e.g., between "Apocrypha" as defined by Protestants and "Deuterocanonical Books (Eastern Orthodox canon)." Automation makes this solution feasible, in terms of both revision of cataloging practice (although cost *will* be involved) and subsequent cataloging routine.

Bias as Reflexive

A point often overlooked, one at least as significant in subject cataloging and classification as in description, is that a bias in favor of one religion actually does a disservice to that religion in addition to other religions. The issue of bias in headings is not only a matter of possible offence, but also of access for the members of different traditions. Solutions are currently available, and they ought to be utilized.

NOTES

1. Stevens, Wallace. "Description without Place." in: *The Collected Poems of Wallace Stevens*. New York: Alfred A. Knopf, 1954, pp. 339-346. Quotation from Section VI, p. 344.
2. Meador, Roy, III; Wittig, Glenn R. "Expert Systems for Automatic Cataloging Based on AACR2: A Survey of Research." *Information Technology and Libraries*, v. 7, no. 2 (June 1988): pp. 166-171.
3. Taylor, Arlene G. *Cataloging with Copy*. 2nd ed. Englewood, Colo.: Libraries Unlimited, 1988.
4. *Anglo-American Cataloguing Rules*. 2nd ed., 1988 Revision. Ottawa: Canadian Library Association; London: Library Association Publishing; Chicago: American Library Association, 1988.
5. Machen, J. Gresham. *The Origin of Paul's Religion*. Grand Rapids, Mich.: Eerdmans, 1947. Originally published: New York: Macmillan, 1921.
6. Tseng, Sally C. *LC Romanization Tables and Cataloging Policies*. Metuchen, N.J.: Scarecrow Press, 1990.
7. *The Holy Bible, containing the Old and New Testaments, with the Apocryphal/Deutero-canonical Books: New Revised Standard Version*. New York: Oxford University Press, 1989.
8. *The New Jerusalem Bible*. Garden City, N.Y.: Doubleday, 1985.
9. *The Old Testament Pseudepigrapha*. Edited by James H. Charlesworth. Garden City, N.Y.: Doubleday, 1983-1985.
10. "Application of the Anglo-American Cataloging Rules at the Library of Congress. Apocryphal Books (AA114)." *Cataloging Service*, bulletin 80 (April 1967): p. 2.
11. *A.L.A. Cataloging Rules for Author and Title Entries*. 2nd ed. Chicago: American Library Association, 1949.
12. *Masorah Gedolah iuxta Codicem Leningradensem B 19a = Masora Magna*. Elaboravit ediditque Gérard E. Weil. Volumen I, Catalogi. Romae: Pontificium Institutum Biblicum, 1971.
13. *Biblia Hebraica Stuttgartensia*. Stuttgart: Deutsche Bibelstiftung, 1977.
14. *Library of Congress Subject Headings*. 9th ed. Washington: Library of Congress, 1980.
15. Anderson, Norman Elliott. *The Cataloging of Pseudepigrapha and New Testament Apocrypha: A Survey of American Cataloging Rules in the Twentieth Century*. South Hamilton, Mass.: Goddard Library, Gordon-Conwell Theological Seminary, 1982.
16. Anderson, Norman Elliott. *Nine Questions Posed to the Library of Congress Regarding the Cata-*

ANDERSON

loging of Pseudepigrapha and New Testament Apocrypha, with Comments and Recommendations. South Hamilton, Mass.: Goddard Library, Gordon-Conwell Theological Seminary, 1982.

17. Sanders, E.P. *Paul and Palestinian Judaism.* London: SCM Press, 1977.

18. Sanders, E.P. *Jesus and Judaism.* Philadelphia: Fortress Press, 1985.

19. Charlesworth, James H. *Jesus within Judaism.* New York: Doubleday, 1988. (The Anchor Bible Reference Library).

20. Anderson, Norman Elliott. *Tools for Bibliographical and Backgrounds Research on the New Testament.* 2nd ed. South Hamilton, Mass.: Gordon-Conwell Theological Seminary, 1987, pp. 27-35.

CATALOGING HERESY   28

THE PUBLIC LIBRARIAN'S PERSPECTIVE: INTRODUCTION

The Library of Congress acquires just about everything that any American public library is likely to acquire. LC serves the American public, yet catalogers in public libraries—notably the author of the next paper—are dissatisfied with the standard bibliographic product.

Sanford Berman, Head Cataloger at Hennepin County Library in Minnetonka, Minnesota since 1973, has found it necessary to modify and augment both descriptive cataloging and subject headings supplied by the Library of Congress in order to serve his patrons' information needs. From time to time, Sandy sends me his cataloging worksheets, with the centrally supplied copy heavily marked up. His critiques of LC cataloging were published in the *Hennepin County Library Cataloging Bulletin* from 1973-1979, and he continues to issue an authority file of alternative subject headings on microfiche.

Sandy Berman has also authored several books. His classic work, *Prejudices and Antipathies: A Tract on the LC Subject Headings Concerning People* brought the cultural biases reflected in LC subject headings to light. Many of Sandy's articles were collected in *The Joy of Cataloging*, published by Oryx Press in 1981. More recently, Mr. Berman has edited several collections, including *Subject Cataloging: Critiques and Innovations*.

In 1981, Sandy garnered ALA's Margaret Mann Citation "for outstanding achievement in cataloging and classification," and in 1989, he won the Equality Award in part for "leadership in the critical field of cataloging." Without question, Sandy Berman is the greatest cataloging heretic of them all.

B.H.W.

Cataloging Tools and "Copy": The Myth of Acceptability— A Public Librarian's Viewpoint

Sanford Berman
Head Cataloger
Hennepin County Library
12601 Ridgedale Drive, Minnetonka, Minnesota 55343

My sole objective is to utterly demolish the reigning myth that because the Library of Congress (LC) did it or you got the cataloging copy through OCLC, WLN [Western Library Network], BroDart, or some other vendor, the data *must* be accurate and useful. A corollary to that is the wonderfully innocent belief— another myth—that major cataloging codes, policies, and tools are at once sensible, functional, and up-to-date.

Subject Cataloging

Subject cataloging problems divide into two basic categories: 1) vocabulary or terminology, and 2) assignment.

Vocabulary is itself a four-fold issue:

First, the failure to contemporize or even correct many awkward, obsolete, and bizarre forms. As examples, LC-directed libraries are still using MEDICINE, MAGIC, MYSTIC AND SPAGIRIC instead of OCCULT MEDICINE; PERSONAL WATERCRAFT for JET SKIS; CESTODA for TAPEWORMS; and SPAIN. EJERCITO POPULAR DE LA REPUBLICA. BRIGADA INTERNACIONAL, XV rather than ABRAHAM LINCOLN BRIGADE.

Second, the failure to promptly create headings when new topics actually appear in books and other media. LCSH does not yet include forms for ARRANGED MARRIAGE, BUSINESS PLANS, FAMILY PLANNING, CLASSISM, CORPORATE POWER, HATE GROUPS, HOME TAPING, RENAISSANCE FAIRS, WINDSOCKS, POWWOWS, YUPPIES, WAGON TRAINS, HOUSEHOLD HINTS, or NATIONAL HEALTH INSURANCE. COLD WAR was only established in 1988, the year after most experts say the period ended, and LC sanctioned APARTHEID in 1986, 16 years later than Hennepin County Library (HCL) started using it, meaning that the earlier 16 years' worth of material is buried, scattered under a number of disparate headings in most catalogs.

Third, the failure to reform many headings that inaccurately denote or represent women's, minority, gay/lesbian and similar themes, and which may actually bias the library patron against either the materials or the topics. For instance, a host of "loaded" PRIMITIVE forms remain; most religion-related headings are unabashedly Christocentric; many sexist terms—like MAN, MANPOWER, and COLOR OF MAN—persist; and several ethnic groups—most notably the Beta Israel, Sami, Inuit, and Romanies are plainly misnamed (FALASHAS, LAPPS, ESKIMOS, and GYPSIES).

Fourth, the failure to make sufficient cross-references and to provide useful subheadings. For example, there should be deliberate *see* references from misspelled variations of primary headings (e.g., "Prostrate gland. *See* Prostate gland"). And we need subheadings for certain concepts or facets of larger topics, like LOBBYING (under names or groups or movements), EMPOWERMENT and RIGHTS (under names of occupations and classes of people), INTERVENTION (under a multitude of human services forms, such as ALCOHOLISM—INTERVENTION), and SUBLIMINAL METHODS (applicable to a host of audiotapes).

A sample page from Hennepin County Library's *Cataloging Bulletin,* illustrating locally established headings, is in Figure 1.

The *assignment* "trouble" is three-fold:

First, single literary works ordinarily enjoy *no* topical nor genre access. Look in your own catalogs under AIDS—FICTION, AIDS—DRAMA, and AIDS—POETRY, and except for the odd collection, you are unlikely to find *anything* listed there, purely as a result of LC assignment policy. What typically happens to an individual play, novel, or book of poetry is NOTHING. Our own Pulitzer Prize-winning playwright from the Twin Cities, August Wilson, last year published *The Piano Lesson.* Unless YOU added them locally, it would be unfindable, irretrievable in your catalogs under a genre heading like AFRO-AMERICAN DRAMA—20TH CENTURY or a subject like AFRO-AMERICAN FAMILIES—DRAMA.

Second, too often there are not enough headings assigned to fairly and helpfully denote what a work is about. As many experts have observed, the average of something less than two subject tracings per nonfiction title simply is not enough to provide suitable subject access for most material. And even for children's books, which frequently *do* get more detailed treatment, we have lately discovered, for instance, that a biography about a Los Angeles Chicana politician got no access point for "Chicana" or "Mexican-American"; another about a Korean-American girl pianist received no subject heading with "Korean-American" in it; and two recent picture books devoted totally to Black people, and featuring Black girls, got no "Afro-American" tracings.

Third, LC—or other contributors—sometimes get it wrong (which YOU cannot possibly know—or do anything about—unless you critically compare the cataloging with the work itself). As examples, a book about "going

```
                                              Cataloging Bulletin #107
                                              page 13
```

→ Fairy tales, Afro-American.

   sf African-American fairy tales
      Black fairy tales

→ Fantasy fiction, Afro-American.

   sf African-American fantasy fiction
      Black fantasy fiction

→ Fantasy fiction--Awards.

   sa August Derleth Fantasy Award Winners
      Balrog Award Winners
      Hugo Award Books
      International Fantasy Award Books
      World Fantasy Award Winners

→ Farm crisis.

   cn Authority: Utne reader subject index: 1984-
      1989 (1990), p. 23.

→ Fear in boys.*

   cn HCL form. Assignment (with --FICTION):
      John Sabraw's I wouldn't be scared (1989).

   sf Boys and fear
      Boys--Fear

   xx Boys--Psychology
      Fear in children

→ Fear in girls.

   sf Girls and fear
      Girls--Fear

   xx Fear in children

→ Feminism and vegetarianism.*

   cn HCL form. Assignment: Carol J. Adams'
      Sexual politics of meat: a feminist-vegetarian
      critical theory (1900).

   sf Feminism/vegetarianism relationship
      Vegetarianism and feminism
      Vegetarianism/feminism relationship

   xx Vegetarianism

→ Feminism--History--20th century.

   sa Feminism--Pakistan--History--20th century
      Feminism--United States--History--20th
      century

→ Feminism--United States--History--20th
century.

   sa Feminism--Greenwich Village, New York
      City--History--20th century

   xx Feminism--History--20th century

→ Fetal research.

   cn LC form: FETUS--RESEARCH.

   sa Human embryology--Research

   sf Research, Fetal

   xx Human embryology--Research
      Human materials in research

→ Fiesta de San Fermin, Pamplona, Spain.

   sf Fiesta of San Fermin, Pamplona, Spain
      Pamplona, Spain, Fiesta de San Fermin
      "Running of the Bulls," Pamplona, Spain

→ Filipino-Americans.

   sf Fil-Ams [authority: "Exotic images help Fil-
      Ams look their best," TM weekly herald,
      Dec. 22, 1989, p. 5]

→ Film--Preservation and storage.

   sa Video tapes--Preservation and storage

   sf Films--Preservation and storage

→ Films, Afro-American.

   sf African-American films

→ Films--Research.**

   cn LC form: MOTION PICTURES--
      RESEARCH. Assignment: Prelinger/
      Hoffnar's Footage 89: North American film

Figure 1. Sample page from Hennepin County Library Cataloging Bulletin (July/ August 1990), listing locally established subject headings.

freelance," geared to *all* sorts of professionals, was assigned the single heading AUTHORSHIP (and, incidentally, was classified in the 800s [literature]), while a title on the Apache Indians, running to some 112 pages, was both classed and subject cataloged as a bibliography—although it contained merely *one page* of bibliographical citations!

Descriptive Cataloging

Turning to descriptive cataloging, I count three major delinquencies:

First, the continued use of punctuation and abbreviations that many people do not understand, including such cherished conventions as "c" for copyright, "ca." for "about," and "v." for volume.

Second, an absence of bibliographic notes, particularly full or partial contents notes which can importantly convey what is actually inside a work and perhaps indicate the author's tone or approach, ultimately saving time for the catalog searcher. And another benefit of notes, amply documented in the literature, is the greater number of keyword "hits" when searching online. But at present, LC only makes content-type notes for about 4% of adult nonfiction titles. For instance, the "copy" for these two items contained no notes whatsoever, which prompted HCL catalogers to clarify their scope and content:

Songs from the alley (1989, nonfiction)
"In-depth account of the . . . life histories of two homeless women."
Sing soft, sing loud: scenes from two lives (1989, fiction)
Fifteen short stories about "the lives of women in prison."
Includes Afterword, "What you can do," and list of organizations for women prisoners.

The latter note also justified or triggered a directory-type subject tracing.

Third, for the particular benefit of non-online catalog users (and some online searchers too), there need to be many more title and other added entries. For instance, *Philippines: fire on the rim* deserved an added title entry for "Fire on the rim," but did not get it. Similarly, *Communication: for and against democracy,* "based on papers presented at a conference of the Union for Democratic Communications," merited an added entry for "Union for Democratic Communications." In fact, it got neither the tracing nor a note indicating the UDC connection.

Figure 2 contains a sample HCL cataloging worksheet, which extensively supplements the LC record.

Copy Quality

Finally, there is the reduction or erosion of usable and credible copy due to what appears to be a severe lack of quality control in the CIP [Cataloging in Publication] program, plus the introduction of LC's new "cataloging priorities."

Despite protestations to the contrary, too many CIP titles are clearly being

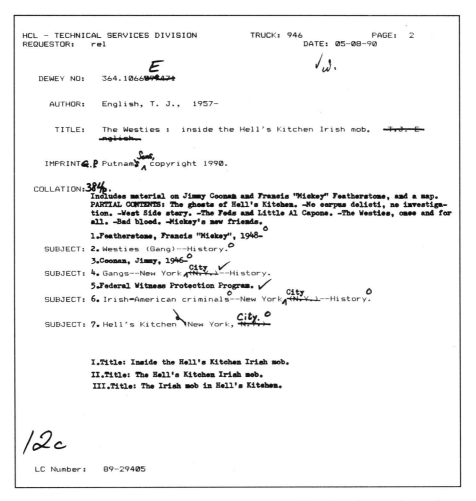

```
HCL - TECHNICAL SERVICES DIVISION          TRUCK: 946              PAGE:  2
REQUESTOR:   rel                                    DATE: 05-08-90

                            E
    DEWEY NO:   364.1066974474                        √ω.

    AUTHOR:   English, T. J.,   1957-

     TITLE:   The Westies :  inside the Hell's Kitchen Irish mob.   T.J. E-
                nglish.

                          Sons,
    IMPRINT G.P Putnam's  copyright 1990.

  COLLATION: 384p.
             Includes material on Jimmy Coonan and Francis "Mickey" Featherstone, and a map.
             PARTIAL CONTENTS: The ghosts of Hell's Kitchen. -No corpus delicti, no investiga-
             tion. -West Side story. -The Feds and Little Al Capone. -The Westies, once and for
             all. -Bad blood. -Mickey's new friends.
                                                           o
             1.Featherstone, Francis "Mickey", 1948-
   SUBJECT: 2.Westies (Gang)--History.
             3.Coonan, Jimmy, 1946-
                                   City    √
   SUBJECT: 4.Gangs--New York --History.
             5.Federal Witness Protection Program. √
                                   o               City          o
   SUBJECT: 6.Irish-American criminals--New York --History.

                                      City. o
   SUBJECT: 7.Hell's Kitchen (New York,


             I.Title: Inside the Hell's Kitchen Irish mob.
             II.Title: The Hell's Kitchen Irish mob.
             III.Title: The Irish mob in Hell's Kitchen.



 /2c

   LC Number:   89-29405
```

Figure 2. Hennepin County Library cataloging worksheet, based on a Library of Congress bibliographic record.

cataloged without looking at the whole book or galley, or even very much of it. That is the only explanation for Vincent Bugliosi's latest work—which includes a substantial photo portfolio—being classed in Fiction, and Sparky Lyle's novel, *The year I owned the Yankees: a baseball fantasy*, getting a 14-digit Dewey number. (Last summer, an HCL cataloger sent a letter to LC's Decimal Classification Division [DCD] questioning its "fiction" treatment of James Corcoran's *Bitter harvest*. Said the DCD respondent: "This is a Cataloging in Publication title which has not yet been seen by this Division. As soon as we see the book, we will consider changing the classification to 364.1'523. It looks like the problem here is that the publisher sent information indicating the book was a work of fiction." Six or seven months later, DCD reported: "The book reached the Division on February 7, 1991, and we do agree that it is not fiction. We have changed the Decimal Classification number to 364.1'523'0978452, which is the number for murder in Stutsman County, North Dakota." Don't bother counting: it's another 14-digit notation, but however long or short, the correction comes much too late to undo the original damage.)

There are doubtless hundreds of libraries that dutifully (and uncritically) accepted LC's initial classification, resulting in a palpably nonfiction book sitting on the fiction shelves— because few, if any, libraries will learn of the mistake and correction.

Again, despite claims that public library representatives were properly consulted before determining the new "priorities" at LC (particularly the de-prioritizing of English-language materials), the fact is that they were not. And what the "priorities" seem to mean, in fact, is that

1. Most CIP titles that previously were upgraded now will not be.

2. Many U.S.-published, English-language titles not covered by CIP get MLC, or Minimal Level Cataloging—essentially a full descriptive paragraph and nothing else. Such "copy" is practically worthless from the standpoint of either shelf or catalog access.

Conclusion

Anyone who genuinely thinks that cataloging tools and copy are okay probably has not looked at them lately.

SUGGESTED READINGS

Berman, Sanford. "Catalog access to health and medical information: new approaches," in *Alternative library literature, 1988-1989* (McFarland, 1990), pp. 211-17.

Berman, Sanford. "Compare and contrast, or, the Unexamined cataloging record isn't worth inputting," in *Alternative library literature, 1988-1989* (McFarland, 1990), pp. 173-81.

Berman, Sanford. "Fiction access: new approaches," in *Worth noting* (McFarland, 1988), pp. 9-17.

Berman, Sanford. "Politics of cataloging," *National Librarian*, August 1990, pp. 2-7.

Berman, Sanford, editor. *Subject cataloging: critiques and innovations* (Haworth, 1984). 252 pp. (Published simultaneously as *Technical Services Quarterly*, vol. 2, nos. 1/2, 1984.)

Berman, Sanford. "Tips on cataloging and classification for library users: a generic handout," *The public image*, October 1990, p.103.

Berman, Sanford. "Where have all the Moonies gone?," in *Worth noting* (McFarland, 1988), pp. 23-31.

Cornog, Martha. "Providing access to materials on sexuality," in *Libraries, erotica, and pornography* (Oryx Press, 1991), pp. 166-87.

Greenblatt, Ellen. "Homosexuality: the evolution of a concept in the Library of Congress Subject Headings," in *Gay and Lesbian library service* (McFarland, 1990), pp. 75-101.

"Who did it when?," Supplement to *HCL* [Hennepin County Library] *cataloging bulletin*, no. 105 (March/April 1990). 20 pp.

THE SPECIAL LIBRARIAN'S
PERSPECTIVE: INTRODUCTION

Centralized cataloging data is not as monolithic as we might think. Standard classification schemes often include alternatives, and in some cases both notations are included in bibliographic records. The Congress packets include a handout, prepared by Professor Alan Thomas, that deals with options in classification.

The Library of Congress provides an alternative set of subject headings for children's materials. For materials in the health sciences, many LC records include both alternative subject headings and classification data provided by the National Library of Medicine (NLM). To what extent can this alternative cataloging serve as a model for other disciplines that have less than optimal subject access in the standard systems?

A top-level staff member of the National Library of Medicine addresses this question in her paper, "The Development of Classification and Subject Heading Systems for Medicine."

Sally Sinn has been Deputy Chief of the Technical Services Division at the National Library of Medicine since 1986. Ms. Sinn came to the National Library of Medicine in 1973 as a Library Associate participating in NLM's postgraduate library training program. In 1974 she joined the staff of NLM's Cataloging Section as a cataloger and systems librarian. From 1978 to 1986 she was Assistant Head of the section and was responsible for a number of automation projects, including the distribution of NLM's cataloging data in MARC format, the development of an online name authority file, and the retrospective conversion of the shelflist. As Deputy Chief of the division that is responsible for the selection, acquisition, and cataloging of materials for NLM's modern collection, Ms. Sinn is currently involved in overseeing the development of a new automated system for technical processing at NLM and an expert system for cataloging.

Sally Sinn received her M.L.S. from the University of Illinois Graduate School of Library Science in 1973 and is a member of the Medical Library Association and the American Library Association. She has served in the past as the NLM representative to the ALA ALCTS/LITA/RASD Machine-Readable Bibliographic Information Committee (MARBI) and as the Medical Library Association's representative to CCDA, the Cataloging Committee on Description and Access.

She has a most appropriate name for a speaker at a Congress on Cataloging Heresy—Sally Sinn!

B.H.W.

THE DEVELOPMENT OF CLASSIFICATION AND SUBJECT HEADING SYSTEMS FOR MEDICINE

Sally K. Sinn
Deputy Chief, Technical Services Division
National Library of Medicine
Bethesda, MD 20894

Classification and Subject Cataloging in Medical Libraries

Medicine is quite possibly the only specialized field of knowledge for which two national, authoritative agencies in the U.S. create and maintain classification schedules and subject heading lists used in cataloging the literature of the field. The National Library of Medicine (NLM) Classification and the Library of Congress (LC) Classification are the two most widely used classification systems in U.S. health sciences libraries today. [1] Medical Subject Headings (MeSH) and Library of Congress Subject Headings (LCSH) are the predominant subject heading authorities used in cataloging the biomedical literature. The National Library of Medicine and the Library of Congress are the two principal sources of authoritative cataloging copy used by health science libraries. The two national libraries currently follow, in almost all details, the same standards for bibliographic description and name authority work.

This uniformity in bibliographic description enables the two libraries to cooperate in the creation of cataloging records for biomedical monographs. It is largely because the two national libraries employ different standards for classification and subject headings in cataloging the biomedical literature that both agencies maintain and distribute their cooperative cataloging products independently.

Although NLM and LC attempt to reduce duplicative acquisitions as much as possible, both libraries collect some of the same materials, especially in subject areas peripheral or related to medicine. [2] As a result, LC and NLM create and distribute cataloging records for some of the same items.

The *NLM Classification Scheme* was first published 40 years ago, and MeSH is now 30 years old. At the time that each of these authorities was developed, other well-established classification and subject heading systems were in use in health science libraries, yet most U.S. health science libraries switched from these earlier systems to use the NLM Classification for shelf arrangement and MeSH for cataloging. This paper examines the development and implementation of cataloging standards by NLM, as well as the adoption of these standards in health science libraries: it also suggests how we might accommodate cataloging records that reflect two national standards for subject headings and classification in local cataloging operations, in library systems, and among cooperative bibliographic databases.

The National Library Role

Among the libraries, bibliographic services, sources, and users of national standard cataloging data and tools represented at this Congress, the National Library of Medicine may have a unique perspective on the conference theme of "challenging the standard bibliographic product." The National Library of Medicine not only provides original cataloging records and standard bibliographic products to a large segment of the health science library community worldwide, but also, like many other libraries, uses Library of Congress copy, which it applies in the cataloging of approximately 30% of its English-language monographs.

As a National Coordinated Cataloging Program (NCCP) participant, NLM follows the *Anglo-American Cataloguing Rules*, 2nd edition, revised (AACR2r), with LC Rule Interpretations (LCRIs) and derives benefit from using LC descriptive cataloging and authority work without modification. The increased use of LC copy, and the reduction in the percentage of materials requiring original cataloging at NLM became possible only after NLM abandoned certain local descriptive options and name heading practices. Compatibility with LC cataloging became the official position of NLM's Cataloging Section with the adoption of AACR2 and the LCRIs in 1981. The decision to follow LC practice allowed NLM to pursue and expand cooperative bibliographic programs with LC, and it was also clearly beneficial to many health science libraries. For these libraries, the differences in descriptive practices and in the forms of name and series headings in the cataloging records distributed by the two national libraries had restricted their use of available LC and NLM copy.

Standardization in Bibliographic Description

A number of factors and events led NLM to adopt descriptive cataloging standards and practices consistent with those of the Library of Congress. These include:

1) The benefits to health science libraries of a single, standard bibliographic record for biomedical materials;

2) The implementation of AACR2 in 1981;

3) The economic benefits to NLM of using LC copy; and

4) NLM's participation in cooperative cataloging with LC through the CIP (Cataloging in Publication) program.

The contribution of each of these factors to the standardization of NLM and LC descriptive cataloging is described below.

1) Single bibliographic record

In 1979, the Medical Library Association (MLA), on behalf of its health science library membership, initiated a series of meetings between the national libraries to urge closer cooperation in technical processing. The Association's original agenda included an investigation of cooperation in all aspects of cataloging—from description and authority work to classification and subject headings. The academic and larger health science libraries, many of which are members of bibliographic utilities such as OCLC, urged NLM and LC to reconcile their differences in cataloging and work toward the creation of a single standard for bibliographic control of the medical literature.

NLM and LC agreed that cooperation in descriptive cataloging and authority work presented the most fruitful area for eliminating redundant cataloging and ensuring that the records distributed by either national library would be usable by the greatest number of health science libraries, regardless of which classification or subject heading system the libraries used. The imminent adoption of AACR2 by both libraries provided the opportunity to change local policies on cataloging rule applications and to follow a single standard in both libraries.

An immediate and practical course of action to address concerns about different subject headings and classification systems was less clear. NLM and LC did agree to establish closer communication in the ongoing maintenance of the two subject heading systems. While NLM and LC do consult each other in developing subject headings in biomedicine for their respective vocabularies, and NLM relies upon the LC classification schedules for classifying materials in subjects peripheral to medicine, there was no serious consideration at the meetings between the national libraries of developing or adopting a single system of classification or subject headings for the medical literature.

2) Implementation of AACR2

Although both NLM and LC had adopted and used the 1967 *Anglo-American Cataloging Rules* and subsequent revised chapters, there were notable differences between the two libraries in the application of that cataloging code. NLM did not adopt LC's policy of superimposition (continuing formerly established name headings) and retained a number of local practices that were expedient for its cataloging operations. In 1981, when LC implemented AACR2, NLM viewed the adoption of new cataloging rules as an opportunity to develop rule applications consistent with those of LC and to abandon its local differences. Most importantly, NLM and LC would apply the same rules in establishing name and series headings, thus removing what had been one of the greatest barriers to the effective use and exchange of NLM and LC cataloging data by health science libraries.

3) *Economic benefits to NLM*
Prior to 1981, NLM had performed original cataloging for all materials that it acquired. Although LC copy was consulted occasionally as a guide, the requirement to perform all name authority work locally, as well as to modify descriptive cataloging and add MeSH and NLM Classification, limited the usefulness of LC copy when it was available. There was little practical benefit to NLM in reconsidering its descriptive cataloging policies, such as the long-standing policy of omitting certain statements of responsibility, as long as the more critical concerns of name headings and authority work for access points could not be resolved easily in light of LC's policy of superimposition. Desuperimposition by LC and the adoption of AACR2 by NLM thus constituted major positive changes.

4) *Cooperative Cataloging-in-Publication*
During the 1970s, NLM and LC established a cooperative arrangement for creating Cataloging-in-Publication data for titles in biomedicine. The CIP packets for titles within NLM's scope and coverage guidelines were sent by LC to NLM, where the titles were fully cataloged with NLM Classification and MeSH. The NLM record was provided to LC, where the NLM call number and MeSH subject headings were added to LC's cataloging record. Under this procedure, both LC and NLM cataloged the title, and both libraries distributed a record for the CIP in their respective cataloging service.

The CIP titles were the most readily identifiable category of items cataloged by both NLM and LC. This group of materials was selected to launch the pilot project in cooperative cataloging between NLM and LC. Under the current arrangement for CIP titles in biomedical subjects, the descriptive cataloging and name authority records are created by NLM and provided to LC for the addition of LC classification and shelflisting, Dewey Decimal Classification, and LC subject headings. The success of the cooperative arrangement between LC and NLM to provide Cataloging-in-Publication data for titles in biomedicine depended on standardization of descriptive cataloging. This standardization ensures that the current cataloging data of both libraries is almost completely interchangeable. Only the classification, subject headings, and occasionally, the tracing practice for series titles remain agency-specific.

The desirability of standardizing descriptive cataloging for LC and NLM as well as for their respective library constituencies is obvious. Why hasn't there been as much interest at the national level or from the health science library community in developing a single standard for classification? The history of the development of the NLM Classification scheme reveals that it actually resulted from the last serious attempt to develop a standard classification system for medicine in this country.

Development of the NLM Classification

In the forty years since the appearance of the first edition of the NLM Classification scheme, it has become the predominant classification system in use in U.S. health science libraries. [3]

It is not by accident or solely for convenience that the NLM Classification resembles so closely the mixed, alphanumeric notation of the Library of Congress classification scheme. In fact, if the goals of the Conference on Medical Classification held at the Library of Congress in 1944 had been fully realized, there would today be one system of classification for medical literature used by both NLM and LC. [4]

In 1943, a survey of the U.S. Army Medical Library was conducted under the sponsorship of the American Library Association; the study was funded by the Rockefeller Foundation. Among the recommendations of the Survey Committee, whose membership included nationally recognized librarians, was the adoption of a modern classification system for the Library. From the descriptions of the state of the card catalog and shelving scheme used in the Army Medical Library at the time, one suspects that the need for systematic classification was apparent to the library's administration before the Survey Committee presented its recommendations. Records for approximately one-fifth of the monograph collection were not in the card catalog. Books were shelved by author under broad subjects, such as anatomy, endocrinology, or surgery, and shelf location was not recorded on the cards, so that finding a book on the shelves was largely a process of guesswork. In some cases, duplicate copies of the same book were found classified and shelved in two different areas of the collection. [5]

A Classification Committee, including librarians and medical specialists, was appointed to formulate a suitable classification for the Army Medical Library. Existing systems of classification for medicine were considered, including the Library of Congress system, the Dewey Decimal Classification, the Barnard system, the Boston Medical Library Classification, and the Cunningham system. [Notes 6 through 10 cite their latest published versions.]

The original directive to the Committee for the preparation of the Army Medical Library Classification specified that the scheme should be broad, simple, and elastic, and that it should allow for the classification of non-medical topics likely to be collected by a medical library. The Committee was advised to consider the basic theory in the Cunningham system, i.e., that the outline for a classification of medical literature should follow the sequence of study in the medical school curriculum, with biology, anatomy, and physiology preceding the classification of the anatomic regions and systems of the body, as well as the phenomenon, study, and treatment of disease.

The Survey report of the Army Medical Library concluded that "The best classification scheme that could be devised for the Library would be one which combined the notation of the Library of Congress system with the basic plan of the Cunningham classification." [11]

The Army Medical Library was then located at 7th and Independence Avenues in Washington, D.C., only a few blocks down Capitol Hill from the Library of Congress. (The Army Medical Library was renamed the Armed Forces Medical Library in 1952, and was officially designated the National Library of Medicine when it was transferred to the Public Health Service in 1956.) Prior to World War II, there were plans to construct a new building for the Army Medical Library on Capitol Hill, close enough to the Library of Congress for the two libraries to be joined by a tunnel. The prospect of such a close connection to LC led to thoughts of cooperative cataloging arrangements, including suggestions of housing the collections together, which made the use of a single classification system for medicine highly desirable. The members of the 1944 Conference on Medical Library Classification unanimously recommended that a broad scheme of classification be developed within the framework of LC's schedules Q (science) and R (medicine). This recommendation was based on the following observations:

1) LC classification notations were printed on LC catalog cards, which could be used in the Army Medical Library catalog.
2) The use of the LC system by the Army Medical Library would foster cooperative cataloging with LC.
3) The LC system was known and recognized by research workers and librarians.
4) LC was interested in revising the medical section of its classification scheme.

The project was endorsed in a letter from Archibald MacLeish, then Librarian of Congress, to Col. Jones of the Army Medical Library, in which MacLeish commented

> The Army Medical Library and the Library of Congress have agreed upon certain cooperative undertakings as regards the service, cataloging and classification of materials in the field of medicine . . . . Since the AML needs a system now and the present system of LC is not adequate, the Library of Congress will be glad to join with the AML in a survey of library classification in the appropriate fields with a view to working out a system of classification satisfactory to the two libraries. [12]

The Classification Committee charged Miss Mary Louise Marshall, librarian at the Tulane University School of Medicine, with the task of compiling an outline of the new classification for medicine using the framework of LC's Q and R schedules, with special schedules to be developed for the history of medicine and military medicine, which were of special importance to the Army Medical Library. Clinical subjects were to be subdivided by body region, system, or organ and further subdivided by a uniform group of headings, such as Anatomy, Physiology, Hygiene, and Surgery. Preclinical subjects were to be classified with the preclinical groups, e.g., bacteria as infectious agents were to be classified in Bacteriology rather than with the diseases they cause. LC classification schedules, without revision, would be accepted for non-medical subjects represented in the collection of the Army Medical Library.

Miss Marshall's work, undertaken in close consultation with Library of Congress representatives to the Classification Committee as well as medical experts invited to submit topical outlines of their specialties, resulted in an outline that would have required substantial revisions to the Library of Congress schedules. The plan to implement a uniform scheme for grouping special anatomy, physiology, and pathology with the specific body system or region was incompatible with the Library of Congress scheme, which classed special anatomy with anatomy, special physiology with physiology, etc.

The exact nature of the review and discussions that led to the announcement that LC could not use the new medical classification are not evident in the official papers of the Classification Committee in the NLM archives, but it is apparent that this outcome, although based on practical considerations, was disappointing. The Library of Congress did agree, however, to reserve the block of letters QS through QZ as well as the letter W, which were undeveloped in the LC schedules, for use in the Army Medical Library Classification.

The NLM Classification contains main schedules for the physiological systems, such as the musculoskeletal system and the cardiovascular system, with subdivision by the morphology, physiology, and pathology of the organs or body regions. The LC Classification, in contrast, contains primary divisions for the disciplines of the health sciences, such as anatomy, physiology, and internal medicine. Table 1 shows the NLM Classification and corresponding LC schedules.

Classification using the NLM scheme results in the grouping of materials on the cardiovascular system in WG, with anatomy of the heart in WG 201, its physiology in WG 202, diseases of the heart and associated structures in WG 240-460, and heart surgery in WG 169. Using the Library of Congress scheme, the anatomy of the heart would be classified in QM—Anatomy, its physiology in QP, cardiac disease in RC, and surgery of the heart in RD. Table 2 charts these contrasting arrangements.

The practical implications of the difference in the two classification systems become evident in the shelving arrangement of biomedical collections. The fact that we classify *books* that can only be shelved in one location, rather than medical *topics*, which can be represented in many places, creates problems for users of either the NLM or LC classification system.

A preliminary edition of the *U.S. Army Medical Library Classification,* as developed by Mary Louise Marshall and the Classification Committee, preceded the publication of the first edition. [13] A prepublication draft of the preliminary edition was used to reclassify the collection of the Army Medical Library in 1946-49. Experience in applying the classification scheme in this project led to significant revisions that simplified the original schedules. The simplification retained most of the basic structure of the classes, but eliminated the very spe-

TABLE 1. GENERAL OUTLINE OF NLM CLASSIFICATION WITH CORRESPONDING LC SCHEDULES

NLM Classification		LC Classification
Preclinical Sciences		
QS	Human Anatomy	QM
QT	Physiology	QP
QU	Biochemistry	QP
QV	Pharmacology	RM
QW	Microbiology and Immunology	QR
QX	Parasitology	QL, QR
QY	Clinical Pathology	RB
QZ	Pathology	RB
Medicine and Related Subjects		
W	Medical Profession	R
WA	Public Health	RA
WB	Practice of Medicine	RC
WC	Infectious Diseases	RC
WD 100	Nutrition Disorders	RC
WD 200	Metabolic Diseases	RC
WD 300	Immunologic Diseases	RC
WD 400	Animal Poisoning	RA
WD 500	Plant Poisoning	RA
WD 600	Diseases by Physical Agents	RC
WD 700	Aviation and Space Medicine	RC
WE	Musculoskeletal System	QM, QP, RC
WF	Respiratory System	QM, QP, RC
WG	Cardiovascular System	QM, QP, RC
WH	Hemic and Lymphatic Systems	QM, QP, RC
WI	Gastrointestinal System	QM, QP, RC
WJ	Urogenital System	QM, QP, RC
WK	Endocrine System	QM, QP, RC
WL	Nervous System	QM, QP, RC
WM	Psychiatry	RC
WM	Radiology	R, RM
WO	Surgery	RD
WP	Gynecology	RG
WQ	Obstetrics	RG
WR	Dermatology	RL
WS	Pediatrics	RJ
WT	Geriatrics, Chronic Disease	RC
WU	Dentistry, Oral Surgery	RK
WV	Otorhinolaryngology	RF
WW	Ophthalmology	RE
WX	Hospitals	RA
WY	Nursing	RT
WZ	History of Medicine	R

cific, 'close' classification that was required in the preliminary edition. The resulting more general classification scheme was easier to apply, expedited the cataloging process, and ensured a more useful grouping of subjects. Forty years and four editions later, the schedules of the current NLM Classification still reflect that broad classification. [14]

Adoption of NLM Classification in Medical Libraries

The NLM scheme, while useful for classifying materials in a large medical library, is less satisfactory for use in libraries covering a special subject area such as dentistry or nursing. The collections of these specialized libraries cover their fields in greater depth than do general medical libraries, and they thus require more detailed classification for specific topics and publication types within these disciplines. The foresight of the librarians and experts who developed a flexible and expandable framework for the NLM Classification more than 50 years ago resulted in schedules with room for expansion and addition of numbers for special topics without introducing long or complicated nota-

TABLE 2. COMPARISON OF NLM AND LC CLASSIFICATION OF PORTIONS OF THE CARDIOVASCULAR SYSTEM AND DISEASES

NLM		LC	
Cardiovascular System		Anatomy, Physiology, Medicine of the Cardiovascular System	
WG			
100	General Works		
101	Anatomy. Histology. Embryology	Anatomy	QM
102	Physiology. Biochemistry	Physiology	QP
140	Electrocardiography. Vectorcardiography. Monitoring	Internal Medicine	RC
141	Examination. Diagnosis	Internal Medicine	RC
142	Pathology	Pathology	RB
166	Therapeutics	Internal Medicine	RC
168	Cardiovascular Surgery	Surgery	RD
169	Heart Surgery	Surgery	RD
200	[Heart] General Works		
201	Anatomy. Histology. Embryology	Anatomy	QM
202	Physiology. Mechanism of the heart beat	Physiology	QP
220	Congenital heart disease	Pediatrics	RJ
300	Coronary vessels. Coronary disease	Internal Medicine	RC

tion. As a result, the trend in these special health science libraries has been to develop expansions and revisions of NLM schedules rather than to develop entirely new schemes.

Prior to the publication of the fourth edition of the NLM Classification, [15] subjects that were to be classified in LC schedules, such as general science, general psychology, and veterinary medicine were referenced in the index to general LC schedules, e.g., Psychology [see] BF. The rationale for this approach, as stated in the introduction to the first edition of the NLM Classification, was: "Specific numbers for LC classes have been omitted on the theory that each library will determine for itself the amount of specificity it desires in its use of the LC Classification tables." [16] Medical libraries using the NLM Classification had to decide whether to assign these selected broad LC numbers or to consult the LC schedules and select the specific class numbers that LC would use. To reduce the guesswork for libraries and to increase the likelihood of consistent classification among health sciences libraries applying only LC classification and those that use LC in conjunction with NLM, the index of the fourth edition of the NLM classification included the specific LC classification number or range of numbers appropriate for each subject.

The NLM Classification provides for the classification of most serial publications strictly by form rather than by subject. In support of NLM's major indexing service and extensive document delivery program for journal articles indexed in *Index Medicus* and MEDLINE, serials are classified and shelflisted at NLM to facilitate rapid retrieval from a central area of the stacks. The policy of classifying serials in form numbers also applies to monographic series; other health science libraries may treat the titles in a series as separate monographic publications, for which they will need a specific subject classification number for shelving each title in the local collection. Recognizing this need, NLM provides an alternate classification number from the NLM schedules in its cataloging records for these serial analytics. The alternate classification number assigned by NLM is further given a book number that is reserved in NLM's shelflist to ensure that another item will not later be assigned the same call number. These subject classification numbers provided for libraries that elect not to use NLM's form numbers are printed in NLM's catalog publications, indexed in CATLINE (the online version of NLM's *Current Catalog*), and distributed in NLM's MARC-formatted catalog records.

When the first edition of the NLM Classification scheme was published in 1951, materials in many health science libraries were already classified according to LC and other existing schemes. Aside from the merits of the NLM scheme for organizing medical publications into a useful shelf arrangement, many other factors were cited by the libraries that switched from other classification schemes to the NLM system. These included:

1) Use by NLM, and the expectation that NLM would catalog more of the medical literature than LC;

C14 - DISEASES-CARDIOVASCULAR

•CARDIOVASCULAR DISEASES	C14	
•HEART DISEASES	C14.280	
ARRHYTHMIA	C14.280.67	
ARRHYTHMIA, SINUS	C14.280.67.93	
ATRIAL FIBRILLATION	C14.280.67.198	
ATRIAL FLUTTER	C14.280.67.248	
BRADYCARDIA	C14.280.67.319	
EXTRASYSTOLE	C14.280.67.470	
HEART BLOCK	C14.280.67.558	
ADAMS-STOKES SYNDROME	C14.280.67.558.137	
BUNDLE-BRANCH BLOCK	C14.280.67.558.323	
SINOATRIAL BLOCK	C14.280.67.558.750	
LONG QT SYNDROME	C14.280.67.565	
PRE-EXCITATION SYNDROMES	C14.280.67.780	
LOWN-GANONG-LEVINE SYNDROME	C14.280.67.780.560	
PRE-EXCITATION, MAHAIM TYPE	C14.280.67.780.770	
WOLFF-PARKINSON-WHITE SYNDROME	C14.280.67.780.977	
SICK SINUS SYNDROME	C14.280.67.829	
TACHYCARDIA	C14.280.67.845	
TACHYCARDIA, PAROXYSMAL	C14.280.67.845.695	
TACHYCARDIA, SUPRAVENTRICULAR	C14.280.67.845.880	
ACCELERATED IDIOVENTRICULAR RHYTHM	C14.280.67.845.880.25	
TACHYCARDIA, ATRIOVENTRICULAR NODAL REENTRY	C14.280.67.845.880.95	
TACHYCARDIA, ECTOPIC ATRIAL	C14.280.67.845.880.315	
TACHYCARDIA, ECTOPIC JUNCTIONAL	C14.280.67.845.880.320	
TACHYCARDIA, SINOATRIAL NODAL REENTRY	C14.280.67.845.880.840	
TACHYCARDIA, SINUS	C14.280.67.845.880.845	
TORSADES DE POINTES	C14.280.67.845.880.900	
VENTRICULAR FIBRILLATION	C14.280.67.932	
CARCINOID HEART DISEASE	C14.280.129	C4.557.112,
CARDIAC OUTPUT, LOW	C14.280.148	
CARDIAC TAMPONADE	C14.280.155	
CORONARY DISEASE	C14.280.211	
ANGINA PECTORIS	C14.280.211.198	
ANGINA PECTORIS, VARIANT	C14.280.211.198.955	C14.280.211.
ANGINA, UNSTABLE	C14.280.211.198.970	
CORONARY ANEURYSM	C14.280.211.205	C14.907.55.
CORONARY ARTERIOSCLEROSIS	C14.280.211.210	C14.907.137.
CORONARY THROMBOSIS	C14.280.211.212	C14.907.854.
CORONARY VASOSPASM	C14.280.211.215	
ANGINA PECTORIS, VARIANT	C14.280.211.215.955	C14.280.211.
MYOCARDIAL INFARCTION	C14.280.211.637	
SHOCK, CARDIOGENIC	C14.280.211.637.667	C23.888.789.

Figure 1. Section of the MeSH Tree Structures for Category C—Diseases.
Source: Medical Subject Headings—Tree Structures, 1991. Bethesda, MD:
National Library of Medicine, 1990.

2) Ease of application;

3) Simplicity of notation;

4) Appropriateness for use in large and small libraries;

5) Correlation with the LC schedules;

6) Currency: use by NLM ensures the issuance of updates and revisions;

7) Feasibility of converting from other systems; because the use of the literature of biomedicine decreases with age, a date cut-off could be established to divide collections by the old and new classification systems. [17]

Many of the reasons given for adopting the NLM Classification scheme are practical considerations. Few libraries listed user preference as the main reason for converting to NLM from another scheme. The case for the use of MeSH as a subject heading authority is somewhat different. Its development as the foundation of the automated subject retrieval system at NLM, the term relationships displayed in its hierarchical structure, its currency, and its comprehensive coverage of the vocabulary of medicine have ensured its continued prevalence in health science libraries.

Subject Headings Used in Medical Libraries

The choice of subject heading systems in health science libraries is primarily between NLM's Medical Subject Headings (MeSH) and Library of Congress Subject Headings (LCSH). In a survey of the subject heading practices in 134 health science libraries, which was published in the *Bulletin of the Medical Library Association* in 1976, 76% of the responding libraries indicated that they used MeSH exclusively or MeSH augmented by terms from other lists, and 22% of the libraries reported using LCSH or LCSH supplemented by MeSH. [18]

Medical Subject Headings (MeSH)

The first edition of *Medical Subject Headings*, published in 1960, had the subtitle "Main headings, subheadings, and cross references used in the Index Medicus and the National Library of Medicine Catalog." MeSH was intended from the outset to be equally applicable to the subject cataloging of books and the indexing of journal articles. The theory of subject cataloging and indexing using MeSH was not to devise a single phrase or label that described the specific topic of a work, but to select a set of appropriate headings or pointers which in combination would define a very specific subject. The use of the first edition of MeSH for subject indexing at NLM in 1960 was primarily for retrieval of citations in the printed tools—*Index Medicus* and the *National Library of Medicine Catalog*, but the advantages of MeSH as a controlled vocabulary in an automated postcoordinate indexing and retrieval system were recognized, and the vocabulary was designed to accommodate the future technology.

When NLM developed its computer-based Medical Literature Analysis and Retrieval System (MEDLARS) in the early 1960s, MeSH became the foundation of computerized subject searching using Boolean operators. Initially, subject retrieval in MEDLARS was done through an offline, on-demand, batch search system. In 1963, the grouping of MeSH terms into a hierarchical structure, under broad categories of terms known as *tree structures*, was introduced to facilitate expanding a search on a heading to include all of the more specific headings grouped under it. The hierarchical structure of MeSH with its categorized lists (see Figure 1) assists catalogers and users in identifying relationships among terms that are not shown through the typical *see also* references.

MeSH features a controlled list of topical subheadings with rules for their proper coordination with main headings. MeSH also includes authorized lists of form, language, and geographic subheadings that are used in cataloging. MeSH is published in several forms. The *Annotated Alphabetic List* contains instructions for indexers, catalogers, and searchers. [19] The *Medical Subject Headings* published as part of the annual *Index Medicus* contains the online search notes and term history notes. [20] The vocabulary is updated annually to add new terms and references and to revise the categorized lists or "trees" as needed.

Many health science libraries have collections in biomedicine that provide extensive coverage of the sciences of biology, botany, and other related sciences. These libraries find it necessary to augment MeSH with terms from LSCH or other lists for adequate subject analysis and retrieval of the works in their collections.

It is interesting to note that while the NLM Classification, with its correlation to the LC Classification for peripheral and non-medical topics, is thought to be better-suited for medium-to-large health science libraries than to smaller, specialized medical collections, MeSH, with its comprehensive and specific coverage of clinical and research medicine, is clearly better suited to describing special medical collections than for the more general collections in medium-to-large health science libraries that include materials in peripheral and related subjects.

The probable reasons for the widespread use of MeSH for subject cataloging in health science libraries, including libraries that classify according to the LC classification system, are:

1) Uniform vocabulary for subject retrieval of both books and journal articles;

2) Use by NLM's Cataloging Section;

3) Comprehensiveness for medicine; and

4) Frequent updates.

Despite the many advantages of MeSH for the subject indexing of the medical literature for automated retrieval, there are some problems with the incorporation of NLM-assigned MeSH headings in manual catalogs, specifically:

1) In smaller catalogs, there are not enough records to warrant the subdivision of main headings by topical, form, language, and geographic subheadings.

2) The annual changes to MeSH are expensive to accommodate in a manual catalog. Especially difficult is the maintenance of *see* and *see also* references.

MeSH is firmly linked to the MEDLARS system at NLM. MeSH terms exist in millions of indexed records in the MEDLARS databases. The subject terms in these records are updated each year to reflect the changes that occur in MeSH annually. As long as MeSH is an effective and responsive tool for the indexing and retrieval of medical literature, it will be used by NLM, and we suspect that as long as NLM continues to use and maintain MeSH, it is unlikely that health science libraries that also use MeSH will adopt a different scheme or urge NLM to do so.

It seems equally unlikely that LC will abandon LCSH for cataloging medical materials. NLM believes that the greatest promise for resolving differences for the user and accommodating different subject heading schemes and terminologies in databases lies in developing links between the systems. There are several projects currently under development to integrate and link multiple thesauri. Northwestern University Libraries is developing a combined index to LCSH and MeSH authority records. Another, longer-term effort to provide links between subject systems in this field is NLM's Unified Medical Language Project, or UMLS.

Accommodating Different Subject Heading Authorities

Many academic health science libraries that follow NLM cataloging policies and practices are part of larger university library systems that use LC Classification and LCSH. The use of different authorities for classification and subject headings within a single library system complicates the integration of records for the medical collection in the main catalog. While the records for items classified according to the NLM Classification can be interfiled in the catalog of a collection classified by the LC system without much problem, the coexistence of MeSH and LCSH in a single catalog is likely to lead to great confusion on the part of users.

The introduction of online catalogs in many academic health science libraries during the 1980s demonstrated clearly the need to develop better methods of guiding users to the alternate headings for the same concept, and made the mapping between equivalent LCSH and MeSH headings a valuable tool for searching catalogs containing both types of subject headings.

Northwestern University has undertaken a project to map LCSH and MeSH headings for searching the online catalog in its local NOTIS system. The mappings were derived from the local authority file containing both MeSH and LCSH records, from bibliographic records, and from a machine-readable file of over 10,000 LCSH-to-MeSH mappings provided by NLM. Using these sources as well as a combination of automated techniques and human editing, Northwestern University Libraries created a combined subject authority file that displays the linkages between equivalent headings in MeSH and LCSH for the online catalog user. [21]

The Unified Medical Language System

One long-term approach to the development of a system to facilitate the retrieval of medical information from a variety of machine-readable sources that are indexed by different terminologies is NLM's Unified Medical Language System (UMLS) project. The goal of the UMLS project is to establish links between the representation of biomedical concepts in different vocabularies to support the mapping of a user's expression of search terms to the controlled vocabularies used in medical literature databases, patient record files, and factual databanks.

The UMLS will include at least three machine-readable knowledge sources, or databases: the Metathesaurus, a Semantic Network, and an Information Sources Map. The Metathesaurus is the knowledge source containing the terms from different vocabularies and the variety of relationships among these terms. The Semantic Network will contain information about the types or categories of terms in the Metathesaurus, e.g., plant, disease, or syndrome, as well as the possible relationships among these terms, e.g., the term "Virus" might be shown to bear a causal relationship to a term that is a disease or syndrome.

The first versions of the UMLS Metathesaurus and Semantic Network became available for experimental use in October 1990. The base set of terms in the Meta-1 includes all terms in MeSH and DSM-III, the American Psychiatric Association's Diagnostic and Statistical Manual of Mental Disorders, terms from the International Classification of Disease, and from SNOMED, the Systematized Nomenclature of Medicine. LCSH terms that have been mapped to equivalent MeSH expressions are also incorporated.

The UMLS project is a long-term effort that will eventually include the functional components to analyze and interpret a user's query, a graphics capability to provide a visual representation of the relationships among terms and semantic types, a search formulater to help translate an expressed information need into the syntax suitable for searching appropriate databases, a search transmitter to send and receive information between computer systems, and an output processor to merge, organize, and evaluate the information retrieved.

The UMLS project is designed to address the information needs of the health professional, but its development and future use in various automated retrieval system applications may serve as a model for projects undertaking similar mappings of concepts in the terminology of other disciplines.

Living with Multiple Standards

Progress has been made by NLM and LC in implementing a single bibliographic standard for descriptive cataloging. This move to standardization was in direct response to the urging of health science libraries. It appears that differences in descriptive cataloging between the two national libraries presented a greater barrier to the effective use of existing cataloging copy by the majority of health science libraries than did differences between local library practices and the national libraries. At least where local practices are concerned, each individual library can take the initiative to examine carefully the costs and benefits of retaining these practices.

The development of AAC2 and the commitment of the national libraries to consistent application of the new rules were key factors in the standardization of descriptive cataloging by NLM and LC. Currently there is no single subject heading list or scheme for the classification of biomedicine. The presence of established subject and classification authorities that are maintained and used by two national libraries, and the size of the collections already organized by one or the other of these systems have hampered any serious consideration of developing a single bibliographic standard for the subject analysis and classification of medicine.

Given the similarities of the two biomedical classification schemes, there might be a greater probability for success in achieving a single standard for classification, especially if we take the view that the principal goal of classification at both NLM and LC is to establish a shelving location based on subject organization. It is unlikely, however, that NLM or LC could seriously contemplate changing subject heading systems. In undertaking a project such as the UMLS, NLM demonstrates its recognition of the fact that medical information exists in many forms and that it is indexed and organized by a variety of systems. MeSH and LCSH constitute two members of a large set of authoritative vocabularies and terminologies in biomedicine. Instead of attempting to reach agreement on a single standard vocabulary, our efforts might be better directed at devising methods to link the systems currently in use.

NOTES

1. Gullion, S.L. "Classification and Subject Cataloging." in *Handbook of Medical Library Practice*, 4th ed. Chicago: Medical Library Association, 1982, v. 2, pp. 253-277.
2. *Collection Development Manual of the National Library of Medicine.* Bethesda, MD: National Library of Medicine, 1985.
3. *U.S. Army Medical Library Classification.* 1st ed., Washington, D.C.: 1951.
4. Meeting of the Conference on Medical Library Classification, Library of Congress, 1944. Unpublished report. Bethesda, MD: National Library of Medicine. NLM MS C 309.
5. Miles, W.D. *History of the National Library of Medicine.* Bethesda, MD: National Library of Medicine, 1982, pp. 293-294.
6. Library of Congress. Subject Cataloging Division. *Classification, Class R: Medicine.* 5th ed. Washington, D.C.: Library of Congress, 1986. —*Class Q: Science.* 7th ed., 1989.
7. Dewey, M. *Dewey Decimal Classification and Relative Index.* J.P. Comaromi, ed. 20th ed. Albany, NY: Forest Press, 1989. 4 v.
8. Barnard, C.C. *A Classification for Medical and Veterinary Libraries.* 2nd ed. London: H.K. Lewis, 1955.

9. Boston Medical Library. *Medical Classification*. 3rd ed., rev. Boston: Boston Medical Library, 1944-46. 2v.

10. Cunningham, E.R. *Classification for Medical Literature*. E. Steinke and M. Gladish, eds. 5th ed., rev. and enl. Nashville, TN: Vanderbilt University Press, 1967.

11. Meeting of the Conference on Medical Library Classification.

12. MacLeish, A. Letter to Col. Jones, May 20, 1944. Bethesda, MD: National Library of Medicine. NLM MS C 309.

13. *U.S. Army Medical Library Classification*. Preliminary ed. Washington, D.C.: Army Medical Library, 1948.

14. *National Library of Medicine Classification*. 4th ed., revised. Bethesda, MD: National Library of Medicine; Washington, D.C.: U.S. Government Printing Office, 1981.

15. *National Library of Medicine Classification:* A scheme for the shelf arrangement of books in the field of medicine and its related sciences. 4th ed. Bethesda, MD: National Library of Medicine; Washington, D.C.: U.S. Government Printing Office, 1978.

16. U.S. Army, 1st ed., p. 7.

17. Scheerer, G.B.; Hines, L.E. Classification Systems Used in Medical Libraries. *Bulletin of the Medical Library Association*. 62 (3) July 1974, pp. 273-280.

18. Fredericksen, R.B.; Michael, H.N. Subject Cataloging Practices in North American Medical School Libraries. *Bulletin of the Medical Library Association*. 64 (4) Oct. 1976, pp. 356-366.

19. *Medical Subject Headings. Annotated Alphabetic List*. Bethesda, MD: National Library of Medicine; Springfield, VA: National Technical Information Service, 1991.

20. *Medical Subject Headings*. Bethesda, MD: National Library of Medicine; Washington, D.C.: U.S. Government Printing Office, 1991.

21. Strawn, G.L. "Mapping the LCSH and MeSH systems." Paper presented at the opening session of the LITA/ALCTS [American Library Association, Library and Information Technology Association/Association for Library Collections and Technical Services] Discussion Group on Authority Control in the Online Environment, June 24, 1990, Chicago, IL.

THE THESAURUS DESIGNER'S PERSPECTIVE: INTRODUCTION

Medical Subject Headings differ from those of the Library of Congress, but they have a similar precoordinate structure in which headings and subheadings are combined by a cataloger or indexer. The *Art and Architecture Thesaurus* (AAT), in contrast, is a very different type of vocabulary from Library of Congress Subject Headings—a thesaurus of unitary concepts. The AAT has been accepted as an official alternative controlled vocabulary by the Research Libraries Information Network and is used in a variety of applications. Should librarians in other disciplines be developing specialized vocabularies in their fields? Thesaurus development is a time-consuming and expensive activity; the *Art and Architecture Thesaurus* is fortunate in having the support of the J. Paul Getty Trust.

The Library of Congress is considered to be especially strong in the humanities. What was wrong with its art vocabulary that warranted a multimillion dollar investment in a new thesaurus? Having consulted for the *Art and Architecture Thesaurus*, I am acquainted with many members of its staff and invited Cathy Whitehead to address this question.

Cathleen Whitehead holds a Master of Library Science degree from the State University of New York at Albany. For the past three years, she has served as User Services Coordinator for the recently published *Art and Architecture Thesaurus* (AAT), a project of the Getty Art History Information Program. She joined the AAT staff in 1984 as Authority Editor and has also served as Production Manager for the project. Ms. Whitehead has recently resigned from her position in order to devote more time to raising her seven-month old daughter, but is continuing to work with the AAT and other projects on a free-lance basis.

Ms. Whitehead is an active member of the Art Libraries Society of North America (ARLIS/NA), in which she serves as Chair of the Visual Resources Division Task Force on Authorities. She is also a member of the Visual Resource Association (VRA), the Museum Computer Network (MCN), and the American Society for Information Science (ASIS). Her articles on the AAT have appeared in *Spectra, ART Documentation,* and newsletters of various professional organizations, such as the Visual Resources Association and the Association of Architectural Librarians. She has presented papers on a variety of topics relating to thesauri and conducted several workshops on using the AAT at various conferences, including those of the Museum Documentation Association, The National Federation of Abstracting and Information Services (NFAIS), the Museum Computer Network, the Art Libraries Society of North America, and the American Society for Information Science. Her most recent publication is "Mapping LCSH into Thesauri: The AAT Model" in *Beyond the Book: Extending MARC for Subject Access*, edited by Toni Petersen and Pat Molholt (Boston: G.K. Hall, 1990).

B. H. W.

The Art and Architecture Thesaurus as an Alternative to Library of Congress Subject Headings

Cathleen K. Whitehead
Consultant
Art and Architecture Thesaurus
62 Stratton Rd.
Williamstown, MA 01267

Uniqueness of the AAT

The development of a thesaurus is by no means a unique or special feat. Thesauri have been used successfully as indexing and retrieval tools in Boolean-based search systems since the end of World War II, and the proliferation of thesauri, especially in scientific and technical fields, is well known. Because they convey the specialized vocabulary of a given field within a semantic network, thesauri are now in vogue as important components of natural-language processing systems.

What is perhaps extraordinary about the *Art and Architecture Thesaurus* (AAT) is the fact that it is an externally-developed, discipline-wide macro–thesaurus that is not tied to any particular application. What is also novel about the AAT is that in 1990 it became the first subject vocabulary control tool to reside next to the *Library of Congress Subject Headings* (LCSH) within the authorities file of the Research Libraries Information Network (RLIN). The depth and scope of the AAT's coverage, its relevance for applications that extend beyond book cataloging, and the principles used in its development make this thesaurus worth considering as an alternative to LCSH for certain applications.

Background of the AAT

A detailed history of the AAT is given in the introduction to the first edition, [1] but for those who are unfamiliar with the project, I shall provide brief background information.

In recognition of the lack of a standard vocabulary for use specifically by art and architectural collections, and of the incompleteness and inadequacy of LCSH and existing authority lists in the field, the AAT was conceived in 1979 by Dora Crouch, an architectural historian, Pat Molholt, and Toni Petersen, then director of the RILA (International Repertory of the Literature of Art) indexing service and currently director of the AAT.

Following a series of grants from the Council on Library Resources, the National Endowment for the Humanities, and other sources, the AAT became an operating entity within the Art History Information Program of the J. Paul Getty Trust in 1983. Currently housed in Williamstown, Massachusetts, with a staff of thirteen full- and part-time employees, the project is expected to join other Trust entities in the Los Angeles area when the new Getty complex is completed. There the AAT is to serve an as ongoing vocabulary coordination project for the visual arts.

In 1984, drafts of the AAT were distributed to a small group of test users. This group grew to over 250 institutions in 1990 when the first edition of the thesaurus was published in both printed and electronic forms by Oxford University Press. To date, nearly 2,000 copies of the first edition have been purchased, and the user base continues to expand. As stated above, the AAT is searchable on RLIN, and a USMARC format version of the AAT is also available.

Applications of the AAT

Thesauri are generally discipline-specific, with a fairly well-defined scope. They are normally developed for a particular application; historically, this application has been document indexing. The AAT is also used for document indexing, but its utilization extends beyond this to the description of drawings, paintings, photographs, prints, slides and other visual materials, sculpture, objects within decorative arts and historical collections, and archival materials, as well as bibliographic and other textual materials. AAT users are therefore quite diverse and include libraries, archives, museums, indexing services, historical societies, and visual collections.

This diversity reflects the nature of information in the visual arts as well as the requirements of scholars and other researchers in this field. It is hoped that the AAT as a standard vocabulary for this discipline will not only enhance subject access to these collections individually, but will also play a major role in the development of information systems that will allow research across these types of collections. The AAT's design reflects its intended use by the museum professional as well as the librarian.

Vocabulary of the Visual Arts

The vocabulary of any discipline has its own characteristics and presents its own challenges. The language of the visual arts is in many cases slippery, imprecise, and open to interpretation. Conveying it within a controlled vocabulary is often difficult, frequently involving heated editorial debate. Some of the choices that art thesaurus builders have to make are summarized in Table 1.

**TABLE 1. PROBLEMS WITH THE LANGUAGE OF
ART AND ARCHITECTURE**

Indigenous vs. Pejorative Terms
    KhoiKhoi / Hottentots
    Inuit / Eskimo

Technical/Scholarly vs. Popular Terms
    diffusion transfer process / instant photography

National vs. Regional Terms
    miniature golf courses / putt putt golf courses

Historical vs. Contemporary Terms
    looking glasses / mirrors

American English vs. Foreign Language Terms
    prayer niches / mihrabs
    lady's writing tables / bonheurs-du-jour

Proliferation of Adjectival Phrases

Victorian houses	painted vases	concrete bridges
Victorian furniture	painted chairs	concrete parking garages

    ⋮   ⋮   ⋮

A primary application of the AAT is in museums, for the naming and description of objects and their components. As shown in Figure 1, even an object as simple as a chair requires numerous terms for its description. This necessitates a vocabulary that is highly specific and enumerative.

To deal with the idiosyncratic problems of the vocabulary of the visual arts and to handle the nearly infinite number of possible object descriptions, the AAT has established criteria for the selection of descriptors. Each term is evaluated according to literary warrant, which the AAT defines as evidence for the use of a term in printed sources. Consultation with subject experts and thesaurus users also informs the decisions on preferred terms.

Structure of the AAT

In its beginnings, the AAT made a commitment to become a discipline-wide standard. The original plan was to cull terms from existing standards such as LCSH and authority lists used in the field of art. Once the terms were gathered, it was thought that current thesaurus construction guidelines could be applied and the terms easily arranged in hierarchies. This quickly proved impossible, primarily

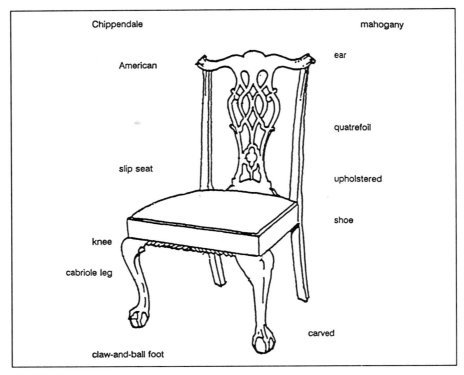

Chippendale

mahogany

American

ear

quatrefoil

slip seat

upholstered

shoe

knee

cabriole leg

carved

claw-and-ball foot

Figure 1. Terms for parts of a chair, illustrating the highly enumerative nature of object description.

because of the incompleteness of these vocabularies for art and architecture and because of the precoordinate and inconsistent forms of headings used in these sources. It seemed that bibliographic systems had bypassed what are now standard approaches to vocabulary control and subject access to online indexes.

The design of the AAT is rooted in the information storage and retrieval techniques developed after World War II, which progressed from uniterm systems to thesauri to rule-based indexing systems as tools to maximize the power of automated retrieval. In keeping with the latest trends in classification, the AAT also has the potential to be used in natural-language processing systems.

The primary display of AAT terms is hierarchical; the basic classification of terms is by *facet*. As defined by the AAT, a facet is a homogeneous class of words sharing common characteristics. Thus far, seven facets in the field of art and architecture have been identified (see Table 2). The facets proceed from abstract concepts to physical artifacts, e.g., the abstract facet "Styles and Periods" precedes the concrete facet "Objects." These fundamental categories have thus far proven to be well suited to the classification of any term selected for inclusion in the thesaurus.

TABLE 2. AAT FACETS AND SAMPLE TERMS WITHIN EACH FACET

Associated Concepts	*Activities*
light	dyeing
opacity	regulating
classicism	bricklaying
	etching
Physical Attributes	typology
	budgeting
oval	surveying
arabesque	auctions
chevron	exhibitions
egg and dart	conferences
gabled	
Styles and Periods	*Materials*
Tudor	sandstone
Medieval	teak
Anatolian	burnt sienna
Late Antique	
American	
Agents	*Objects*
artists	ribbed vaults
acoustical engineers	letters
sculptors	pavilions
patrons	folding chairs
leatherworkers	pictographs
presidents	portraits
	relief maps
	cookbooks

Table 2 also illustrates the type of term that one will find in each facet. As is evident from the table, the AAT includes nouns (in both singular and plural forms), gerunds (verbal nouns), and adjectives. Table 3 gives an overview of the conceptual structure of the AAT. Terms within the facets are further subdivided into 41 hierarchies, which are graphic displays of terms linked according to genus/species or class/subclass relationships. The hierarchical displays are used instead of the BT/NT (broader term/narrower term) notation that one finds in alphabetically arranged thesauri. Shown in Figure 2 is a sample page from the Furniture hierarchy as it appears in the first edition of the AAT.

To the left of each facet and hierarchy listed in Table 3 is an alphabetic code, for example, "M" for the Materials facet and "V.VD" for the Drawings hierarchy. These codes serve as the prefix for the classification notation (CN) of each descriptor in the thesaurus. The CN is a unique code assigned to each

TABLE 3. AAT FACETS AND HIERARCHIES

B	**ASSOCIATED CONCEPTS FACET**	**V**	**OBJECTS FACET**
B.BM	Associated Concepts		**Built Environment**
		V.RD	Settlements, Systems and Landscapes
D	**PHYSICAL ATTRIBUTES FACET**	V.RG	Built Complexes and Districts
		V.RK	Single Built Works and Open Spaces
D.DC	Design Attributes	V.RM	Building Divisions and Site Elements
D.DG	Design Elements		
D.DL	Colors	V.RT	Built Works Components
			Furnishings and Equipment
F	**STYLES AND PERIODS FACET**	V.TB	Tools and Equipment
		V.TD	Measuring Devices
F.FL	Styles and Periods	V.TF	Hardware and Joints
H	**AGENTS FACET**	V.TG	Furniture
		V.T	Lighting Devices
		V.T	Furnishings
H.HG	People and Organizations	V.T	Personal Artifacts
		V.T	Containers
K	**ACTIVITIES FACET**	V.T	Culinary Artifacts
		V.T	Musical Instruments
K.KD	Disciplines	V.T	Recreational Artifacts
K.KG	Functions	V.T	Armament
K.KM	Events	V.T	Transportation Artifacts
K.KT	Processes and Techniques	V.T	Communication Artifacts
M	**MATERIALS FACET**		**Visual and Verbal Communication**
		V.VB	Image and Object Genres
M.MT	Materials	V.VD	Drawings
		V.V	Paintings
		V.V	Prints
		V.VJ	Photographs
		V.V	Sculpture
		V.V	Multi-Media Art Forms
		V.V	Communication Design
		V.V	Exchange Media
		V.V	Book Arts
		V.VW	Document Types

```
        <storage and display furniture>
        case furniture
          cabinets
            <cabinets by function>
```

TG.442	spice cabinets
TG.443	thread cabinets
TG.444	utility cabinets
TG.445	chests
TG.446	arcae
TG.447	blanket chests
TG.448	board chests
TG.449	bottle cases
TG.450	campaign chests
TG.451	caskets (chests)
TG.452	cassoni
TG.453	cellerets
TG.454	chests with drawers
TG.455	clothes chests
TG.456	coffers (furniture)
TG.457	armada chests
TG.458	bahuts
TG.459	trussing coffers
TG.460	dower chests
TG.461	hembras
TG.462	machos
TG.463	dug-out chests
TG.464	lobby chests
TG.465	medicine chests
TG.466	mule chests
TG.467	Nonsuch chests
TG.468	sea chests
TG.469	spice chests
TG.470	sugar chests
TG.471	taquillónes
TG.472	tea chests
TG.473	tea caddies
TG.474	tilting chests
TG.475	chests of drawers
TG.476	bachelor's chests
TG.477	butler's desks
TG.478	chest-on-chests
TG.479	chests on frames
TG.480	cheval dressers
TG.481	chiffonniers
TG.482	chiffonnières
TG.483	chifforobes
TG.484	commodes
TG.485	commodes à encoignures
TG.486	commodes à la régence
TG.487	commodes à vantaux
TG.488	commodes en console
TG.489	corner commodes
TG.490	demi-commodes

May be used in combination with other descriptors (e.g., mahogany +
pedestals; turned + legs; serpentine–front + chests of drawers;
Louis XIV + pier tables).

Figure 2. AAT sample hierarchical display.

descriptor that indicates its relative position within a hierarchy and which may substitute for the term in automated systems. The classification notation for the term *chests of drawers* is shown in Figure 3, which features a complete entry for this term from the alphabetic portion of the AAT.

---

chests of drawers

      TG.475   (L,N)

ALT   chest of drawers

SN   Type of case furniture usually having four drawers but sometimes made with three, five or more; generally supported on feet and sometimes resting directly on the floor.

            Use commodes for similar case pieces generally supported on short legs. Use chests with drawers for chests with one or more tiers of drawers below a deep storage space.

UF   bureaus (chests of drawers)

            chests, dressing (chests of drawers)

            drawers, chests of

            dressers (chests of drawers)

            dressing chests (chests of drawers)

CN   V.TG.AFU.AFU.AXC.ALO.BCW

Figure 3. AAT sample alphabetical entry.

The AAT follows the tree structure of MeSH [Medical Subject Headings] as a model for its hierarchies, though AAT hierarchies are expandable, rather than having a fixed depth as do the MeSH trees. The deepest hierarchy in the AAT currently goes to sixteen levels, whereas MeSH trees are fixed at seven levels.

The sample page shown in Figure 2 illustrates the enumerative nature of the thesaurus. While many sections of the AAT are quite exhaustive, its notation allows for the easy assimilation of new terms.

The hierarchical approach to thesaurus construction is expedient for both indexing and retrieval. Hierarchies facilitate the assignment of the most appropriate terms by indexers and catalogers, and allow researchers more readily to retrieve information to a greater degree of specificity. In an application that uses the hierarchies for retrieval, one could search for records that deal specifically with *blanket chests*, for example, but could also expand the search by selecting the broader term *chests*. The expressive nature of the classification notation (i.e., the fact that a longer CN is indicative of greater specificity) allows the automatic retrieval of records dealing with chests and all of its narrower terms.

The first edition of the AAT contains 23 of 41 planned hierarchies. These include hierarchies in the first six facets, as well as Tools and Equipment, Hardware and Joints, Furniture, Image and Object Genres, Drawings, Photographs, and Document Types. The remaining hierarchies are expected to be issued in 1992 along with updates to the first edition.

As well as the hierarchical display, the AAT includes an alphabetical listing of terms that serves as an index to the hierarchies and provides other information about each term, as shown in Figure 3. Included in the alphabetic display are standard thesaurus conventions such as Scope Notes (SN) and synonyms of the descriptor (UF). Also included to the right of each descriptor are codes indicating whether the term appears in one of five major sources; in this case, "L" is LCSH and "N" is *Revised Nomenclature for Museum Cataloging.* [2]

The AAT allows the use of the singular form of descriptors for certain applications, such as the description of objects in museum catalogs. The singular form, tagged ALT, i.e., alternate term, is shown in Figure 3. The alternate term convention is also used to provide a different part of speech for some terms (e.g., *Impressionist* ALT: *Impressionism; painting* ALT: *painted).* This is useful for combining adjectives from one facet with nouns from another facet.

Postcoordination vs. Precoordination

The British Standards Institution's thesaurus construction guidelines recommend that "terms should represent simple or unitary concepts as far as possible, and compound terms should be factored into simpler elements except when this is likely to affect the user's understanding". [3] Following this principle, the AAT is constructed in such a way that each descriptor can be used as an access point in its own right or as a building block of indexing terms as needed.

As a general rule, compound phrases that contain descriptors from two or more facets are not enumerated in the AAT. For example, the phrase "Byzantine churches" contains descriptors from the "Styles and Periods" and "Objects" facets. Given the nearly infinite number of possible term combinations, even phrases that occur frequently in the field, such as "painted Greek vases," are factored into single-word descriptors.

This policy has proven beneficial to many object and visual collections databases that often apply the AAT in a postcoordinate fashion, with separate fields for style, object name, and material. As a result of collaboration between the AAT and the Library of Congress MARC Network and Development Office, a new subject field, 654—Faceted Topical Term, allows users of thesauri like the AAT to enter faceted indexing terms into a MARC record.

The AAT may be used in precoordinate systems, in which descriptors are combined syntactically by the indexer at the time of indexing, or it may be used in postcoordinate systems, in which terms are assigned separately by the indexer and combined at the time of searching. In either case, the building-block approach to thesaurus construction allows greater precision in cataloging and retrieval, since new combinations of terms can be made as needed rather than being governed by a fixed universe of precoordinated headings as one finds in LCSH.

For precoordinate indexing, the faceted structure of the AAT forms the basis of the syntactic rules according to which indexing statements are created. A protocol for combining descriptors and for coding them in MARC is given in the first edition of the AAT.

LCSH and the AAT

Some of the basic differences between subject heading systems like LCSH and thesauri were clearly explained in Mary Dykstra's [4] series of articles. The most significant difference between the AAT and LCSH is that the former, following BSI [5] and the draft NISO [National Information Standards Organization] thesaurus standard, [6] contains no precoordinated subject headings. Each descriptor is a single semantic unit. Other differences between the AAT and LCSH are summarized in Table 4.

TABLE 4. COMPARISON OF AAT AND LCSH

AAT	LCSH
Hierarchical Arrangement	Alphabetical Arrangement
Single Concepts	Single & Composite
Faceted Terms	Precoordinated Terms
Consistent Term Form	Inconsistency in Heading Form
Direct Word Order	Inverted & Direct Word Order
Strict Literary Warrant & Expert Review	Headings Established by Precedent
Use Fors are Synonyms	*Use Fors* are Synonyms or Narrower Concepts
Qualifiers Used to Distinguish Homographs	Qualifiers Used to Distinguish Homographs & Indicate Context
Complete Syndetic Structure	Incomplete Syndetic Structure
Strong User Input Process	Weak User Input Process

The AAT strives for compatibility with LCSH as far as is possible, but because of the extent of divergence between the two controlled vocabularies, the number of descriptors that the AAT can derive from LCSH is limited. What the AAT has done, however, is to maintain online all source information on each of its descriptors. This data is part of the term record within the AAT database and is distributed in the 670 field of the AAT/MARC RLIN authority record.

Nearly 2000 sources have been used in the development of the thesaurus, but five major sources, including LCSH, are systematically tracked. The form of the LC heading as well as its status, i.e., whether it is an established heading or a USE reference, is recorded.

In my study of AAT's mapping policy, which appears in the recently published *Beyond the Book: Extending MARC for Subject Access*, I reported that AAT terms map in some way to about 5 percent of LC subject headings, and that approximately 17 percent of AAT terms have a match in LCSH. [7] The types of matches are summarized in Table 5.

TABLE 5. TYPES OF MATCHING BETWEEN LCSH AND AAT

- *Established Heading to Descriptor:*
  - LCSH: **Abbeys**
  - AAT: **abbeys**
- *See/USE Reference to Descriptor:*
  - LCSH: Working drawings
    - USE **Architecture— Designs and plans —Working drawings**
  - AAT: **working drawings**
- *Established Heading to AAT Use For:*
  - LCSH: **Sugar factories**
  - AAT: **sugar refineries**
    - UF sugar factories
- *See/USE Reference to AAT Use For:*
  - LCSH: Chapels royal
    - USE **Chapels, Court**
  - AAT: chapels royal
    - USE **royal chapels**
- *Precoordinate Heading to Focus Term:*
  - LCSH: **Roads, Brick**
  - AAT: **roads**
    - **(+ brick)**

If this study of the AAT database were repeated today, I am convinced that I would find an even greater percentage of mapping. I say this because the boundaries of the discipline covered by the AAT are not clear. The new art history, for example, requires information from many disciplines—history, sociology, psychology, and even science. In addition, user input has led to the incorporation of many terms that may seem outside the scope of the AAT, but are necessary to our users nonetheless.

Recognizing that LCSH is the de facto standard for subject access in the library world, mapping processes such as those undertaken by the AAT are necessary to ease the transition from subject heading systems to thesauri, and to allow for the coexistence of multiple vocabularies.

Over the years, LCSH has been criticized as inconsistent, unpredictable, outdated, and unresponsive to user needs. It is widely held that LCSH generally lacks any applied linguistic basis. The introduction to the eleventh edition itself clearly states that the form of headings follows policy in place at a particular time. [8] While LCSH acknowledges the problem of lack of consistency, it is difficult to implement changes in the structure of the vocabulary given the thousands of LCSH users and the millions of records containing LC subject headings.

One is no longer limited to LCSH for subject description and access, however. The *USMARC Code List for Relators, Sources, Description Conventions*, published by the Library of Congress, identifies all of the thesauri and subject headings or term lists approved for use in the subject fields of the USMARC formats. [9] About thirty lists, including the AAT, have been authorized for cataloging and indexing purposes.

Object Cataloging and the AAT

With few exceptions, the AAT was first applied not in libraries by users of LCSH and the MARC format, but rather by curators of object and visual collections trying to modernize access to their collections, which had formerly been inventoried in rather rudimentary and idiosyncratic ways.

Many of these initial users were novices at automation and had no training in library or information science. Instead, they were individuals with a high level of subject expertise working in museum and original document cataloging environments. Needless to say, the AAT staff had to overcome the culture shock that these groups felt when confronted with the ways of the library world. We also had to form close ties with these groups during the development of the thesaurus. One of the ways we do so is through the Candidate Term process. This provides a formal opportunity for user groups to contribute to the AAT. A Candidate Term Form submitted by one user institution is shown in Figure 4.

To foster the sharing of information among art-related institutions, a growing number of constituencies have been looking to the MARC format itself or towards developing MARC-compatible databases. PC-based systems like Mina-

---

Architecture
Thesaurus

AAT
Candidate Term
FAX # 413 - 458 - 3757 **Form**

AAT · Getty Art History Information Program · 62 Stratton Road · Williamstown, MA 01267 · 413-458-2151

Please use this form to submit Candidate Terms to the AAT office. Be sure to complete section I. Section II is optional. Section III is for AAT staff use.

Submitting organization: Guggenheim Museum

Contact person: Nancy Spector   Date: 2/5/90

SECTION I	**SECTION II [Optional]**
Suggested Term: Situationist (Post 1945 Styles & Periods)	Suggested definition: _____ _____
Source of Term: (please give specific indication of at least one place where the term was found; if in text, give full citation, including page numbers; include photocopy if possible.)	Suggested Lead-in Term(s): _____ _____
Phillips, Christopher, "Hommage to a Phantom Avant-Garde: The Situationist avant-garde"	Suggested Broader Term: _____ _____
ART IN AMERICA vol 77, No 10 (October '89)	Suggested Related Term(s): _____ _____
pp 182-113, 239 _____ _____	Comments: (continue on reverse or attach sheet if necessary) An important French avant-garde, post-war movement. Precursors to today's

SECTION III [For AAT Office Use]

AAT Editor(s): EB Sanders   Date: 2/21/93

☒ Accepted form of term: Situationist   AAT hier.: SP

AAT Broader Term: < post 1945 fine arts styles & movements > Spc. Thes.: _____

AAT Scope Note:

☐ Accepted as Lead-in Term to AAT Term: _____

☐ Not accepted: ☐ Use existing AAT Term(s): _____
           ☐ Postcoordinate from AAT Term(s): _____
           ☐ Sufficient literary warrant not found. Please supply further information.
           ☐ Term is outside scope of AAT   ☐ Other

AAT Comments:

Figure 4. AAT Candidate Term Form.

ret and MicroMarc AMC [Archives and Manuscripts Control] are beginning to appear on the market; these systems have MARC conversion capabilities for both importing and exporting MARC records. In addition, the Library of Congress MARC Network and Development Office is very open to modifying the MARC format to meet the needs of these nonbook constituencies.

Complexity of the AAT

I have painted a rosy picture of the AAT because I strongly believe in the methodology by which the thesaurus has been constructed and is being maintained. Its application, however, is a complex process to which much of the AAT staff's energy is currently being devoted.

For many areas of application of the AAT, cataloging rules are either nonexistent or idiosyncratic. Indeed, the crafts of subject analysis and descriptive cataloging, which were once the exclusive domain of librarians, are experiencing a revival of interest among curators of museums, archivists, slide curators, and other groups, as they begin to identify the requirements of access to their collections.

A potential problem with the faceted approach of the AAT is that common compound phrases are not included in the thesaurus and are left to the cataloger to formulate. The open-ended nature of the vocabulary can be problematic in terms of consistency in indexing. The AAT is considering the addition of certain compound phrases as lead-in vocabulary to the component terms, which would provide some degree of control over the formulation of indexing terms.

The AAT manual of editorial policy, which explains the rules and guidelines used in its development, is being made available. The "Guide to Use" section of the first edition of the thesaurus also describes some of these policies.

The existing application rules for combining terms are quite general and have yet to be refined for constituencies using the AAT. The AAT staff plays an active role in professional organizations, providing workshops and orientations on using the thesaurus. The staff also works with institutions on an individual level to offer advice on how the AAT might fit into their collections management systems. We are confident that media-specific application guidelines will be developed as the AAT continues these practices.

The art library community has been supportive of the work of the AAT, but for varying reasons, mainly economic, is reluctant to commit itself to using the AAT. AAT staff members are trying to portray the thesaurus not so much as an alternative to LCSH, but rather as a challenge and an opportunity to the library community and others involved in providing art information to their constituencies. Thesauri and subject heading systems should be more than mere housekeeping tools serving the needs of catalogers; they should rather be tools that first and foremost serve the end-user.

Advice on Thesaurus Development

I was asked to provide you with some advice on undertaking such a project, i.e., developing a controlled vocabulary in a specialized domain. Let me first say that it has taken over ten years and annual budgets often over half-a-million dollars to produce the first edition of the *Art and Architecture Thesaurus*. This time and money have allowed for, among other things, rigorous expert review of the terminology, the use of state-of-the-art technology, and the development of a multilingual project and training programs in the use of the thesaurus.

In addition to the prerequisite of stable funding, I offer the following advice to anyone developing a thesaurus.

1) *Consult subject experts.* It is essential to establish a core advisory group of people with subject expertise in the discipline covered by the thesaurus. No one will be an expert in all areas of the terminology, so it is important to maintain a list of people who can be called upon to review not only the choice of a descriptor, but also the hierarchical structure of the vocabulary. An extensive bibliography of published sources is also important.

2) *Follow thesaurus construction standards.* The guidelines published by BSI and NISO are excellent starting points in understanding how a thesaurus should be constructed and are essential reading for any thesaurus developer. [10, 11]

3) *Consult thesaurus experts and people who have built thesauri.* Thesaurus standards cannot address the individual nuances of a particular subject area, and so most thesauri are interpretations of the standards. A good printed thesaurus will have a wealth of information in its introductory material, but it is also important to talk with thesaurus developers about their editorial practices as well as to those who have used and studied thesauri.

4) *Establish a base of "test" users.* It is important to maintain a close relationship with those who will be using the final product. They will provide invaluable comment on the thesaurus as they apply the terminology in indexing and searching.

5) *Incorporate existing term lists/authorities.* National standards like LCSH and controlled vocabularies that are already in use in the field are good sources of terms for the thesaurus. It is important to maintain compatibility with such lists whenever possible.

6) *Develop application rules.* Developing good terminology and a sound structure for the thesaurus really constitute just half the battle. The application of the thesaurus in a consistent and optimal manner is an elusive goal. Application guidelines are essential, as is editorial review of indexing based on the thesaurus.

NOTES

1. *Art and Architecture Thesaurus.* New York: Oxford University Press, 1990.

2. *Revised Nomenclature for Museum Cataloging: A Revised and Expanded Version of Robert G. Chenhall's System for Classifying Man-Made Objects.* Nashville, Tenn.: American Association for State and Local History, 1989.

3. British Standards Institution. *Guidelines for the Establishment and Development of Monolingual Thesauri.* London: BSI, 1987. (BS 5723), p. 9.

4. Dykstra, Mary, "LC Subject Headings Disguised as a Thesaurus," *Library Journal* 113, no. 4 (March 1, 1988), pp. 42-46; "Can Subject Headings Be Saved?" *Library Journal* 113, no. 15 (September 15, 1988), pp. 55-58.

5. British Standards Institution.

6. National Information Standards Organization. *Proposed American National Standard Guidelines for Thesaurus Construction, Structure, and Use.* Gaithersburg, MD: NISO, 1990.

7. Whitehead, Cathleen, "Mapping LCSH into Thesauri: The AAT Model" in Toni Petersen and Pat Molholt, eds., *Beyond the Book: Extending MARC for Subject Access.* Boston: G.K. Hall, 1990, pp. 81-95.

8. *Library of Congress Subject Headings.* 11th ed. Washington, D.C.: Library of Congress, 1988, Vol. 1, p. viii.

9. Library of Congress, Network Development and MARC Standards Office. *USMARC Code List for Relators, Sources, Description Conventions.* Washington, D.C.: Library of Congress, 1988.

10. British Standards Institution.

11. National Information Standards Organization.

THE TECHNICAL
SERVICES MANAGER'S PERSPECTIVE:
INTRODUCTION

University libraries have a research orientation similar to that of the Library of Congress. Their patrons are educated, and the choice between laymen's and scholars' terminology is generally not an issue. Do catalogers in academic libraries accept the standard bibliographic product uncritically? The number of them that registered for the Congress leads me to believe that many would prefer not to, but are forced to by their technical services managers.

In seeking a speaker to present the manager's perspective, I did not have to go very far, as we have an expert on the St. John's campus.

Mary Parr is Assistant Dean for Technical Services at St. John's University Libraries. A couple of decades ago, she served as chairman of the Department of Library Science at St. John's, and is now on the adjunct faculty of both St. John's and Columbia's library schools. During the past three decades, she has taught in just about every library school on the east coast.

The credit for the title of this Congress is probably due to Mary. In 1984, she presented a colloquium at St. John's entitled "The Quintessence and the Quagmire of Serials." I vividly recall her first words: "I preach heresy." I also recall bursting with laughter as she recounted tales of monthly serials that appear 13 times per year and other librarians' delights. A particularly memorable observation made by Mary that I found worth recording was "More serials catalogers than any other group commit suicide."

I am sure that you will find Mary Parr's heretical words entertaining and stimulating, as she is one of the brightest and funniest ladies in the cataloging business.

B.H.W.

STANDARD CATALOGING DATA
AND THE ACADEMIC LIBRARY:
THE TECHNICAL SERVICES MANAGER'S
POINT OF VIEW

Mary Y. Parr
Assistant Dean for Technical Services
St. John's University Libraries
Jamaica, New York 11439

It is my intention to question, which in itself may be considered heresy. Were I to answer the questions which I am about to ask, certainly some would dislike the replies sufficiently to consider them heresy. I would like to quote Thomas Hobbes in this regard. In chapter eleven of *Leviathan* (1651), he wrote, "They that approve a private opinion, call it opinion; but they that dislike it, heresy."

One reason I do not propose to answer what I ask is that I believe that libraries are much like apples. They have many common properties; however, they also have differences. I do not know the size, shape, texture, or color of your "apple"; therefore, each of you must answer these and other hard questions based on the unique as well as the common properties of your library.

Inconsistencies and Errors in Cataloging Copy

The following questions are based on some obvious and recurring inconsistencies and/or downright errors in standard bibliographic data.

Question 1:

A man named Marvin Richard O'Connell wrote a book entitled *The Counter Reformation, 1559-1610*, which is volume four (4) of *The Rise of Modern Europe*. Originally this book was classified and Cuttered as follows: D 228 .R4. When additional copies of this title were purchased, the classification and Cutter appeared as follows: D 228 .O26 1974. The questions are these. Do you pull the original and redo? Do you put additional copies under the same call number as the first? Do you hold copies of the same title under two classification numbers? Does it bother you that if you do, copies of the same title will not shelve together?

Question 2:

A well known and long-lived index was originally classed AI 3. Somewhere along the line, it became Z. The question is: Do you go back to the first volume and relabel and change all other parts of the equation, or do you simply continue to use AI 3?

Question 3:

Selections from the Koran was produced by Ikbal Ali Shah. It was published by Octagon Press in 1980. When the bibliographic record is searched, it is noted that the book has been given the number BP 110 1980. In consulting the Library of Congress classification schedule, we learn that Cuttering should not be used either for selections from or for the complete work, which is classed in BP 109. In practice, however, LC has assigned Cutter numbers to about twenty-five percent (25%) of works classified in both BP 109 and BP 110. Do you leave this number alone, as the schedule says you should, or do you Cutter?

Question 4:

What do you do when series are sometimes traced? When titles and authors in a series are unique, how can you locate which parts of the series you own, other than by securing a list of the titles and authors in the series and checking them one by one? Are you willing to spend this kind of time/money on this kind of verification?

Question 5:

You have the book in your hand, the pages are clearly numbered, and there are 171. The bibliographic record says 117. This is obviously a typographical error. Will you change it?

Question 6:

Downloading/Uploading Online Databases and Catalogs is the title of the proceedings of the 1985 Congress for Librarians, which was published by Pierian Press. The LC class number printed in the Cataloging in Publication Data on the verso of the title page is Z6374.7. In the Fifth edition (1980) of the LC schedules for *Bibliography and Library Science*, we learn that Z6374 is to be assigned to "Other special topics" in subject bibliography relating to Jews. The first-named editor of the book, Bella Hass Weinberg, writes extensively on Judaica librarianship. Is it useful to your user community to class downloading as a special topic in Judaica bibliography? Or should you look for the correct number in the schedule for library science? Although the LC MARC record may be revised, the erroneous class number is permanently printed in the book, and many paraprofessionals will copy it without questioning it. Is there an advantage to having the same incorrect class number throughout the nation's libraries?

Question 7:

Cataloging Service Bulletin (Number 51, Winter 1991, p. 57) says that "The

Library [i.e., the Library of Congress] has discontinued making additional changes to the call number field (050) of MARC book records and to its shelflist to adjust either Cutter numbers for subsequent changes in main entry or title or publication dates as originally assigned at the time of CIP cataloging." My question to you is: Can you/will you live with this?

The first four of these examples are inconsistencies. And while one of my colleagues tells me with some regularity that consistency is the hobgoblin of little minds, he misquotes Emerson who wrote "A foolish consistency is the hobgoblin of little minds" ("Self-Reliance," in: Ralph Waldo Emerson, *Essays*, 1841). Another and perhaps a more useful quotation in terms of inconsistencies in bibliographic data can be found in No. 162 of the *Spectator*, in which Joseph Addison wrote, "Nothing that is not a real crime makes a man appear so contemptible and little in the eyes of the world as inconsistency."

Questions for the Technical Services Manager

The ways in which you answer the questions I have posed as well as other questions and their corollaries may well be based on another series of questions, such as: How competent is the head of cataloging? Do you trust his/her judgment? How pragmatic is he/she? Do you have a sufficient number of senior/competent catalog librarians? What is the caliber of the support staff in your copy cataloging unit? How much training time have you put into that staff? How much more are you willing to put? Based on the answers to these questions, how much authority are you willing to give in regard to "editing" and to whom? What does it cost your organization to revise standard data? How much are you willing/able to spend? Where is the break-even point?

All these and a myriad of others are the questions that managers must ask themselves and others on an almost daily basis. The eventual answers must produce the satisfaction of a job well done, while minimizing the frustration of do and redo. In order to determine whether to accept or reject standard bibliographic data, each manager must ask and answer the question posed by Lewis Carroll in Chapter 6 of *Through The Looking-Glass*: "The question is," said Humpty Dumpty, "which is to be master—that's all." Does the central bibliographic record control you, or do you control the record?

Addendum

Personal Opinion Only:

It was my intent to ask rather than answer questions based on examples of problems created by standard bibliographic data; however, I have been requested to answer them in this addendum. I do so using my own philosophy, being guided, at least in part, by the unique characteristics of the libraries for which I am responsible: main and branch collections of a university library with holdings of 1,000,000 volumes.

Question 1:

The first question raised concerned the variation in the Cuttering of Marvin Richard O'Connell's book entitled *The Counter Reformation, 1559-1610.* It was first given the Cutter .R4 and subsequently .O26. On a quick first glance it might be assumed that .R4 came from the author's middle name, but on more thorough investigation it is obvious that it came from the series title, *The Rise of Modern Europe*, as *The Counter Reformation* is volume four of that series. The fact that the feature heading for the class number D228 is *Modern History. General Works. Compends* confirms this.

In conscience, there is no quick fix. It needs to be determined whether this book came to the library as a result of a series standing order, or whether there was a firm order for this specific title, quite independent of any others of the series. If it proves to be part of a standing order, each title in the series should be checked to determine how it has been handled *and* the standing order file should be marked in such a way that all of the time and effort now being expended does not have to be expended again when questions arise about other volumes.

Because I find it difficult to shelve copies of the same book in different locations, I would settle on one Cutter or another (not both), basing my selection almost entirely on the findings in order file records and holdings information. (Obviously the additional copy could simply be recorded on the .R4 Cutter record, but, more likely, earlier copies would be pulled and changed to .O26.)

Question 2:

A well known and long-lived index originally classed AI3 became Z. For me, this is one of the easier questions with one of the most expensive answers. Since I hold no brief for indexes in AI3, and because standard bibliographic data now uses Z primarily for indexes, I would pull *all* volumes, relabel, and reshelve them in the Z class (despite the current dissatisfaction with materials classed Z rather than in their specific subject classification).

Question 3:

Selections from the Koran was prepared by Ikbal Ali Shah. The LC bibliographic record gives it the number BP 110 1980. A non-Cuttered call number is a dilemma to staff and users, especially when many titles in the same class *are* Cuttered. Another consideration in my situation (a larger library with extensive holdings in B) is that many religious texts are published without dates, making subarrangement of the class number by a Cutter for editor's name preferable. A related point is that several editions of a classic text may be published within one year, making the assignment of a unique call number based on date cumbersome (1980a, 1980b, etc.). Other holdings in our library in this class would be examined, and local past practice would determine the decision.

Question 4:

The whole issue of tracing series is a knotty one. All serials catalogers will be quick to detail the problems involved. In general I accept the record, traced or not, as it stands, although on occasions, particularly in the sciences, it is a regrettable decision.

Question 5:

The book in your hand has 171 pages. The record says it has 117. Would I change it? Probably the answer is yes, although it is far from a top priority.

Question 6:

In St. John's University Libraries, a trip to the catalog or to the shelves will reveal that *Downloading/Uploading Online Databases and Catalogs* has been classed Z 674.7, for which the feature heading in the LC schedules is "Library information networks—General works." Obviously, the CIP information printed in the book has been ignored. This is a reflection of both a local policy and the fact that the LC MARC record was revised. The printed LC card features the class number Z 674.7 as well, so it is possible that the one in the book represents a misprint introduced by the publisher rather than an LC error. While LC often revises its MARC records and its printed cards, publishers have not been known to recall books with errors in CIP data.

In response to the question, "Is there an advantage to having the same incorrect class number throughout the nation's libraries?" I would have to observe that such a consistency would be a foolish one.

Question 7:

Cataloging Service Bulletin says that "The Library has discontinued making additional changes to the call number field (050) of MARC book records and to its shelflist to adjust either Cutter numbers for subsequent changes in main entry or title or publication dates as originally assigned at the time of CIP cataloging." This information was provided by the Library of Congress at the beginning of 1991. It is too soon to see the full impact of this decision. A good guess would be that smaller libraries may not be bothered much by it. Larger libraries that acquire more esoteric and/or scholarly materials may find it a policy which is difficult to accept.

The OCLC Perspective:
Introduction

OCLC, the Online Computer Library Center, was the first bibliographic utility and is currently the largest. Its founder, Frederick Kilgour, did not believe in the need for authority control, but in recent years there has been an attempt to create a consistent bibliographic database. In searching OCLC online, only one master record—usually that of the Library of Congress—is displayed for each work, regardless of the number of libraries that have input records for it. OCLC allows for local modification of the master bibliographic record, but the changes made are not accessible to all users of the system.

If tampering with the standard bibliographic product were to become widespread, what would be the implications for a bibliographic utility such as OCLC? We are fortunate to have a top-level staff member of OCLC addressing this question.

Liz Bishoff is Director, OCLC Online Union Catalog Product Management Division. She is responsible for strategic product planning and product management for the OCLC Cataloging, Interlibrary Loan and Union List systems. Prior to coming to OCLC, Ms. Bishoff was the Principal Librarian for Support Services at Pasadena, California Public Library, with responsibility for management of technical services, circulation, and automated services. Liz has also been a public library director, school media specialist and cataloger in her 20-year library career.

Liz holds an MLS from Rosary College and has done post-graduate work in public administration.

Ms. Bishoff was unable to present her paper at the Congress, and OCLC sent a very able substitute.

Glenn Patton is Consulting Product Support Specialist in the Cataloging and Database Services Group at OCLC. He has spent 10 years engaged in support, training, and product development activities for the OCLC Cataloging Subsystem. These activities have included preparation and presentation of training workshops for the MARC formats, preparation of documentation for OCLC users, and participation in the design process for enhancements to the OCLC Online System. He has had a major role in the incorporation of changes to the USMARC format into the Online System.

He is currently involved in the project which will completely redesign and reimplement the OCLC Online System. He had primary responsibility for user-apparent aspects of OCLC's activities in the Authorities Implementation of the Linked Systems Project. He is OCLC's representative to the Linked Systems Project Applications Committee and worked with various national and international standards activities related to bibliographic data and data exchange.

Mr. Patton serves as OCLC's liaison to the ALA ALCTS Committee on Cataloging: Description and Access and to the ALCTS AV Committee. He is completing a term as a member of the MARBI Committee. He is also OCLC's liaison to the Online Audiovisual Catalogers and has recently served as Chair of that organization.

Prior to coming to OCLC in 1980, he spent 11 years as Music and Fine Arts Librarian at Illinois Wesleyan University in Bloomington, Illinois.

B.H.W.

MASTER BIBLIOGRAPHIC RECORD VS. LOCAL BIBLIOGRAPHIC RECORD— WHO NEEDS WHAT?: AN OCLC PERSPECTIVE

Liz Bishoff [1]
Director, Online Union Catalog
Product Management

Glenn Patton
Consulting Product Support Specialist
Cataloging Services Section
OCLC
6565 Frantz Road, Dublin, OH 43017-0702

Master Record Architecture

The issue of which approach to bibliographic database architecture is best may be as old as the breath mint battle—"Is it a breath mint or is it a candy?" The question of whether a master record architecture or a local-copy database architecture best meets the cataloging needs of U.S. libraries has been discussed or, one might say, argued for nearly two decades. Both approaches have been successfully implemented in both bibliographic utilities and local systems. OCLC and many local systems have implemented the master record architecture, where a single bibliographic record exists for each unique item. Libraries modify the master record for local use and add holdings information to it, but the master record remains as initially created. RLIN, Utlas, and Autographics are networks that, in contrast to OCLC, have developed systems based on retaining the local copy of a bibliographic record, which the source library can retrieve online for future modification and reuse.

The decision regarding whether to build a bibliographic system based on a master record or local copy depends on user need, the cataloging environment, technical capabilities, and economics. In the late sixties, when Fred Kilgour and the pioneering librarians from the original Ohio college libraries that formed the Ohio College Library Center were developing the OCLC shared cataloging system, disk storage space was costly, database management systems were primitive, and use of the MARC [machine-readable cataloging] communication format was a pioneering effort. No one was making use of MARC records in a shared environment at that time. The model of shared cataloging proposed by the Ohio college libraries was new. The user community was homogeneous, with similar needs. They were all academic libraries, they were all using Library of Congress cataloging copy, they all used catalog cards, and most important, they all wanted and needed to reduce the amount of original cataloging they were doing. A system that allowed libraries to share cataloging, produce cards, and reduce staff in a cost-effective manner could be built in the late sixties using the computer technology of the time. That system was based on the single master record architecture.

Systems that followed in the footsteps of OCLC built on the pioneering efforts of those original Ohio college libraries. They learned from what the OCLC system did; they provided many of the same basic capabilities and were able to offer new ones—enhanced searching, new displays, and retention of local cataloging information. By the mid-seventies, competing bibliographic services emerged. These services were developed based on the library needs and environment of that period. Catalog cards were still the dominant form of bibliographic retrieval in libraries. Use of bibliographic utilities was expanding beyond academic and research libraries to all types of libraries. Retrospective conversion and reclassification programs were growing. Computer technology was changing rapidly, with the cost of disk storage dropping. Database management software to support complex bibliographic search requirements and large databases became more readily available.

We certainly could continue to discuss whether OCLC's decision to base the Online System on a master record architecture was the best approach for the network to take. Rather than do that, I think we should be asking if the approach has allowed libraries to accomplish what they need to do and, perhaps a more important question: Will a master record architecture serve the future bibliographic needs of OCLC member libraries? To both questions, we would respond a resounding 'yes.'

Growth of OCLC

In the past 20 years, OCLC membership has grown from those original Ohio libraries to over 4,400 cataloging libraries. OCLC member libraries use its cataloging subsystem to process more than 16 million items each year. The database has grown to 23 million records, and there are more than 350 million holding symbols attached to those bibliographic records. [2] OCLC records support thousands of local systems, are the foundation of book catalogs, COM [computer output microfilm] catalogs, and CD-ROM [compact disk-read only memory] catalogs. The records are used by several national libraries, including the Library of Congress, the Government Printing Office, the National Agricultural Library, and the British Library. The initial goal of reducing original cataloging by member libraries has been met, with the majority of OCLC libraries realizing a 94% hit rate. [3] Member libraries are sharing cataloging and are able to obtain pre-filed catalog cards, as well as machine-readable copies of their cataloging.

Beyond the original goals, the OCLC system has evolved into the world's largest bibliographic database, supporting not only the member libraries' cataloging needs, but also resource-sharing activities, all based on the single master bibliographic record architecture.

Customizing OCLC Records

Recognizing that the master record puts constraints on some activities, OCLC has introduced system capabilities that reduce the limitations of the master record. The CONSER and Enhance programs allow participating libraries to make permanent changes to the master record through special authorization. [4] Minimal-level records can be upgraded. Medical libraries are able to add NLM [National Library of Medicine] classification and MeSH [medical] subject headings to the master record. CJK [Chinese, Japanese and Korean script] users can add vernacular data, and a group of French university libraries are authorized to add French subject headings.

With the introduction of the PRISM service, all OCLC cataloging libraries will be able to add classification numbers and subject headings to master records that lack this data. [5] Several new projects are underway, including a pilot project to allow member libraries to add table-of-contents information to monographic records, and a cooperative project with the Library of Congress and member libraries to add subject headings to individual works of fiction. Over the years, tapeload capabilities have been enhanced to allow for the merger of specific data into the master record, thus enriching that bibliographic record.

Even with all these changes, the needs of some libraries were not met by the single master record architecture. While 4,000 libraries use the OCLC system with a 95% satisfaction rating, [6] some libraries felt that access to their local cataloging was necessary. Those libraries had to look to other options.

Changing Needs of Libraries

Let us now turn to the question: Will the master bibliographic record meet libraries' cataloging needs during the next decade? As indicated earlier, we feel that it will. Not only will it continue to meet the needs of the libraries who have used it for the last two decades, but it will also meet the changing needs of those libraries who have required online access to a local record. Why are we so confident in this position? You might say, "Well, you have to be, after all, you work for OCLC." Certainly there has to be some truth to that, but let us share with you some evidence that supports our position that the master record will be the best option for U.S. libraries into the nineties.

In 1989, Jerry Lowell of the Yale University Library surveyed the technical services directors of the 25 largest research libraries on the topic of local systems and bibliographic utilities in 1992. The results of his survey were published in the July 1990 issue of *The Journal of Academic Librarianship*. [7] Some of the findings are:

- by 1992, the majority of the respondents will be using multiple bibliographic utilities, seeking the highest hit rate at the lowest possible cost;
- by 1992, the majority of the respondents indicated, their official bibliographic record will be the record on their local system, not the record on the bibliographic utility;
- respondents indicated that they will be acquiring bibliographic information at the time that an item is ordered, rather than after it is received; and
- by 1992, the majority of the respondents expect to be creating original cataloging on their local system and uploading that information to a bibliographic utility.

Jerry Lowell goes on to explain that the introduction of the online public access catalog and the closing of card catalogs has allowed libraries to use multiple sources of bibliographic information more easily. The bibliographic record on the local system replaces the catalog card. The bibliographic maintenance component of the local system supports timely revision and updating of bibliographic records at little or no additional cost. It is no longer important to store the most up-to-date version of the library's local bibliographic record on a bibliographic utility. The importance of participating in the national database has shifted from providing local cataloging information, which is generally important only to the owning library, to supporting cooperative programs and resource-sharing activities. The bibliographic utility no longer serves as the library's official catalog, but rather as a source of cataloging copy, as a means of sharing cataloging copy, and as a means of supporting cooperative programs.

Local Systems Survey

If we know where the largest of our libraries are going, can we expect that other libraries will follow the same pattern? Because OCLC has a diverse user population, we have to be careful not to assume that all libraries have the same needs. To help determine member library cataloging needs, OCLC surveyed 600 member libraries that use the cataloging subsystem regarding their use of local systems and the OCLC cataloging system. As of May 1990, 48% of all OCLC libraries had installed a local system. An additional 26% of the responding libraries indicated that they will have installed a local system within three years. By 1993, 100% of the academic research libraries expect to have a local system, while 80% of academic, 86% of public, and 69% of the other libraries expect to own a local system. Eighty-six percent of the libraries expect to export/download records from OCLC to their local system. Twenty-eight percent of libraries that own local systems currently transfer bibliographic records as part of the acquisition process. Nearly 100% of the libraries have catalog maintenance functions in their local system, and most indicated that their local system supports local record creation and editing functions. Across the different types of libraries, there is little variance in these patterns.

During the design process for the PRISM service, we discussed the issue of retention of local data in the Online Union Catalog with the various advisory committees who provide input to the development process at OCLC. While many committee members are ardent supporters of the idea of making available more holdings and locations information—local call numbers, specific location of the item, and more detailed holdings data—they are equally firm in their view that the idea of making locally edited versions of records available online in the central system is an idea whose time has come and gone.

Subsequent Updates on OCLC

We have also looked at the current system as a predictor of future use. One characteristic we study from time to time is the amount of editing done—the number of fields edited for the "produce" or "update" functions of OCLC. The last time we examined this characteristic, it was "holding steady" at between three and four edits per transaction. If one considers that two of those may be related to call number and location, and that the total number of edits includes those related to tne creation of new records, one may conclude that editing does not constitute a lot of activity on OCLC.

Equally important in this regard is the revision of a record that a library has already used—as a subsequent "update" or a subsequent "produce." Over the last three years, we have seen a 27% decline in the use of the subsequent update function on OCLC. Libraries are not coming back to modify a record that they have already used. When we ask libraries why they are not using the subsequent update function, they indicate that they are revising the record on their local system. They do not need nor can they afford to update the record on both their local system and the bibliographic utility.

Conclusions

Will many libraries find their need for local copy on the bibliographic utility reduced? Probably. It is important to note, however, that certain cooperative programs, such as preservation programs, can best be supported by the presence of specific local information in the national databases. The library community is still coming to grips with the question of what information must be stored nationally and what information is appropriate for the local system.

Within that discussion must be the issue of how to support these specialized needs within a system that everyone can afford to support and maintain.

OCLC staff will continue to enhance the network's capabilities within the master record architecture, based on what we know and continue to learn about the current and future cataloging needs of OCLC member libraries.

Improving productivity while controlling costs was what brought the original Ohio college libraries together two decades ago. The growing importance of local systems in our libraries and our lives has changed many aspects of the ways member libraries use OCLC services, but at OCLC we continue to work together with our members toward the goal of cost-effective, value-added cataloging services that enhance libraries' use of their local systems.

NOTES

1. The paper was originally scheduled to be presented by Liz Bishoff. Glenn Patton delivered the paper at the Congress, but both contributed to the text for publication.
2. The 23 millionth bibliographic record was added by the University of Illinois-Urbana/ Champaign in January 1991.
3. "OCLC Cataloging and Database Services" fact sheet, publication no. 412, October 1990.
4. The CONSER (Cooperative Online Serials) program is a cooperative effort by the library community to build a machine-readable database of authoritative serials cataloging information. Institutions participating in CONSER can upgrade serials records in the OCLC Online Union Catalog. The Enhance program allows selected OCLC users to add data to and correct data in member-input bibliographic records, and replace those records in the Online Union Catalog.
5. The PRISM Service is the name for the new OCLC Online System. Release 1 of the PRISM Service has enhanced cataloging and searching functions; other OCLC online capabilities will be migrated to the PRISM Service later.
6. OCLC Customer Satisfaction Survey, September 1990.
7. Lowell, Gerald R. "Local Systems and Bibliographic Utilities in 1992: A Large Library Perspective." *The Journal of Academic Librarianship*, 16 (July 1990): 140-144.

THE RLIN PERSPECTIVE:
INTRODUCTION

The Research Libraries Information Network is a bibliographic utility that has many different features from OCLC. One of these is the fact that all local libraries' modifications of the Library of Congress's bibliographic record can be displayed online. The Library of Congress record is, however, generally designated the "primary cluster member" or the *primum inter pares*.

RLIN's philosophy regarding local cataloging data is clearly relevant to the theme of this Congress. Having served as a technical consultant on RLIN's Hebrew capability, I have quite a few contacts on the staff; I was assured that Ed Glazier, the Bibliographic Quality Assurance Officer of the Research Libraries Group, is the most qualified person to address this topic.

Ed Glazier holds a bachelor's degree in Classical Studies from Michigan State University and a Masters in Library Science from the University of Michigan. From 1970 to 1980 he held positions of increasing responsibility at the University of Michigan Library, including Head of Serials Cataloging. (In light of Mary Parr's observation cited earlier, we are glad that he did not commit suicide!)

For the past decade, Mr. Glazier has been with RLG. Besides ensuring the quality of RLIN's bibliographic data, he serves as the network's liaison to the Bibliographic Control Committee of the Music Library Association and to Online Audiovisual Catalogers, Inc. He is also an ex-officio member of ALA's Cataloging Committee: Description and Access. Ed has contributed chapters to three books: *Retrospective Conversion of Music Materials*, *The Linked Systems Project*, and *Authority Control in Music Libraries*.

Mr. Glazier came to the Congress by way of Indianapolis, after participating in the conference of the Music Library Association.

B.H.W.

THE DISPLAY AND INDEXING
OF CUSTOMIZED CATALOG
RECORDS IN RLIN

Ed Glazier

Bibliographic Quality Assurance Officer
Research Libraries Group
1200 Villa St.
Mountain View, CA 94041-1100

Introduction

The Research Libraries Information Network (RLIN), unlike OCLC, is not a master record database. In the RLIN database, each institution's full record, reflecting any customization done by that institution, is retained online and can be maintained by the owner and viewed by all users. Records for copies of the same item at different institutions are grouped together in entities called *clusters,* based on elements of the bibliographic description. Different access points from any record within a cluster can be used to retrieve the entire cluster. The following sections provide the rationale for this architecture and details of the network's operation.

Diversity of Users

The RLIN user community is not homogeneous. While many RLIN users are located in large research libraries, many are smaller, more specialized institutions, such as the art and museum libraries that belong to the Research Libraries Group (RLG) Art and Architecture Program Committee. In addition, one must not overlook the numerous public and special libraries that also create catalog records in RLIN.

Customized Catalog Records

Many institutions strive to make their catalogs responsive to their distinct user communities. The ways in which such customization is achieved differs from catalog to catalog. A library may use subject headings that do not follow RLG standards. Such nonstandard subject headings may be used to supplement standard headings, or they may be used in place of standard headings. In this context, "nonstandard" headings are those that do not follow the RLG standards (see following section), even though they may come from a consistent, published list. Many institutions choose to add entries that are of local significance, e.g., for the fifth author of a book, who may be a faculty member, but who would not customarily receive an added entry if one followed cataloging rules and national practices strictly.

Inputting bibliographic data into a bibliographic utility allows its use by others for copy cataloging and various kinds of resource sharing, such as interlibrary loan and cooperative activities in acquisitions and preservation. Customization of the data may have positive benefits outside the institution for which it was intended. Other institutions of the same type (e.g., museum libraries) may find that a customized record created in a peer institution meets their own needs better than a record following strict national standards.

The retention of customized catalog records in RLIN is beneficial even for an institution that has a local online system. Many such institutions have not acquired a methodology for system backup (e.g., book catalog, microform) because the amount of local data present in their RLIN records permits them to rely upon RLIN as their backup catalog.

Individual researchers using a bibliographic utility may benefit from all types of customization. Serendipity often plays a part in using library catalogs, especially for users who are not very familiar with standard library practice. RLIN users may retrieve records by means of another institution's enhanced access points.

Each institution's record for the same item is retained in the RLIN database, and can be maintained by the owner and viewed by all users. Each record contains basic bibliographic data, and may also contain holdings and call number information; acquisitions data; local notes, including copy-specific notes; and additional access points, either in standard or nonstandard form.

Standards

The members of The Research Libraries Group have adopted a set of bibliographic standards outlining what may be labeled by a cataloger as a *full standard record* in the RLIN database. The RLG standards for full-level records basically follow national standards, which are usually geared towards general rather than specialized collections.

In brief, the RLG standards follow the provisions of the National Level Record requirements as laid out in the *USMARC Format for Bibliographic Data* (1988 + updates). Name and name-title access points for current input follow *Anglo-American Cataloguing Rules*, 2nd ed. (AACR2). Subject headings are required for full-level cataloging; they must come either from the Library of Congress subject heading list, the National Library of Medicine's Medical Subject Headings (MeSH), or as of February 1991, the Art and Architecture Thesaurus or other standard source, when that source has been identified at the field level.

There are no requirements for classification numbers or the use of any particular classification scheme.

As has often been stated, accepting existing bibliographic records for copy cataloging without extensive verification and modification results in substantial savings in cataloging costs by allowing paraprofessional staff to process materials with copy. This frees professional cataloging staff to concentrate on problem solving and cataloging materials for which catalog data is not available. Following standards in description and access points is a means to achieve consistency in and comprehensiveness of retrieval for the end users of catalogs.

Records meeting the RLG standards can be supplemented by additional local information. Many records contain large amounts of useful information, but the choices made in customizing may result in the records' not meeting RLG standards. While RLG and the RLIN User Services Division encourage all users to create full standard records when cataloging in RLIN, the creation of nonstandard records is permitted, so long as the record is not labeled as meeting the full standards.

RLIN Extensions to MARC

How is nonstandard data recorded and identified in RLIN records? In addition to the set of fixed and variable fields of the USMARC format, RLIN has defined a number of special extensions. Of particular importance are the extensions for access points. Each of the subject added entry fields (600-651), added entry fields (700-730), and series added entry fields (800-830) has a parallel RLIN-defined field in which a user can input subject headings, added entries, and series added entries that do not conform to national or RLG standards (see Table 1).

TABLE 1. RLIN-DEFINED FIELDS FOR LOCAL ACCESS POINTS

690	Local Subject Added Entry - Topical Term
691	Local Subject Added Entry - Geographic Name
696	Local Subject Added Entry - Personal Name
697	Local Subject Added Entry - Corporate Name
698	Local Subject Added Entry - Meeting Name
699	Local Subject Added Entry - Uniform Title
796	Local Added Entry - Personal Name
797	Local Added Entry - Corporate Name
798	Local Added Entry - Meeting Name
799	Local Added Entry - Uniform Title
896	Local Series Added Entry - Personal Name
897	Local Series Added Entry - Corporate Name
898	Local Series Added Entry - Meeting Name
899	Local Series Added Entry - Uniform Title

In addition, RLIN provides local fields for institution- or copy-specific notes and holdings data. Data entered into any of the RLIN local fields is assumed to be institution-specific and is therefore not carried over to another user's derived record during copy cataloging.

Clustering

Records for the same item are stored together in a group called a *cluster*. Clusters are created by examining certain elements of the bibliographic description of each record and combining the records that match in the defined categories into a single cluster. Table 2 lists the fields that are used for clustering in the RLIN Books file.

It is important to emphasize that records for the same item from different institutions are clustered together based on data elements from the bibliographic description, not from the access points. Most of the elements in the clustering algorithm are pieces of information that are customarily *transcribed* from an item in cataloging, such as the title, imprint, pagination, and standard numbers like ISBN (International Standard Book Number) and ISSN (International Standard Serial Number)—not elements subject to manipulation by the cataloger, such as choice and form of main entry.

The clustering process begins with *normalization* of these elements to minimize or eliminate differences in capitalization, spacing, punctuation, and tagging that have occurred over the years as a result of changes in cataloging rules. After the elements have been normalized, a series of comparisons is performed. For each data element, there is a set of rules determining what constitutes a match. Not all elements require an exact match. For example, in the Books format, the

---

TABLE 2. RLIN CLUSTERING FIELDS, BOOKS FILE

Title (245 $a $b $n $p)
($a = title; $b = remainder of title; $n = number of part/section; $p = name of part/section)

Edition statement (250 $a)

Place of publication and publisher (260 $a $b)
($a = place of publication; $b = name of publisher

Physical description (300 $a)
($a = extent [of item])

Date of publication (008/7-14 and/or 260 $c)

Library of Congress Control Number (010 $a $z)
($a = LC control number; $z = canceled/invalid LC control number)

International Standard Book Number (ISBN) (020 $a $z)
($a = ISBN; $z = canceled/invalid ISBN)

---

245 title fields are compared only on the shorter of two strings. Thus, for example, the title proper *Cataloging special materials* will match the title proper plus sub-title *Cataloging special materials : critiques and innovations.*

The combination of data elements compared for each pair of records has been designed insofar as possible to put records for the same item in one cluster and to keep records for different items out of the cluster, although neither of these goals is perfectly realized. Occasionally, some records for a single item do not cluster together, and sometimes records for different items appear in the same cluster.

Multiple Record Display (MUL)

A successful search of RLIN by most of the general indexes to the database (i.e., personal or corporate name, title word or phrase, subject word or phrase, standard numbers like ISBN, etc.) will produce a result of one or more clusters. The multiple record display (MUL) shows the main entry, title, place of publication, publisher, and date of the item in each cluster. In addition, the brief display for each record in the cluster includes indications of the following:

- the owning library (a four-character symbol for the RLIN Library Identifier (LI) plus the NUC symbol; this identifies which record belongs to which institution);[1]

- whether the record contains *cataloging data* (coded c), *acquisitions* data (a), or *both* cataloging and acquisitions data (b); (this indicates whether there is a record that can be used for copy cataloging);

- the RLIN Cataloging Category (a four-digit number indicating the degree to which a record meets the RLG standards);

- the presence of vernacular data ([CJK] - Chinese, Japanese, or Korean; [HBR] - Hebrew; [CYR] - Cyrillic; [ARB] - Arabic);

- the generation of microform—preservation master, printing master, or service copy—held by an institution (coded "a", "b", and/or "c", respectively, enclosed between asterisks);

- whether the item has been queued for preservation microfilming ("+").

This information allows a user to determine which records he may wish to see rather than having to examine every record in a cluster. The first four data elements may help an institution searching for cataloging copy to find the most useful record. For example, catalogers generally know which other institutions use the same subject heading and/or classification schemes, and they can tell from the MUL display whether a record meets their needs for inclusion or exclusion of non-roman data.

---

[1] The RLIN Library Identifier (LI) is used to request display of a particular record in a cluster. The National Union Catalog (NUC) symbol for the library may be more familiar to users than the LI; therefore both are included in the display. RLIN now has a "sho LI" command that tells a user which institution is represented by a particular LI.

Figure 1 shows an example of a MUL display. Table 3 explains the codes used in each institution's record on the MUL and primary record (PRI) displays.

FIN TW KAOTSUNG - 37 clusters

11) Chang, Chun-jung. NAN SUNG KAO–TSUNG PIEN AN CHIANG TSO YUAN
    YIN CHIH TAN TAO / Chu pan. (Tai-pei shih : Wen shih che chu pan she,
    min kuo 75 [1986])

    DCLP   (c-9118 DLC [CJK])   CASX (c-9118 CU-SB)
    CTYO   (c-9118 CtY [CJK])   CUDG (c-9118 CU-A)
    ILCO   (c-9118 ICU-FE [CJK])   MIUO (c-9118 MiU-A [CJK])

12) Li, Tang. SUNG KAO-TSUNG / Tsai pan. (Tai-pei shih : Ho lo tu
    shu chu pan she, min kuo 69 [1979])
    IAUO (c-9114 IaU [CJK]) NJRO (c-9114 NjR [CJK])

13) Lo, Yun-chih. CH'ING KAO-TSUNG T'UNG CHIH HSIN-CHIANG
    CHENG TS'E TI T'AN T'AO. (Taipei : Li jen shu chu, Min-kuo 72 [1983].)
    NYPO (a-9668 NN)

Figure 1. Portion of RLIN Multiple Record Display. Each LI-NUC group represents a separate record in the cluster. LI is the RLIN library identifier, and NUC is the National Union Catalog symbol. The presence of "[CJK]" in some LI-NUC groups indicates that the record contains Chinese, Japanese, or Korean characters. (The numeric codes are explained in Table 3.)

**TABLE 3. CODES IN RLIN MULTIPLE RECORD AND
PRIMARY RECORD DISPLAYS**

CTYO (c-9114 CtY *cba*   [CJK])

CTYO - RLIN 4-character library identifier for holding library
    (Yale East Asian Library)

c - Record type: cataloging

9114 - RLIN cataloging category

Position 1-level of authority control;   "9" – no authority control

Position 2-level of cataloging;   "1" – full level of cataloging

Position 3-level of content designation;   "1" – full level of content designation

Position 4-source of machine-readable record. "4" – RLG member online cataloging in RLIN

CtY - NUC symbol for holding library
    (Yale University)

cba - Microform generation code: service copy (c), printing master (b), and
    preservation master (a)

[CJK] - Non-Roman script indicator

The record belongs to Yale, contains cataloging data, three generations of microform, and Chinese, Japanese, or Korean data.

Primary Record Display

The primary record display (PRI) shows a brief bibliographic description of one of the records in a cluster. That record is called the *primary cluster member* (PCM) and represents what can be determined as being the most complete record in the cluster.

In addition, the PRI display includes, for each record in the cluster, the same elements that are present in the MUL display, as outlined above, i.e., the library identifier, NUC symbol, microform generation, preservation information, etc. (see Figure 2).

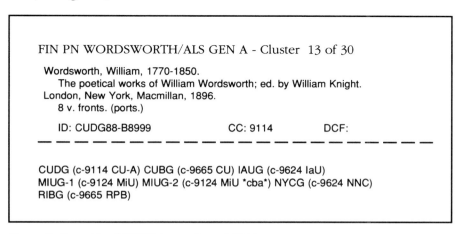

```
FIN PN WORDSWORTH/ALS GEN A - Cluster  13 of 30

Wordsworth, William, 1770-1850.
    The poetical works of William Wordsworth; ed. by William Knight.
London, New York, Macmillan, 1896.
    8 v. fronts. (ports.)

    ID: CUDG88-B8999              CC: 9114              DCF:
    ─── ── ── ── ── ── ── ── ── ── ── ── ── ── ── ── ── ── ──

CUDG (c-9114 CU-A) CUBG (c-9665 CU) IAUG (c-9624 IaU)
MIUG-1 (c-9124 MiU) MIUG-2 (c-9124 MiU *cba*) NYCG (c-9624 NNC)
RIBG (c-9665 RPB)
```

Figure 2. Example of RLIN Primary Record Display.

Any record represented in this display by an LI-NUC group can be individually displayed. The search statement chains together two search commands, separated by the slash ("/"). The command "FIN PN WORDSWORTH" translates into "Search (Find) the personal name (PN) index for the surname 'Wordsworth'." The search=qualifying command "ALS GEN A" translates into "Examine the result set of the previous search (ALSO) for any clusters in which a record has a microform generation (GEN) code of "a" for 'preservation master'."

Impact of Levels of Cataloging and Customized Records on Clustering

In an RLIN search, a cluster of records can be retrieved by any of the indexed access points within any record in the cluster. The effects of various levels of cataloging and of different types of customization on clustering are described below.

Acquisitions and Cataloging Data

RLIN is a complete technical processing system and supports acquisitions as well as cataloging. Even institutions that do not use RLIN for acquisitions may enter brief records for in-process items or for backlog control. Assuming that enough accurate bibliographic data is present, these brief records will cluster with full cataloging records. The access points in the catalog records of one institution can provide access to in-process material at another institution.

In addition, a user entering a brief record in RLIN can indicate that he wishes to be notified when a fuller record for the same item enters the database. This is done using a feature called *fuller record notification*. This feature permits users to have some degree of bibliographic control over uncataloged items while waiting for what is, in essence, automatic searching for cataloging copy when none is available at the time of the initial search.

Full Records and Minimal Level Records

An institution may choose to do minimal-level cataloging for some classes of material in order to provide some level of access to more materials. If an institution has chosen to do minimal-level cataloging for an item, the resulting record should still cluster with a full-level record for the same item. Thus, although the minimal-level record has no subject headings or added entries, the cluster containing that record will be retrieved by a search for a heading that appears only in the full-level record. The RLIN cataloging category (element cc) can be examined to determine which records in a cluster are full level (second position value "1") and which are minimal level (second position value "5").

AACR2 versus pre-AACR2

The RLIN database includes records created following the adoption of AACR2, records that predate AACR2, and records that were created following no particular cataloging code. RLG standards for retrospective conversion permit the input of standard AACR records without upgrading to AACR2. (It is generally not possible to determine from the PRI and MUL displays which record was cataloged using which set of rules.) Provided that the descriptive elements are sufficiently consistent and the records cluster together, a searcher can retrieve a cluster using either the current authorized form of a name or earlier authorized forms, as well as the name in nonstandard form. This is important in a database in which there is no authority control, and searches are not directed first through an authority file.

Microforms and Hard Copy: Preservation Information

Because the clustering algorithm is based on the descriptive elements in the cataloging record, and because Library of Congress cataloging policy for microreproductions describes the original item in the title paragraph, records for hard-copy originals and microform reproductions will cluster together. This is useful for several constituencies.

Interlibrary Loan: If someone is searching for a particular item for interlibrary loan, the RLIN display of the cluster will indicate which institutions hold hard-copy originals, and which hold microform reproductions. If format is not significant, the searcher may choose to borrow from the most convenient source. Transmitting call number and location information in interlibrary loan requests generated in RLIN saves searching time at the lending institution. Staff may proceed directly to the stacks to retrieve materials being borrowed, without having to ascertain locations and call numbers in the local catalog.

Preservation: RLIN displays indicate which generation of microform is held at each institution. This is useful in preservation work because it enables a librarian to determine whether a microform preservation master has already been produced. As mentioned above, the PRI and MUL displays contain a plus sign symbol (+) to show that an item has been queued for preservation microfilming; this is designed to obviate redundant, costly activity in this area.

If different institutions have chosen to preserve items in different ways, such as microfilming and deacidification, only a database like RLIN that retains local data can communicate the information for all institutions participating in cooperative preservation programs such as the RLG Preservation Program Committee.

Non-roman Data

Users can create RLIN records using Chinese, Japanese, Korean, Cyrillic, and Hebrew scripts; Arabic script will soon be available. However, for all records containing vernacular data, RLG standards require that some basic fields be entered also in romanized form, particularly title and imprint. The clustering of records for non-roman works is based on the data in the roman fields, since this data is common to both the roman and non-roman records in the cluster. If an institution chooses not to enter vernacular data, searching with non-roman access points will still retrieve a cluster containing its record if another institution has input a non-roman record that clusters with it. (The PRI and MUL displays enable a user to determine which records in a cluster contain non-roman characters.)

Variant Subject Headings

A search using any subject heading in any record in a cluster will retrieve the whole cluster. Assume that one institution uses LC subject headings exclusively while another uses MeSH headings. If the records cluster together on the basis of the descriptive data, a user can retrieve the entire cluster, with both of these records in it, by using either LCSH or MeSH terms in a subject search. The same holds true for two records clustered together when one contains LC subject headings and the other contains headings from the Art and Architecture Thesaurus. A search using local forms of subject headings will retrieve the cluster containing the record with the local forms as well as the records containing standard subject terms. (There is, however, no way to tell from the PRI or MUL display which record contains which headings. Subject heading information is not explicitly coded in the RLIN cataloging category: full level requires standard subject headings; base/minimal level does not.)

GLAZIER

The RLIN Database

The RLIN database is divided into nine separate bibliographic files based on the different material types encompassed by the USMARC format. The files are:

- Archives and Manuscript Control (AMC)
- Books
- Computer Files
- Maps
- Serials
- Scores (part of the USMARC Music format)
- Sound Recordings (part of the USMARC Music format)
- Visual Materials
- Citations (a clone of the USMARC Books format, containing article-level information rather than monographic data).

The features of RLIN that have been described are available for all of the above formats, with the exception of the AMC file, which contains primarily unique materials, and the Computer Files database, which is currently unclustered. To simplify the discussion, however, the examples have been drawn from the RLIN Books file, the file that contains primarily monographic textual materials.

Conclusions

RLIN was designed to accommodate a certain degree of customization in cataloging. Since all records that are clustered together can be retrieved by a search on an access point input by a single institution, users can benefit from each other's customization. This is only possible because RLIN retains the full catalog record for each institution. Although many institutions have already acquired local systems and many more are actively planning to do so, the retention of customized records and local information in the RLIN database continues to be significant to the members of the Research Libraries Group and other users of RLIN.

ACKNOWLEDGMENTS

My thanks to my colleagues in the RLIN User Services Division for their assistance in preparing this paper: Jackie Casselli, Bruce Washburn, and Gregory Whitfield for finding RLIN examples, and Arnold Arcolio and LaVonne Gallo for reviewing the text.

POSTSCRIPT

In March 1991, shortly after the conference at which this paper was delivered, several changes in the organization and direction of the Research Libraries Group were proposed. In June 1991, some of the organizational changes were approved, including a new governance structure, simplified membership categories, and the elimination of the program committee structure. The paper refers specifically to the Art & Architecture Program Committee and the Preservation Program Committee; their activities will be continued under a new administrative structure. It is of primary importance to note, however, that the decisions of the RLG Board of Governors resulted in a reaffirmation of the importance of the RLIN database and the ability to create and maintain customized records as described in this paper.

—Ed Glazier
July 1991

THE LIBRARY OF CONGRESS' PERSPECTIVE: INTRODUCTION

The Library of Congress takes a lot of flak from catalogers at other institutions, and it sometimes seems that we are all ungrateful for the great effort and expense that goes into creating LC cataloging data.

Although this conference was designed to address a theoretical question, many specific criticisms of LC cataloging have been leveled. What does the Library of Congress think about all of this? Does it view its cataloging data as standard? Does LC feel obligated to attempt to satisfy the demands of all user communities?

When I developed the initial list of speakers for this Congress, Lucia Rather, LC's Director for Cataloging, accepted my invitation. Several months ago, however, she wrote me that she was resigning her position at LC to complete her doctorate, and indicated that her representative, John D. Byrum, was willing to present the LC position. We are very honored that LC sent such a high-level staff member to address the Congress.

John Byrum has been chief of the Descriptive Cataloging Division at the Library of Congress since November 1976. He has held concurrently for the past two years the position of acting chief of the Subject Cataloging Division. His responsibilities include administrative oversight of the Library's monographic cooperative cataloging projects. Prior to his appointment at LC, Mr. Byrum worked for ten years at the Princeton University Library, first as descriptive cataloger and then as head cataloger. He holds a B.A. from Harvard College and an M.L.S. from Rutgers University.

Mr. Byrum has a longstanding interest in the profession. He served as chair of the ALA committee to create rules for the descriptive cataloging of machine-readable data files, as chairman of the Cataloging Code Revision Committee, and twice as a member of the Margaret Mann Award Citation Committee. He was also the first chair of the Resources and Technical Services Committee on International Relations, and continues to serve on that group as the LC liaison. In addition to ALA work, Mr. Byrum has been active in IFLA since the mid-1970s, contributing to the creation or revision of several International Bibliographic Standards. He is currently chair of the ISBD Review Committee and of the Section on Cataloguing's Working Group for ISBD Simplification.

Mr. Byrum has also contributed to the program of the National Information Standards Organization and is now engaged in a project to formulate an ISO standard for three-character language codes. His publications include several articles concerning the Anglo-American Cataloguing Rules, among them three resulting from an investigation sponsored by the Council on Library Resources. John Byrum is also a recipient of ALA's Esther J. Piercy Award.

B.H.W.

STANDARD CATALOGING DATA: THE VIEW FROM THE LIBRARY OF CONGRESS

John D. Byrum, Jr.
Chief, Descriptive Cataloging Division
Library of Congress
Washington, D.C. 20540

The Uses of Bibliographic Records

In August 1990, in conjunction with the annual IFLA (International Federation of Library Associations) Conference, a Seminar on Bibliographic Records was held in Stockholm, with participants from 22 countries. At the conclusion of this two-day meeting, which focused on "the uses of bibliographic information" and "links in the information chain," the conferees adopted a series of recommendations, some of which are relevant to the topic of this Congress:

1. "The national bibliographic agency should be responsible for ensuring the recording of the national published output in all media, whilst taking into account the needs of the variety of groups of users."

2. "A study should be commissioned to define the functional requirements for bibliographic records in relation to the variety of user needs and the variety of media."

3. "A study should be commissioned to identify the means for an incremental approach to record extension, improvement, and enhancement."

It is within the context of these concepts that I shall discuss the Library of Congress view of standardized cataloging data. Although I have developed much of what follows on the basis of discussions with a number of my colleagues at LC (see Acknowledgments), my remarks represent my personal views and are not an official institutional statement.

The National Bibliographic Agency

In relation to the Seminar's recommendation that the national bibliographic agency be responsible for recording the national published output in all media, I observe that the Library of Congress's cataloging output—currently, in the vicinity of 200,000 titles annually (not including MLC [minimal level cataloging])—at once both exceeds and falls short of this goal. That is, we produce bibliographic records for much of the national imprint in some media and very little in others, while also covering many titles that might be considered the responsibility of foreign national libraries. We estimate that LC's centralized cataloging program saves the nation's libraries $370 million annually.

Not unexpectedly, the nature of the cataloging standards that are in effect, among other factors, has an immediate bearing on this bibliographic output. The more elaborate and extensive the requirements, the fewer the bibliographic units that are produced, and the longer it takes to get items under bibliographic control. Yet, national libraries are finding themselves asked to catalog more and do it faster. The tension of this situation has prompted some agencies to respond by reconsidering formerly observed standards. Indeed, one major national library has within the past two or three years undertaken major cutbacks in all aspects of the cataloging its staff produces. Surely, the possibility that there might be a trend in this direction—that is, unilateral redefinition of cataloging policy and abandonment of existing standards—explains the Seminar's strong urging that national libraries continue to be responsible for recording the national bibliography.

User Needs

This, then, brings us to that part of the Seminar's recommendation which urges the national library to "take into account . . . the needs of the variety of groups of users." I believe that a case can be made very easily that LC does inform and consult widely in the development and maintenance of cataloging policies, and that as a result these standards reflect a consensus in terms of both data content and content designation.

As a publicly funded agency, LC is expected not only to be responsive to its divergent constituencies, but also to inform them about its cataloging policies and practices. These are well documented and kept up to date in such publications as the *Rule Interpretations* and *Subject Cataloging Manual*, to name the most important—with changes and proposals announced in *Cataloging Service Bulletin*. LC staff members also have participated in outward-reaching institutes such as those that ALA (American Library Association) has organized from time to time, in order to deal with questions face to face. As a recent example of how LC communicates its implementation of cataloging standards, we are now in the process of publishing a commissioned study in which Lois Mai Chan has defined for the first time in a single statement the "Principles of Structure and Policies for Application" of the LC subject headings system.

Consultative Techniques

The mechanisms by which consultation proceeds vary. In many cases, the procedures for obtaining input involve formalized relationships with user groups—for example, with subunits of ALA and any other organization having an identifiable interest in cataloging policy. Indeed, it is by virtue of our commitment to consultation that one can explain why it often seems to take so long to accomplish even a minor change in cataloging policy or practice. Another recently developed and well received approach has been to assemble a group of experts and representatives of differing types of libraries and end-users to discuss a cataloging issue and attempt to reach a consensus as to the preferred policy. The 1990 meeting to discuss the handling of multiple versions and the forthcoming conference (May 1991) on subject subdivisions illustrate this approach. In this regard, I am reminded of the recent letter from a college librarian in Wisconsin who wrote: "Thanks for the opportunity to get involved in direction-setting decisions on the subject heading list; you're certainly trying to work against the feeling that some in cataloging have [that] LC decisions are just 'set down from on high'."

To further illustrate consultative techniques, twice in the past decade the Library has canvased its cooperative cataloging partners to identify ways of reducing costs through cataloging simplification, and then invited them to meetings for discussion of the suggestions made. In addition, the Library frequently announces in *Cataloging Service Bulletin* its own proposals to modify standards or those put forward by others in order to stimulate reaction. A recent example of this approach was our call for responses to a suggestion to simplify Hebraica vernacular cataloging by omitting certain romanized data elements. [1]

The Library has a strong commitment to international consultation as well. Today, its bibliographic products are distributed worldwide. Here the major focus is on IFLA and ISO (International Organization for Standardization), although LC confers directly with other national libraries in areas of common interest, such as with the British Library and the National Libraries of Canada and Australia in regard to the *AACR2* (*Anglo-American Cataloguing Rules*). The implementation of Universal Bibliographic Control (UBC) is proceeding, even if progress is slowly incremental, which should not be surprising given the grand scheme of the UBC concept. For example, just now work is underway to enable loading of foreign MARC (machine-readable cataloging) data to LC's online database, so that the bibliographic output of other national libraries might be available as a resource to our staff and thereby potentially facilitate cataloging operations. Many other steps remain to be taken, with the result that LC will continue its commitment to international cooperation in the cataloging standards area.

Conflicting Views

Out of the consultative decision-making process, however, have come countervailing views as to the directions that LC should be pursuing in cataloging standards. One major theme of the past few years is a call for cataloging simplification, so that bibliographic records can be created more easily, quickly, and cheaply; advocating this view are many national agencies as well as research libraries. On the other hand, a significant number of special-interest libraries and groups ask for the elaboration of cataloging standards and data, in order to take into account the requirements of their users. Another example is the tug and pull between "growth" and "stability" in subject heading and classification practice—between keeping up with new concepts and the cost of changing large files in order to do so. Further, we have to consider the needs of catalog card users, but at the expense of realizing fully the capabilities of the machine-readable catalog. And, looming ahead is the problem of reconciling local systems that reflect local needs and national systems that emphasize interchangeability of data.

The dynamics of this situation should be kept in mind in assessing some decisions which by hindsight may not seem to have been wisely made. For example, when LC considered adoption of the Pinyin romanization scheme, the specialists consulted, although divided, were mostly in favor of retaining Wade-Giles. Now, some ten years later, after many thousands of bibliographic records have been introduced into online catalogs in accordance with that policy, the Library is being asked to reconsider and switch to Pinyin. It appears that the influence of Wade-Giles has greatly diminished over time. But, unfortunately, the costs of conversion now are beyond existing resources, and the state of automation is not yet such as to ease the task. As another example, it now appears that for ease of application and in terms of machine validation, there is a much stronger case for direct subdivision in the geographic components of subject headings than was foreseen when the decision was made to set these up indirectly. Fortunately, however, problematic decisions are rather rare as results of the consultative process.

Successful Collaboration

Given the potential for conflicting interests, it is reassuring to find that in the area of descriptive cataloging, consultation appears to be well established and functions generally to the satisfaction of all involved. (I do not mean to imply that every stakeholder consulted is always satisfied with the outcome of particular policy decisions!) This may be explained by the long tradition of collaboration in this area and by the wide acceptance of *AACR2*, including its articulation of the International Standard Bibliographic Descriptions (ISBD). In the absence of controversy, alternatives to *AACR* such as the COSATI (Committee on Scientific and Technical Information) rules have all but disappeared, as has most of the hostility to some aspects of ISBD, particularly regarding its use of punctuation marks, which were unfamiliar when introduced nearly a generation ago.

Two other areas in which consultation is generally judged to work effectively in relation to cataloging standards are the development and application of the Dewey Decimal Classification and the MARC standards.

By way of contrast, subject cataloging is not an area where consultative decision-making is as regularized or gratifying. This may be true because subject cataloging itself lacks an internationally agreed-upon basis for national or local applications—if that is even possible. However, because of the already pervasive influence that *LCSH* (*Library of Congress Subject Headings*) has on the online catalog and the growing international interest in *LCSH*, many at the Library of Congress view the development of this subject headings list and the principles controlling its application as likely to come under the increasing influence of outside users. Certainly, the subject subdivisions conference mentioned above is a move in that direction.

Special User Needs

Given the involvement of the user community in the definition of the Library's cataloging standards, does LC then conclude that its bibliographic products are "appropriate for all types of libraries and users"? The answer, of course, is "no." We recognize that, while our cataloging is of sufficient value to most users as is, in certain environments it is necessary or desirable to provide more elaborate or even different data.

No more than anyone else can LC cataloging policymakers claim a certain knowledge as to what comprises the full range of functional requirements in relation to the variety of user needs and the variety of media—you will recall my quote at the outset of the Seminar on Bibliographic Records' recommendation that study to determine these is, in fact, a matter of high priority. LC's recognition that such needs exist, however, explains our cooperation with specialists in projects to create cataloging manuals for rare books, prints and photographs, archival films, manuscripts, newspapers, cartographic materials, legal publications, East Asian and Hebraica imprints, government documents, audiovisual materials, and computer files, among others. [2] These manuals help specialist catalogers provide for the needs of users in areas where we presume the basic LC cataloging standards may need amplification or modification. This realization also explains the investment that the Library makes (jointly with Forest Press) in developing and applying the Dewey Decimal Classification, both full and abridged versions, although neither is used for classifying LC's collections. And, it accounts for such practices as the inclusion of summary notes and additional subject headings for both fiction and nonfiction juvenile publications.

Enhancing LC Bibliographic Records

If the Library of Congress recognizes that, exceptionally, others are willing and able to modify and customize centrally supplied cataloging, by what means does it recommend that such record extension and enhancement be pursued?

To be of more than local benefit, customizing and extending bibliographic data should operate within the framework of existing standards. For example, in matters of bibliographic description, the specialized manuals mentioned above are based on *AACR2*. This cataloging code and the International Standard Bibliographic Descriptions from which it is partly derived are replete with opportunities for "optional additions" within a stipulated approach. In the area of subject cataloging, the opportunities for providing access points are limited only by an institution's resources and its ability to observe policies that make such access helpful to users. The latter consideration is of utmost importance in an online catalog to which many catalogers contribute records.

Of equal significance is the recommendation that record extension and enhancement should reflect a valid application of the MARC formats, which by design provide opportunities to modify or extend LC cataloging. For example, there are several fields for data which we do not ordinarily supply, such as 653 for index terms or uncontrolled subject headings—a field LC uses primarily in its minimal-level cataloging of foreign-language titles to enable keyword retrieval. Another field, tagged 654, provides for subject added entries that are faceted topical terms. And, of course, there are defined fields set aside for local call numbers and subject use and definition. The point is that standard and non-standard data elements need to be clearly delineated and not intermingled.

Thus there are many opportunities—for those who can afford to undertake to do so—to "customize" LC and other standard cataloging to meet local needs when entering these records in a local OPAC (online public access catalog) without having to sacrifice adherence to cataloging standards.

Taking a more cost-effective and comprehensive approach, LC has begun to help organize efforts to enhance its cataloging output through its cooperative cataloging programs. For example, when the ALA Subject Analysis Committee completed work on its *Guidelines on Subject Access to Individual Works of Fiction, Drama, Etc.* (1990), it asked the Library of Congress to consider implementation of these guidelines. We undertook a cost study and determined that we could not afford to do so. As a positive response, however, we offered to sponsor training and technical oversight of other libraries that were willing and able to make such enhancements. Subsequently, OCLC agreed to provide a funnel through which genre terms and additional headings will be added to existing LC records for such individual works, and is currently developing a project involving about a dozen libraries to meet this goal.

As another example, the Library of Congress has recently begun discussions with a few law libraries that are about to undertake retrospective conversion in order to implement the now-developed K schedule. According to this proposal, we will encode and reissue LC records to make available the call numbers assigned by these libraries to reduce the cost to other law librarians who will subsequently reclassify such collections.

In response to yet another suggestion, the Library is preparing to determine whether publishers participating in the CIP (Cataloging in Publication) program are willing to provide genre information for appropriate titles when submitting prepublication information needed for cataloging. If so, we will encode this in the 653 field of the MARC record for the benefit of public librarians and others who find such information useful in planning for collection development. Our cooperative cataloging staff will oversee the implementation of these programs; it is hoped that many other such initiatives will follow.

Enhancing the LC product, as just described, is a possibility that would not exist were it not for the availability of effective standards and for the willingness of others to follow them in the same way as does LC. This is also true in relation to extending the national database to include records that LC itself did not produce, but which otherwise are indistinguishable in terms of fullness and quality. Here I am referring to large-scale database development through cooperative cataloging programs such as CONSER (Cooperative Online Serials), NACO (Name Authority Cooperative), and NCCP (National Coordinated Cataloging Program).

Since the mid-1970s, LC has actively solicited the contributions of other librarians who are willing and able to generate and update authority and bibliographic records. Those who undertake to participate in such activities agree to fully apply LC cataloging policy and practice. They receive training, have access through electronic mail to our cataloging staff for questions and feedback, receive all pertinent documentation including "drafts for comments," and their records undergo quality-assurance monitoring. And, as noted, these librarians also have a firsthand opportunity to influence our operations directly through suggestions for improvement of our policies and procedures.

Since the first name authority record was contributed by the Government Printing Office Library in October 1977, cooperative cataloging efforts have expanded dramatically. As a result, the 43 libraries now participating in the Library's cooperative programs have contributed more than 450,000 name authority records, 7,000 series authority records, and 100,000 bibliographic records for monographs. All of these have been made widely available. In addition, many of the participating libraries initiate or execute changes to existing records; indeed, as a result of cooperative programs, a total of 70,000 authority records and 35,000 bibliographic records have been modified during the past decade alone. Another major cooperative program, CONSER, is now at the half-million record mark.

It is instructive to consider also the nature of the data produced and distributed through these programs. Some cooperating libraries produce authority records that would not be created at LC, for example, for access points on records for the individual titles in microform sets. In this area, cooperating libraries have contributed thousands of headings for authors represented in ESTC (Eighteenth Century Short Title Catalogue), Wing, [3] Goldsmiths'-Kress Library of Economic Literature, Pollard and Redgrave, [4] Nineteenth Century Legal Treatises, and others. One library is undertaking a project to make authority records for each element in the uniform title headings for certain composers.

This initiative will be especially appreciated by libraries that are dependent on machine validation of authority data. Another project involved creation of bibliographic records for a large collection of rare books in science and technology. One major art library has submitted authority records to upgrade to *AACR2* form the personal name headings found in compilations such as the *International Repertory of the Literature of Art*. A recent undertaking by another will bring into the national authority file large quantities of records from such special collections and archival sources as the Academy of Natural Sciences and the American Philosophical Society.

Very recently, in an effort to expand the activities of our cooperative partners, we asked them to consider submitting proposals for new subject headings and changes to existing headings, including all types of references, as well as for new and revised class numbers, by way of developing *LCSH* and *LCC* (*Library of Congress Classification*) to take account of needs which have not arisen in the course of LC's current cataloging.

Conclusions

It therefore seems reasonable to conclude that the recommendations of the Seminar on Bibliographic Records are already implemented to a large extent in the case of the United States. The Library of Congress catalogs much of the national imprint and many other works as well. It strives to determine and meet the functional requirements of its users through a program of regular consultation. It coordinates cooperative projects to extend and enhance the national database. The standardization of cataloging has played a significant role in enabling this progress towards Universal Bibliographic Control.

The impetus that has led us to place so much emphasis on standardized cataloging during these past decades has not diminished. The need to minimize duplicate cataloging and to work cooperatively are today's economic realities. Indeed, as a practical consideration, the investment the profession has made in developing today's standards has been enormous—so great, in fact, that we cannot foresee any but gradual change. As Klaus-Dieter Lehmann recently observed, "The need to follow revisions to standards is costly in terms of: training of staff, programme-changing, [and] coping with possible incompatibility in databases." [5]

Experience so far suggests that automation locks us into standards. It is not likely that advancing technology will provide an impetus to overturn existing standards, although presumably change will be easier to accomplish when linked authority and bibliographic files are the norm, when global update exists widely, and when machine catalogs have greater standardization in such features as commands for information retrieval. Meanwhile, the increasing number of OPACs might enable orderly reconsideration of some prevailing conventions—for example, the necessity of requiring choice of main entry, the provision of certain cross-references which simply transpose terms within a heading, or the inclusion of redundant data in a bibliographic record through fixed-field coding and natural language. But, I know of no impending indications that existing standards in any cataloging area are about to be abandoned— unless the proliferation of local systems leads to such a development.

For all of these reasons, if we can view heresy as does Webster as "an opinion, doctrine or practice contrary to . . . generally accepted beliefs or standards," then there appears to be little room for it in today's bibliographic setting. At least, this is how many of us at LC view current circumstances. This does not mean that prevailing policy is beyond improvement. At the Library of Congress, we believe it is through the continuation of the well established practice of working together to produce the best bibliographic standards and products that catalog users will reap the greatest rewards of our professional services.

NOTES

1. "Hebrew Cataloging Proposal." *Cataloging Service Bulletin* No. 49 (Summer 1990), p. 45.
2. See Library of Congress, Cataloging Distribution Service. *The Complete Catalog, 1991* for information concerning availability of these guides.
3. Wing, Donald Goddard. *Short Title Catalogue of Books Printed in England, Scotland, Ireland, Wales, and British America, and of English Books Printed in Other Countries, 1641-1700.*
4. Pollard, Alfred William; Redgrave, G.R. *A Short-Title Catalog of Books Printed in England, Scotland and Ireland, and of English Books Printed Abroad, 1475-1640.* (Known as *STC.*)
5. Lehmann, Klaus-Dieter. "Links in the Information Chain," p. 5. Paper for the Seminar on Bibliographic Records (1990: Stockholm), to be published in late 1991 or 1992.

ACKNOWLEDGMENTS

I am pleased to have this opportunity to thank the following for sharing with me information and views concerning the topic of this paper: Henriette Avram, Dorothy Glasby, Jeffrey Heynen, Sally McCallum, Mary Kay Pietris, Lucia Rather, David Smith, Ben Tucker, and Glen Zimmerman. I am especially grateful to Philip Melzer, my research assistant, for his contributions to this paper.

THE EDUCATOR'S
PERSPECTIVE: INTRODUCTION

In the past two decades, since the introduction of the bibliographic utilities, there has been a decline in cataloging course requirements in American library schools. The assumption has been that centrally supplied cataloging data can simply be copied, and that the copying can be done by paraprofessionals. Cataloging has become a dying art.

There is now a vast literature on the limitations of standard subject access concomitant with experimentation in online classified displays. How many of our recent library school graduates are competent to evaluate a so-called standard bibliographic record? Can they develop and maintain an alternative set of subject headings? Do they know enough about classification notation to tamper with centrally supplied data?

The final paper of the Congress focuses on the implications for the education of catalogers rejecting standard cataloging copy. We are fortunate to have one of the best-known cataloging educators in the U.S. addressing this topic.

Sheila S. Intner is a Professor at the Graduate School of Library and Information Science, Simmons College, in Boston, where she teaches beginning and advanced classes in cataloging and classification, collection development, and bibliographic instruction. Formerly Music Librarian and Coordinator of Automated Services at Great Neck Library (NY), Dr. Intner taught at Emory, Columbia, and UCLA before joining the Simmons faculty. She received a doctorate from Columbia University in 1982.

Dr. Intner does research in cataloging and collection development, with a special focus on videos and computer software. Recent research articles of hers include "A Field Test of the Library of Congress's *Training the Trainer* Course," in *Education for Information* (1991), and "Quality in Bibliographic Databases: An Analysis of Member-Contributed Cataloging in OCLC and RLIN," in *Advances in Library Administration and Organization* (1989). Dr. Intner edited *Library Resources & Technical Services* from 1987 to 1990, and now is series editor of *Frontiers of Access to Library Materials* for ALA Books. She serves on the editorial boards of *Judaica Librarianship, Resource Sharing & Information Networks,* and *Technicalities.* Dr. Intner writes the "Interfaces" column for *Technicalities* and among her recent books are *Cataloging, The Professional Development Cycle* (Greenwood, 1991), *Library Education and Leadership* (Scarecrow, 1991), *Standard Cataloging for School and Public Libraries* (Greenwood, 1989), *The Library Microcomputer Environment* (Oryx, 1988), and *Policy and Practice in Bibliographic Control of Nonbook Media* (ALA, 1987).

Dr. Intner is secretary-treasurer of the Library Research Round Table and chair of the Margaret Mann Award Citation Committee of ALA. She also serves on the education committees of the Massachusetts Library Association and the Association for Library Collections and Technical Services' Cataloging and Classification Section.

B.H.W.

REJECTING STANDARD CATALOGING COPY: IMPLICATIONS FOR THE EDUCATION OF CATALOGERS

Sheila S. Intner

Professor
Graduate School of Library and Information Science
Simmons College
300 The Fenway, Boston, MA 02115-5898

"Question: How many catalogers does it take to change a lightbulb?
Answer: It only takes one, but he or she has to wait to see
how LC did it."—Author unknown.

Some Preliminary Observations on Cataloging, Standards, and Tradition

The goal of libraries is to serve their patrons is a familiar platitude to which a good many present-day librarians pay lip service and consider it a job well-done. A more powerful influence on cataloging than how well it provides service to the patron appears to be tradition—the tradition of Panizzi [1] and of Cutter. [2] Preserving the status quo and protecting job descriptions from major changes seem to be much more compelling than responding to the changing needs of patrons (or, alternatively, to the needs of changing patrons). At least, that might explain why catalogers tend to perpetuate their traditional practices, whether the practices conform to standards or not. In fact, catalogers may even believe that what they do is "standard," regardless of the actual truth of the claim. [3]

Where cataloging is concerned, standards are set by a relatively small coterie of leaders, and when changes occur, they often are made in response to problems important to members of this leadership cohort. A standard that contravenes the desires of the leaders is not likely to remain in force for long. [4] (The standards to which this paper refers are for descriptive cataloging, i.e., the *Anglo-American Cataloguing Rules* [AACR], and for subject analysis, i.e., subject heading lists and classifications.)

In the United States, what the Library of Congress does has always set a standard of excellence toward which other libraries might strive. Few other places can compare with the Library of Congress, with its large numbers of highly-credentialed, well-trained professional staff members covering numerous specializations in disciplines, languages, and materials, or its enormous resources in facilities, collections, and budgets.

In recent years, however, Library of Congress descriptive cataloging practices have been designated officially as the *only* acceptable standard by OCLC (Online Computer Library Center), RLIN (Research Libraries Information Network), WLN (Western Library Network), and others among the nation's cataloging leadership. These official rulings may be the result of the networks' adoption of the MARC (machine-readable cataloging) standard for computer communication of bibliographic information, developed by the Library of Congress for its own computer systems, and of the understandable desire to ensure the most uniform products possible in network databases. And it is not a bad standard, either, since the Library of Congress exercises great care in devising its policies, conducting scholarly studies before establishing authoritative decisions or choosing particular methods of operation.

Logic, however, would indicate that what the Library of Congress does for itself is not necessarily the best thing for all other libraries in the nation. In many ways, the Library of Congress is unique. The environments, patrons, resources, and goals of most individual libraries differ considerably from those of the Library of Congress. Yet, through the bibliographic input standards of all of the major cataloging networks, catalogers all across the country have adopted the Library of Congress's descriptive cataloging policies as well as its name and subject authority files, and indexing practices. Catalogers whose institutions are national network members also have adopted Library of Congress classification in large numbers, regardless of its match with their collections or its suitability for their users' needs.

Where Library of Congress practice is not a de jure standard, it operates as a de facto standard. To maximize their market appeal, local systems must link with the databases of the national networks. To be able to do so, they must support the MARC standard and, by definition, Library of Congress interpretations of and policy decisions for other cataloging standards. Although the descriptive cataloging code—the most restrictive of the several standards used for library cataloging—permits three levels of description, MARC-based networks endorse only the levels adopted by the Library of Congress, although each network also accommodates briefer types of records that do not quite match the alternative bibliographic level offered by the descriptive cataloging code, AACR2.

Libraries that opt for subject authorities other than *Library of Congress Subject Headings*, and classification schemes other than the Library of Congress classification do so knowing that these decisions decrease the likelihood that they can copy subject headings and class numbers from other libraries' records, or find vendors willing to provide them with bibliographic records using the less-popular schemes.

The Educational Issues

This paper, however, has not set out to discuss the value of standards based on Library of Congress policies and practices. Others at this Cataloging Heresy Congress have done that quite thoroughly. The issues to be analyzed and explored in this paper are the implications for the education of cataloging librarians of (a) continuing the status quo, and (b) the consequences of rejecting the standard record paradigm. To put it in more concrete educational terms, the issues involve the effects of accepting or rejecting what this paper has chosen to call "standard catalog copy" on library school program objectives, curriculum, and instruction.

Focusing on program goals raises an eternal debate: Are program goals to prepare persons for their first jobs, or to arm them with a body of knowledge that they may use in responding to the demands of different jobs over a career lifetime? U.S. library schools since Dewey's original School of Library Economy have tried to strike a balance between these opposing poles, some coming down a little more on the side of entry into the profession, while others are a little more on the side of education for the longer term.

People may view the dichotomy in more simplified terms as a debate between practice and theory, with the proponents of practice emphasizing what a beginning librarian must know to maximize readiness for a job, and the proponents of theory emphasizing principles in general, without regard to the needs of any particular type of job. [5] Clearly, the dominant goal will determine the range of potential responses to the other two questions, i.e., "What will be taught?" and "How shall it be taught?" The sections that follow explore the educational requirements, first, of supporting current cataloging standards; second, of rejecting them; and, then, attempt to analyze the differences between the two.

Education To Support The Status Quo

What are the educational requirements of continuing to support the current cataloging paradigm, i.e., the standard catalog record found in network databases? They must include, at the least, knowledge of the standards themselves and currently accepted methods of their application; understanding of various network environments on national/international and regional levels; and, finally, specific knowledge of local systems currently employed in library operations. All of this material—and it includes large amounts of data of several disparate types—must be crammed into a total curriculum that averages 36 hours of credit (usually, twelve 3-credit hour courses) for one-year master's degree programs.

This raises another issue: Can this material be taught in one course? Most professors believe that it cannot, [6] and most library schools offer more than one course to accommodate the large and constantly growing cataloging and classification curriculum. The basic cataloging curriculum may be divided in different ways, e.g., one course in descriptive cataloging, another in subject analysis; or, one course in book cataloging and classification, another in nonbook cataloging and classification; or, one course in bibliographic control, another in applications (i.e., rules and tools); or, one course in simple cataloging such as the kind that might be appropriate to small public or school libraries (i.e., mostly books, using "level one" bibliographic description, Dewey [classification], and Sears [subject headings]) and another in more complex cataloging such as that required by research libraries (i.e., books, serials, microforms, etc., using "level two" bibliographic description, and Library of Congress classification numbers and subject headings). But setting this problem aside for the moment, let us examine these requirements more closely.

Knowledge of the standards and applications—These are the rules and tools: for descriptive cataloging, the *Anglo-American Cataloguing Rules*, second edition, 1988 revision and Library of Congress rule interpretations; for indexing, *Library of Congress Subject Headings* and *Subject Cataloging Manual: Subject Headings*; for classification, the Dewey Decimal or Library of Congress classification; and for communicating the data by computer, the Library of Congress's Machine-Readable Cataloging protocols. Known by their acronyms, AACR2R, LCRIs, LCSH, SCM:SH, DDC or LCC, and MARC, respectively, they are a familiar alphabet soup to catalogers.

A practical approach might be to simply teach the current version of each standard, not worrying about the changes that might occur before the student begins using them in practice. Such an approach might emphasize learning (perhaps, even, memorizing) the descriptive cataloging rules, class numbers and subject headings for commonly collected types of materials, and lists of MARC content designators, along with the Library of Congress policies. Exceptions to the rules might be discussed in general or in detail, depending on the time available and the professor's perception of how important it is to learn the details. This approach focuses on "how," not "why" library cataloging is done.

A theoretical approach would identify and explain the principles that underlie the organization of information in addition to teaching the specific rules, classification numbers, subject headings, and protocols contained in the current standards. (This author's experience shows that there is a natural tendency to emphasize the principles supported by current standards, and to gloss over the ones that appear to be contravened by particular rules or policies, which can create confusion for the students who discover the conflicts, but are unable to find adequate resolutions.) This approach focuses on "why" as well as "how" cataloging is done, but offers few answers in response to questions about why principles and standards are allowed to remain in a state of discord. Practicing catalogers who teach in library schools may turn immediately to cost and time factors that influence the course of library operations to explain standard-theory conflicts but theoreticians are less apt to use such justifications. "Because that is the rule" may be the sole explanation offered because it is all that is available. ("Because" may be the only reasonable explanation for certain problems, such as why *bough, rough,* and *trough* do not rhyme, but have three entirely different pronunciations.)

Understanding of network environments—A program that aims to prepare students for their first jobs might translate "understanding of network environments" as being able to identify records from the various national networks, to search the databases and match online records with items in hand, and to edit or input original records into the databases. While this does not explore the larger issues, such as network architecture, storage and retrieval alternatives, quality control, etc., it will prepare the student to sit down at a terminal with minimal on-the-job training, to search for and recognize desired records, and to perform various database maintenance tasks. Time might be considered well-spent having the student input records into different databases using various types of terminals and editing or inputting techniques.

A theoretical approach would have to explore the larger issues mentioned above as well as the tradeoffs for the library between editing existing records and inputting original records, the implications of following various bibliographic input standards, the potential benefits of different search strategies for professional searchers, i.e., catalogers or other library staff members, and for lay searchers with different levels of expertise.

Knowledge of current local systems—The purely practical, first-job-preparation approach to local systems would be to provide students with cataloging experience using as many different local system products as could be made available. The theoretical approach would not preclude providing such experiences, but, in addition, it would have to include comparison of different local systems and discussion of database design principles, screen display alternatives, searching options, etc., and the findings of available research on user interfaces, searching behavior, and potential uses of retrieved data—both bibliographic records and the full texts of documents.

The theoretical approach covers more territory and, thus, takes longer to teach, even though it has a smaller payoff in the short run. Its strength lies in the enduring applicability of principles to more than the immediate situation or a particular network or local system, and the greater benefit a practitioner might derive from using this knowledge over a career lifetime. Given the dynamic nature of these standards, all of which undergo a continuing revision process, such knowledge is necessary to deal with the changes that are bound to occur, and, ideally, to enable a librarian to be a contributor to the process of change.

Rejecting Standard Cataloging Copy: Educational Needs

What are the educational requirements for rejecting current standards and the kinds of records found in network databases? They must include the same fundamental knowledge of current standards as was outlined in the preceding section, for one can hardly reject something that one does not know and understand. In fact, to support rejection of standard records, one must go beyond the minimal knowledge of standards required for practical first-job-preparation to thorough understanding of the principles that underlie them, with special emphasis on the conflicts between principles and rules. At the outset, then, rejecting standards begins with the requirement that the student be exposed to the larger body of theoretical knowledge required for accepting standards. In addition, the thorny problems of theory-rule conflicts must be studied, if not to resolve them, at least to identify and analyze the problems in order to achieve a complete understanding of the issues they involve.

Once the student thoroughly understands the status quo, a deeper study of the organization of knowledge begins. To the basic information about cataloging standards and their underlying principles, knowledge of generic principles of information production, alternatives for organizing information, and the processes of human communication and information transfer must be added. This more general study of information generation, processing, and use, which sounds a great deal like the definition of "information science," is needed to build new and different organizational paradigms.

Special attention to the different manifestations in which information appears would be warranted, since the medium determines, or, at least, influences, potential perceptions of informational messages, and organizational structures and systems might be expected to recognize and address the resulting differences. Deep knowledge of human behavior with regard to the recognition, absorption, and integration of information—a process we might deem "turning information into knowledge"—would be important, also. The ways in which humans perceive and internalize information ought to influence how information is presented to them. Methods used to arrange and structure information for use should take into account and enhance people's behavioral tendencies. If organizational structures cannot provide enhancement for every variation in behavior, which surely must be extremely difficult if not impossible to anticipate, at least they should not work against commonly encountered patterns of behavior or erect barriers to the use of information by people exhibiting recognized and expected behaviors.

A legitimate question is: Why would a cataloger require knowledge of information production? The answer is simple: Organizational systems anticipate the type of material that is to be organized. When that material does not meet expectations, the systems break down. One example of such a breakdown was encountered with the introduction in the early 1980s of microcomputer software into libraries, for which the descriptive cataloging rules for computer files (then called *machine-readable data files*) were inadequate. After a groundswell of dissatisfaction and agitation for change, new rules had to be written, which appeared in the 1988 revision of AACR. [7]

Another example is the way microform copies of printed originals are described (see note 4). The system of descriptive cataloging rules, aiming for consistent treatment of all materials, mandated identical treatment for all microforms whether they were original micropublications or microreproductions of titles that had originally appeared as books or journals. The resulting records were unacceptable to the librarians in U.S. research libraries who had to use them, however, and, eventually, the obnoxious rules were overturned (at least in the U.S.), destroying the symmetry that was fundamental to the code.

Further examples of disaffection with descriptive cataloging rules are cropping up as new technologies develop and the new forms of informational materials to which they give rise differ from AACR's anticipated media types (e.g., music videos and interactive media). While the intention of AACR is to "cover the description of, and the provision of access points for, all library materials commonly collected at the present time," and its recommendation is to use "the general rules . . . as a basis for cataloguing uncommonly collected materials of all kinds and library materials yet unknown," the system does not work well in practice. [8] Catalogers are reluctant to apply existing rules in new ways without precedents, and such precedents are lacking when the Library of Congress does not provide them.

Another question that can be raised is: Why should catalogers worry about material use? Once the collection is organized, one might think, the problems of how it is used are the province of other librarians—reference specialists, bibliographers, and readers' advisors. However, knowledge of material use patterns is an important feedback mechanism for catalogers to evaluate the efficacy of their cataloging, indexing, and classification systems. When material use patterns reflect anomalies, e.g., low circulation of philosophy materials, although term paper assignments in large, beginning philosophy classes would have indicated heavy use; or reports of interlibrary loan requests for works that are available in the library's own collection, then catalogers need to examine the organizational systems they have constructed to identify any potential retrieval barriers for these materials.

Underlying many of the skills needed by catalogers who undertake to reject standards is comprehensive knowledge of the conduct of research in order to develop plans, weigh alternatives, and evaluate outcomes. Catalogers need to learn systematic methods of evaluating the performance of catalogs, indexes, and other organizational systems. Systematic evaluations that can provide input for future planning and improvement may include identifying relevant evaluative criteria, gathering data to measure the extent to which each criterion is met, analyzing and interpreting the data that is collected, and employing the findings in improving these bibliographic systems.

Speaking about the U.S. Department of Education's study of the future of the library, Director Anne Mathews said, "The key issue is the passive position that the profession has taken toward the importance of research." [9] Deanna

Marcum, Catholic University's Dean of the School of Library and Information Science echoed this theme, suggesting that credibility for the profession as a whole will come from the pursuit of applied research, while educators take responsibility for basic research. Toni Carbo Bearman, Dean of the School of Library and Information Science at the University of Pittsburgh, summed up the skills needed by librarians, including managerial skills, knowledge of technology, and critical thinking, i.e., the ability to analyze and synthesize, and to move quickly and assertively in responding to information needs. [10]

The power of the cataloger who is not bound by standards to make direct contributions to the effectiveness of library services in a local institution is immense; but, at the same time, the risks of making poor choices that could result in negative impacts on service are a clear and present danger. By making decisions based on the advantages for local library users instead of nationally mandated standards, catalogers shoulder the lonely burden of being accountable for the impact of their decisions. (Imagine how individual catalogers might have fared had they had to bear the full responsibility in their libraries for the shift from the first to the second edition of AACR in the late 1970s. Being able to place the blame for the costly change on an anonymous standard may have saved catalogers from public hangings.)

Bibliographic control specialists might benefit greatly from a pre-graduation internship or a post-graduation residency requirement in which they work with an experienced master specialist, performing, in an apprentice role, the activities associated with database and system design, planning and goal setting, data gathering and analysis, and experimentation with storage and retrieval alternatives in a real library. Apprenticeships would be needed to bridge the gap between classroom learning and real world practice, to protect the neophyte specialist from making unfortunate decisions with disastrous results out of sheer inexperience, and to give them opportunities to learn how to operate successfully in the political environment of libraries.

A Comparison of Educational Needs

It is obvious that the cataloger who is not bound by standards needs to draw upon a much larger body of knowledge in order to make organizational decisions on the basis of what is best for an individual library and its community of users. "Best" is not an absolute term, of course, but it is defined here to mean that decisions are made on the basis of user needs for particular types of information and are consistent with the expected behaviors of members of the community in searching, retrieving, and using the information. The determination of a unique local standard challenges the cataloger's ability to assess the situation and translate it into bibliographic terms, and since the situation inevitably will change over time, new assessments must continually be made and systems altered to address the changes.

Knowledge required to maintain standards must begin with identification of the standards and understanding of their applications. Because of the information explosion, which fuels the production of larger amounts of more complex materials, and the use of advanced technology in information handling, standards are growing in number and complexity, and this basic body of knowledge is growing. Because the standards are dynamic, knowledge of the theories and principles on which they are based also is essential for more than rote compliance.

The knowledge required to reject standards is even greater than that outlined above, however, and includes the following general areas:

1) current standards and their applications, i.e., the same basic body of knowledge already mentioned;
2) information production, i.e., what information is, where it comes from, and how it is produced;
3) generic principles of information organization and use, i.e., the principles of information science;
4) managerial skills of planning, decision making, communicating, training, etc., including systems analysis and methods of recognizing the implications and outcomes of particular practices and the tradeoffs they involve, cost-benefit analysis to determine when it is more advantageous to follow a standard and when it is better to reject it;
5) statistics and research methods;
6) calculation of risks and the attractions of the challenge of risk-taking;
7) assumption of an overall perspective, not only the cataloging department, but the good of the whole organization; and, lastly,
8) assumption of professional responsibility and accountability for one's judgments and decisions as well as the understanding that this is what separates librarians from lay people.

Summary and Conclusions

Rejecting standards may appear on the surface to be easy, but it is not. It is far more difficult and challenging, albeit it can be more rewarding and productive than conformity. As might be expected for something difficult, it takes more knowledge as well as something rarely found among cataloging librarians: willingness to assume the risks associated with setting precedents, not following them.

Teaching cataloging as following standards is merely teaching students to identify and execute the correct rule or policy. Teaching cataloging as rejecting standards means educators must teach students to perceive problems, recognize needs, and design a variety of alternatives (including the standard method) that would resolve or address them, and then to take the risk of choosing the alternative most appropriate for the library. The curriculum for the latter, being larger, would occupy a larger proportion of the total curriculum, perhaps needing to be chosen at the outset of a student's program. The crowded library and information science curriculum would have to be augmented to include requirements in information science, research methods and statistics, systems analysis, communications, and risk management in addition to a minimum of two beginning cataloging courses (bibliographic control theory and current standard cataloging and classification systems) and at least as many advanced-level courses.

To earn the rewards of contributing to better services by choosing to ignore standards that appear to work to the library's disadvantage, catalogers also must accept the downside of risk-taking. Risk-taking is not something taught in library schools or encouraged much by the profession. Along with other skills identified as necessary to reject standards such as planning, decision-making, and evaluating, risk-taking is associated with leadership.

Leadership in developing more relevant and effective bibliographic systems will be costly to the student-librarians, who must bear the expense of the larger curriculum with which they must prepare themselves; to the library schools, who must teach it; and to the libraries in which they work, which will have to undertake the added expense of maintaining the entire infrastructure unique to their systems. Some libraries already are aware of the magnitude of the investment and the ultimate value of positive results, but one cannot expect all students, library schools, or libraries to be persuaded that major investments in new nonstandard bibliographic systems will have large returns in more efficient or effective local library services. The question is, Will such a demand ever develop? Unless a great many potential employers of cataloging librarians capable of designing nonstandard, but better, bibliographic systems are willing to pay for this expertise, larger educational programs may not be warranted. [11]

Improvements in technology allow libraries to have highly individualized systems designed to meet their particular needs and objectives. Realizing these capabilities, however, requires appropriately trained cataloging librarians willing to explore new territory. If administrators turn for help to catalogers bound by tradition and precedent, they will find the restrictions on their creativity prohibitive. If, on the other hand, they turn to computer programmers and other non-library analysts, they might find that the resulting systems throw out the baby with the bathwater, making them difficult to integrate into library settings. The middle ground, i.e., cataloging specialists with the requisite knowledge and willingness to combine nonstandard elements into bibliographic systems, has been lacking.

The truly compleat cataloger will be someone who has both the knowledge and the will to meet the challenge of making a better catalog. Should making a better catalog be perceived as a worthy effort of which a librarian can be proud? The answer, and the power to act, rests with each one of us.

NOTES

1. The tradition of Anthony Panizzi, Keeper of the Books at the British Museum in the early nineteenth century, was the primacy of the author's name as the "main" entry for an item being cataloged. His legacy stems from the codification of his ideas into 91 rules established for the preparation of the British Museum catalog, which became a model for subsequent U.S. codes. See: Anthony Panizzi, *Rules for the Compiling of the Catalogue* (London: British Museum, 1841).

2. The tradition of Charles Ammi Cutter, librarian of the Boston Athenaeum and creator of a prototype U.S. cataloging code in 1876, was the establishment of a dictionary catalog in which each cataloged item had three access points: its author, title, and subject or literary genre. See: Charles Ammi Cutter, *Rules for a Dictionary Catalog*, 4th ed. (Washington, DC: USGPO, 1904).

   Both Panizzi and Cutter deserve the acclaim they have received, and they are rightfully lauded for their ideas, which were constructive and innovative in their own times and far beyond. But more than 150 years later, in an environment that operates with fundamentally different technologies, new ideas are needed that account for the changes in materials, use and users, and the potential of contemporary organizational systems. Holding fast to these traditional ideas now may be inappropriate and counterproductive.

3. This conclusion is based on this author's direct experiences teaching workshops to hundreds of practitioners, many of whom believed they were doing standard cataloging even though they had never heard of *Library of Congress Rule Interpretations* or the Library of Congress Name Authority File; others who thought they were doing standard indexing because they used an edition of the *Library of Congress Subject Headings* (not necessarily the current one) to select terms, but had no idea that they also needed to consult a policy manual called *Standard Cataloging Manual: Subject Headings*; and a very small minority who thought that their emulation of OCLC records was sufficient to perform standard cataloging—they had never heard of the *Anglo-American Cataloguing Rules*.

4. A case in point is the standard for describing microform copies of printed materials. The second edition of *Anglo-American Cataloguing Rules*, the international standard for description, states that such items are to be treated first as microforms, and only secondarily as copies of something else (following the principle of cataloging the item in hand). Catalogers are to give in the main body of the record the appropriate title, responsibility, edition, publication details, physical description, etc. for the microform; and put the details for the original in a note. This approach was a change from the first edition of the rules, in which such an item was treated *as if it were the original*, giving in the main body of the record the appropriate title, etc. for the printed item, and putting the details for the microform in hand in a note.

   Members of the Association of Research Libraries were disturbed by the change and refused to follow it, claiming that their users were interested solely in the original and did not care about the physical manifestation. They continued to treat microform copies as originals and relegated information about the item in hand to the notes. After two fruitless attempts to rescind the offending rules at the international level, this powerful group settled for a rule interpretation that reestablished the first-edition [of AACR] practice at the Library of Congress and, by local agreement to follow LC, throughout the nation!

5. See, for example, some recent publications on practical vs. theoretical education in library/information science: A.J. Anderson, "They Never Taught Me How to Do This in Library School: Some Reflections on the Theory/Practice Nexus," *Journal of Library Administration* 6 (Summer 1985): 1-6; Kathryn Luther Henderson, "Some Persistent Issues in the Education of Catalogers and Classifiers," *Cataloging & Classification Quarterly* 7 (Summer 1987): 6-12; Robert M. Hiatt, "Education and Training of Cataloging Staff at the Library of Congress," *Cataloging & Classification Quarterly* 7 (Summer 1987): 121-129; Sheila S. Intner, "Theory *and* Practice or Theory *versus* Practice: Fundamental Issues and Questions," *Library Education and Leadership: Essays in Honor of Jane Ann Hannigan*, edited by Sheila S. Intner and Kay E. Vandergrift (Metuchen, NJ: Scarecrow Press, 1990): 153-165; and J. Bradford Young, "The Teaching of Cataloging: Education or Training," *Cataloging & Classification Quarterly* 7 (Summer 1987): 149-163.

In May 1988, a three-day conference was devoted entirely to the topic of bridging the gap between theory and practice in information science education. Intner's paper at this conference focused on cataloging: "Practical and Theoretical Knowledge in Cataloging: What We Should Teach and Why," *Bridging the Gap Between Theory and Practice: Proceedings of the First Joint Meeting Between the Association Internationale des Ecoles de Sciences de l'Information (AIESI) and the Association for Library and Information Science Education (ALISE)*, 25-26-27 May 1988, edited by Rejean Savard (Montreal: The Meeting, 1988), pp. 259-273.

6. Responding to the survey instrument on which "Practical and Theoretical Knowledge in Cataloging" was based, one library educator wrote: "As in real life, this paper-and-pencil exercise shows that it is just plain impossible to squeeze all the essential topics into *one single* introductory course. None of them [i.e., the suggested topics] can be given 15% or more, all are shortchanged, and so are the students. My solution: not *one* but *two* full-semester introductory courses: one on *bibliographic control* (not just descriptive cataloging) and one on *subject indexing*, totally 60 semester hours [of contact time] or more and worth 6 credits. The subjects have become so vast and so important and complex that they cannot any longer be taught as they were some 20 years ago. I would go so far as to propose that ALA [the American Library Association] deny accreditation to any school that does not provide for *at least* 60 hours of introduction (compulsory) to these topics which are, after all, at the heart of information storage and retrieval." Intner, "Practical and Theoretical Knowledge in Cataloging," (note 5), p. 272. [Emphasis in the original.]

7. A detailed history of the development of cataloging rules for computer software may be found in the following publications: *The Library Microcomputer Environment: Management Issues*, edited by Sheila S. Intner and Jane Anne Hannigan (Phoenix, AZ: Oryx Press, 1987), pp. 22-44; and/or Nancy B. Olson, *Cataloging Microcomputer Software*, 3rd ed. (Englewood, CO: Libraries Unlimited, 1990), pp. 1-30.

8. *Anglo-American Cataloguing Rules*, 2nd ed., 1988 rev., edited by Michael Gorman and Paul W. Winkler (Chicago: American Library Association, 1988), p. 1.

9. Gail Stahl, "Rethinking the Library in the Information Age," [report of a program held at the June 1990 Special Libraries Association Conference] *Library Management Quarterly* 13 (Summer 1990): 8.

10. Ibid., pp. 9-10.

11. There is a parallel in the development of computer-based bibliographic systems. A few pioneering libraries began unilateral efforts to computerize their bibliographic records in the 1960s and early 1970s, assuming the costs of system design, development, and implementation for the benefit of their own operations and services. Some of these unilateral efforts subsequently became the basis for multi-institutional networks, e.g., Stanford University's BALLOTS system became the basis for the Research Libraries Information Network (RLIN), and the University of Toronto's UTLAS system became the first Canadian bibliographic utility. Other systems were eventually generalized so they could be employed by other libraries individually, e.g., Northwestern University's NOTIS system. Few libraries undertake to develop such systems solely to help their colleagues. The initial investments have to be worthwhile for the developers alone, without the potential for entrepreneurial growth beyond the local library.

ACKNOWLEDGMENTS

The author wishes to acknowledge the assistance of Linda Watkins and Charlotte Hegyi, librarians at the Library and Information Science Library of Simmons College, in the preparation of this paper.

CONCLUDING REMARKS

Bella Hass Weinberg, Chair

We have examined the concept of standard cataloging data from a variety of perspectives. We began with general theoretical critiques and continued with public, academic, and special librarians' points of view. These were followed by position papers of the bibliographic utilities and of the Library of Congress. We concluded with an educator's perspective.

I hope that you have found the papers stimulating. Perhaps they will lead to changes in cataloging for your user community.

The great interest in the theme of this Congress is rewarding to me because these are questions that have been in my mind for many years, and I see that they have spoken to many people in the library world.

Postscript: Jay Lambrecht concluded his review of the 1990 literature of descriptive cataloging by noting that " . . . it reflects a complacent discipline . . . [W]e . . . hope that more questions will be asked and answered in 1991." [1]

I believe that the 1991 Congress for Librarians did pose important questions in cataloging, and that the invited speakers provided thought-provoking responses.

NOTE

1. Lambrecht, Jay H. "Ours Should Be to Reason Why: Descriptive Cataloging Research in 1990." *Library Resources & Technical Services* Vol. 35, No. 3 (July 1991), p. 257-264. Quotation from p. 262.

CALL FOR PAPERS

"Cataloging Heresy: Challenging the Standard Bibliographic Product" will be the theme of the Congress for Librarians scheduled to be held at St. John's University in Jamaica, New York, on Presidents' Day, Monday, Feb. 18, 1991. With support from a grant by the H.W. Wilson Foundation, nationally known librarians, thesaurus designers, and representatives of bibliographic utilities have been invited to address the theme. The papers scheduled for presentation at the Congress are:

A Theory of Relativity for Catalogers (Bella Hass Weinberg, St. John's University)

The Non-Neutrality of Descriptive Cataloging (Norman Anderson, Gordon-Conwell Theological Seminary)

The Art & Architecture Thesaurus as an Alternative to LCSH (Kathy Whitehead, AAT)

The Development of Classification and Subject Heading Systems for Medicine (Sally Sinn, NLM)

Cataloging Tools and 'Copy': The Myth of Acceptability—A Public Librarian's Point of View (Sanford Berman, Hennepin County Library)

Standard Cataloging Data and the Academic Library: The Technical Services Manager's Point of View (Mary Parr, St. John's University)

OCLC and the Master Record Concept (Liz Bishoff, OCLC)

The Display and Indexing of Customized Catalog Records in RLIN (Ed Glazier, RLG)

Standard Cataloging Data: The View from the Library of Congress (Lucia Rather, LC)

Rejecting Standard Cataloging Copy: Implications for the Education of Catalogers (Sheila Intner, Simmons College)

Because the acceptability of standard cataloging data concerns all types of libraries and all subject specialties, this call is for additional papers for inclusion in the volume to be published by Learned Information. Papers of varying length are acceptable. Manuscripts should be double spaced, with ample margins, and should use the author-date system of citation. The deadline for submission is Dec. 15, 1990. All contributed papers will be refereed by a committee of experts in the theory and practice of cataloging. Contributors will be notified of the referees' decision by January 15, 1991.

Authors of accepted papers will receive complimentary registration for the full-day Congress (which includes lunch) and a copy of the book upon publication. A list of the authors and titles of accepted papers will be distributed to attendees at the Congress.

For further information, contact:

Dr. Bella Hass Weinberg
Division of Library and Information Science
Tel: (718) 990-6200   St. John's University
Fax: (718) 380-0353   Jamaica, New York 11439   5/29/90

EDITOR'S NOTE

The Call for Papers, which is reproduced on the facing page, was distributed to library schools in North America and published in many journals and newsletters in the field of library and information science. This document generated great interest in the Congress and in this publication.

The following referees devoted their time and expertise to the selection and editing of the contributed papers:

Prof. Sheila Intner, Simmons College
Dean Mary Parr, St. John's University Libraries
Prof. Alan Thomas, Division of Library and Information
Science, St. John's University

The papers treat issues in descriptive cataloging, subject cataloging, and classification. They represent a variety of disciplines and types of libraries. While some of the papers describe local deviations from the standard cataloging product, we trust that the considerations and innovations are relevant to a wide audience. It is hoped that readers will find these contributed papers a valuable complement to the invited papers.

B.H.W.

SPECIAL COLLECTIONS AND CATALOGING STANDARDS: ISSUES AND COMPROMISES AT THE STEINBECK RESEARCH CENTER AND THE CENTER FOR BEETHOVEN STUDIES

Patricia Elliott
Curator, Ira F. Brilliant Center for Beethoven Studies
San Jose State University
San Jose, CA 95192-0171

Celia Bakke
Head, Cataloging Department
Clark Library, San Jose State University Library
San Jose, CA 95192-0028

The standard cataloging practices of general libraries present problems for special collections, particularly those in narrow subject areas. At San Jose State University, two such collections exist which are administered independently from the University Library. The Steinbeck Research Center, established in 1974, currently contains a collection of resource materials in various formats totalling more than 4,000 items, including first editions, manuscripts, letters, film scripts, films, photographs, and memorabilia. In 1985 the University established the Ira F. Brilliant Center for Beethoven Studies after receiving a major gift of first editions of Beethoven's scores. The Beethoven collection now includes nearly 1,600 books on Beethoven and related subjects, 1,300 first and early editions of his scores, and two original manuscripts. The issue of whether these collections should be represented in the general library's catalog (recently converted to online) has been addressed differently by these two centers.

The Steinbeck Research Center

Several factors influenced the decision not to incorporate the cataloging records of the Steinbeck collection into the library catalog. In general, the catalog's primary function was to represent ownership of materials, with less emphasis on access to resources. The Steinbeck Research Center was established as a unique, separate entity, not as an integral part of the library. Rather than adhere to existing cataloging rules and standards, the Center elected to describe the editions of Steinbeck's works according to the principles of descriptive bibliography, formulated by Fredson Bowers [1] and his disciples. Since John Steinbeck is the focus of the collection, main entry under Steinbeck was abandoned in favor of access by the title of the work, a decision which was not compatible with the cataloging practices of the general library.

Since its inception, the Center has developed an extensive collection of secondary materials, including complete issues of periodicals containing book and film reviews, articles, and editorials as well as special issues devoted to Steinbeck. Articles and newspaper clippings (original or photocopy) are maintained in a vertical file and are represented by author, title, and subject entries in the Center's catalog. The Center also created analytical catalog entries for individual essays in books as well as entries for articles and other materials pertinent to the study of Steinbeck but not contained in its collections. At that time, it was not the general library's policy to represent such materials in its catalog.

Initially, because the collection focuses on Steinbeck, the Center did not assign the standard subject heading, "Steinbeck, John, 1902-1968" with the appropriate free-floating or uniform title subdivisions for discussions of his life and works. The Center did not envision the retrieval power of the online catalog and therefore did not consider in-depth subject analysis of works about or relating to Steinbeck. Consequently, subject access is extremely limited or nonexistent for all the materials in the collection. In addition to author and title entries, the articles and clippings in the vertical file are retrieved primarily by title of the appropriate Steinbeck work (e.g., *Cup of Gold* or *Of Mice and Men*) or by very general terms (e.g., Activities—Travels, Biography, Steinbeck Country).

The Steinbeck Center was established in the early 1970s, when issues of access and the enhancement of standardized cataloging records were not clearly defined. In 1974, the general library at San Jose State was not yet cataloging its holdings on OCLC. The decision to isolate the cataloging records of the Steinbeck Center has profoundly affected access to the collection. For students and Steinbeck scholars, access is restricted to those who consult the catalog located in the Center or printed bibliographies of its holdings, such as the descriptive catalog compiled by Robert Woodward. [2] A page from the catalog is reproduced in Figure 1. [All figures for this chapter begin on page 141.]

The Center for Beethoven Studies

The curators of the Beethoven Center decided at the outset to increase the collection's visibility and accessibility. Rather than publish a printed descriptive bibliography, the Center opted for making its cataloging records available through the library's online public access catalog. With that choice came the problem of providing cataloging records that would be acceptable to the gen-

eral library, to the cataloging utility (in this case, OCLC), as well as to the patrons and staff of the collection itself. The major issues that needed to be resolved included what cataloging rules to use, how OCLC requirements would
affect the cataloging process, and how to provide more in-depth subject access
to the collections without conflicting with the subject authorities standards of
the general collection.

Catalogers of special collections and archives may find themselves torn
between loyalties to different sets of rules and user groups. A bibliographer
who caters to the needs of scholars in a particular field may decide to abandon
AACR2 [3] altogether in favor of the principles of descriptive bibliography. The
latter allow catalogers to treat each item as a unique gem of which every facet
can be examined and described. To researchers, slight variations in copies of
an edition, denoting differences in *issue* or *state*, [4, 5] are important. Unfortunately, descriptive bibliography does not transfer well to bibliographic utilities
for which AACR2 is the only acceptable standard. AACR2 insists on uniformity
in describing copies of an edition, ignoring the diversity that so interests textual critics. Lacking from most standard cataloging records for music, for example, are lengthy dedication statements, publishers' addresses, and price of
the issue, all of which are usually found on the title page (see Figure 2a). For
the Beethoven Center, original cataloging is often preferable to using existing
online records (see Figure 2b), which almost never meet the needs of the
collection's users and must be heavily edited (see Figure 2c).

Most frustrating about this time-consuming task of editing standard cataloging to an enhanced level is the knowledge that none of these details will be
retained in the master record on OCLC, which will merely show a holdings
code for the host library. Recently, the Beethoven Center cataloged a very rare
copy of the first edition of Beethoven's song cycle, "An die ferne Geliebte,"
which is not only from the earliest issue of the work, but also contains significant alterations in the music plates on one page. A photocopy from the Library
of Congress revealed that its copy of the same issue did not contain these alterations. OCLC's bibliographic input standards require that holdings for both copies be attached to the same master record, which would not indicate the differences between the two copies. (Figure 3 shows the Beethoven Center's original
record for the variant state.) Librarians using OCLC to assist scholars in locating
this edition would assume that these two copies are identical and would thus
overlook an important research source.

In spite of the inefficiencies of using OCLC for original and copy cataloging,
the Beethoven Center has found some acceptable solutions to the problems of
providing online access to the collection and the correlated standards for descriptive cataloging and subject access. While these solutions may not be ideal, they
serve the needs of the collection while staying within the restrictions of AACR2.
The Beethoven Center's practices may serve as a model for catalogers of special
collections who find themselves faced with the same dilemmas.

From the outset, the Beethoven Center adopted rules for *Descriptive Cataloging of Rare Books and Other Special Materials*, which were formulated under AACR2 and ISBD(A) [6] by the Office for Descriptive Cataloging Policy of the Library of Congress in 1981. These rules expand the guidelines for cataloging older printed materials, originally presented in AACR2 Chapter 2, by following many of the principles of descriptive bibliography. The Center catalogs all of its first and early editions of music scores (most of which were published between 1795 and 1850) in accordance with these rules, even though the rules do not specifically deal with music. There appear to be no precedents for systematically using these rules for scores published after 1800, particularly those cataloged on online networks.

A fundamental principle of the rules for rare-book cataloging that departs from AACR2 practice allows for all elements of data from a publication to be "generally transcribed as they appear, frequently without transposition or other forms of intervention practiced by catalogers of ordinary books under AACR2." [7] Because the order of information on the title page can be maintained, a textual scholar viewing the Center's cataloging records will obtain a reasonably good impression of the layout of a title page without examining the material itself. By following this principle, however, the Beethoven Center ignores one of the standard practices of music catalogers of transposing the opus number of a work to the title proper or other title information, as it usually appears on the title page after the statement of responsibility (see Figure 2).

Using ISBD punctuation, which is inseparable from AACR2, is a more troublesome compromise. The rare-book rules generally allow for precise transcription of punctuation that appears on the title page, as long as the prescribed punctuation is also added (rule 0E). Even slight changes in punctuation may indicate a different edition; the punctuation on the title page should therefore be transcribed as precisely as possible. Adding prescribed punctuation may confuse a textual scholar, who will not understand the difference between symbols that actually appear on the title page and those that are added by the cataloger to separate elements of the description. Symbols that textual scholars expect to see in descriptive bibliographies, such as the vertical slashes used to indicate line endings, also conflict with ISBD punctuation and are rarely seen in MARC records, which also do not attempt to reproduce exact title-page capitalization or unique printers' symbols.

To temper these compromises, the Beethoven Center makes heavy use of notes to describe details that cannot be transcribed exactly, most frequently comprising information that appears below the statement of responsibility. The OCLC records in Figures 2-4 illustrate how the Center describes engraved music plate numbers, publishers' rights statements ("Eigenthum der Verleger"), price indications, title page illustrations, and any details which may indicate a variant issue or state. Extremely long and detailed publishers' statements may be transcribed in a note. Most important to the research scholar are the many references to other catalogs and printed descriptive bibliographies, particularly when they give a more detailed description of the material than the online record can accommodate.

For music scores, the Beethoven Center has found a fairly successful means of working within the standards for description without compromising the needs of the collection's users. For the Center's books, the issues of standards revolved not around description, but around subject access. Most of the Center's books are not considered rare and therefore do not require the precise bibliographic descriptions demanded by the scores. Standard cataloging practice simply calls for establishing a name subject heading for books on Beethoven, occasionally adding a free-floating subdivision (e.g., Beethoven, Ludwig van Beethoven, 1770-1827—Friends and associates) or a uniform-title subheading for a book discussing a composition (e.g., Beethoven, Ludwig van Beethoven, 1770-1827—Symphonies, no. 5, op. 67, C minor). However, because the collection focuses entirely on one subject—the life and works of Ludwig van Beethoven—the Center is in a unique position to provide much more sophisticated access to its contents.

After consulting with Dr. Elaine Svenonius, an expert on thesaurus construction who worked with the Art and Architecture Thesaurus project, the Center chose to develop its own list of subject headings, taking LC terms as a starting point. The Center's subject headings list is being built fundamentally from general terms in Library of Congress Subject Headings (LCSH), used in very specific applications to Beethoven's life and music, and free-floating subdivisions that apply specifically to Beethoven as a person. Local headings are added for terms not in LCSH that music researchers are expected to use. Cumbersome uniform titles are replaced by opus numbers (e.g., "opus 21" replaces "Symphonies, no. 1, op. 21, C major), which are more readily searchable in online catalogs, to provide access to individual compositions. For example, the standard cataloging record for the book *Beethoven's Nine Symphonies Correlated with the Nine Spiritual Mysteries*, by Corrine Heline (Black Mountain, N.C.: New Age Press, 1971) offers two subject headings: "Beethoven, Ludwig van, 1770-1827—Symphonies" and "Occultism." The Center retained these two headings, but also added eight headings taken from LCSH, plus eleven local headings:

LCSH: Beethoven, Ludwig van, 1770-1827—Psychology
       Beethoven, Ludwig van, 1770-1827—Philosophy
       Spiritualism (Bible)
       Masculinity (Psychology)
       Femininity (Psychology)
       Symbolism
       Astrology
       Religion

        Mystical union
        Mysticism

Local headings: Musical criticism—Symphonies
                Analysis—Symphonies
                Opus 21, Opus 36, Opus 55, Opus 60, Opus 67,
                Opus 68, Opus 92, Opus 93, Opus 125

This in-depth subject analysis allows the Center to retrieve materials for patrons with complex research questions. The headings listed above will enable the Center's reference staff to locate this book by performing Boolean searches with the appropriate terms in response to questions about symbolism in Beethoven's ninth symphony (Opus 125), Beethoven's philosophies, or the concept of femininity in Beethoven's works.

Future Plans

The Beethoven Center's goal is to provide a unique and readily-accessible bibliographic database of Beethoven materials built of enhanced bibliographic data and sophisticated subject indexing. To avoid the problem of conflicts with the general library, the Beethoven Center is creating an alternate database in the library's online catalog which will maintain the integrity of the records with a corresponding local authority file. The staff of the Steinbeck Center now recognizes that knowledge of their collection's existence is too restricted, and that even those students and scholars who visit the Center are hampered by the limitations of the cataloging records. A priority of the Steinbeck Center is to catalog the collection through OCLC in order to be represented in the online catalog. The Center is now faced with the issues of cataloging standards and online system requirements.

Summary and Conclusion

Providing online access to bibliographic information in accordance with standard codes presents problems for the cataloging of special collections. AACR2 alone is often not adequate for the provision of the level of detail required by such collections. Some special collections catalogers have instituted practices that do not follow an official standard of description. Until there is a formal solution to the issues of national standards vs. local needs, compromises will continue to be necessary in order to properly serve the community of users of special collections.

German

B2-4 JOHN STEINBECK | DER ROTE PONY | STEINBERG VERLAG ZÜ RICH

Copyright 1945 by Steinberg Verlag Zürich. Printed in Switzerland. No translator listed. *Pagination:* [1-10], 11-343 (text), [344]. 189 x 114 mm. *Binding:* Gray cloth, printed in red on front cover and spine. Edges trimmed; top edges stained blue. Colored pictorial dust jacket. *Notes:* G&P D192. P. [4] notes original title: *The Long Valley.*

The Grapes of Wrath
AMERICAN EDITIONS

A7-1 [*Enclosed within an Oxford rule*] THE GRAPES | OF WRATH | [*ornament*] | JOHN STEINBECK | [*publisher's emblem*] | [*ornamental rule*] | THE VIKING PRESS·NEW YORK | 1939

Pre-publication dummy. No copyright information. *Pagination:* [i-vi], [1-2], 3-10 (text ends with "He stood in the sun, peeling the"). Remaining pages blank. 202 x 136 mm. *Binding:* Buff cloth, stamped in blue on cover and spine. Edges trimmed. Top edges stained green. Plain endpapers. *Notes:* Notation on right-front endpaper: prepublication Dummy copy.

A7-2 [*Enclosed within an Oxford rule*] The | Grapes | of Wrath | JOHN STEINBECK | [*ornamental rule*] | *THE VIKING PRESS·NEW YORK*

First edition. First published in April 1939. *Pagination:* [i-vi], [1-2], 3-619 (text), [620-622]. 202 x 136 mm. *Binding:* Beige cloth, with line drawing in reddish-brown on front cover and spine. Spine printed in reddish-brown. Buff endpapers printed with portion of "Battle Hymn of the Republic." Edges trimmed. Top edges stained yellow. Illustrated dust jacket; illustration by Elmer Hader. Printed on bottom right of front flap: FIRST | EDITION. *Notes:* G&P A12a. Inscription on right front endpaper: "As He died to make | men holy | Let us die to make men | free" | John Steinbeck

A7-3 Same as A7-2, except as noted. 203 x 138 mm.

A7-15 Same as A7-2, except as noted. Third Printing Before Publication. Printed at bottom right of front flap of dust jacket: *Third Printing.*

A7-4 [*Enclosed within a double rule, the upper portion illustrated, the lower portion a yellow background*] | The Grapes | of | WRATH | *by* JOHN STEINBECK | WITH LITHOGRAPHS *by* Thomas Hart Benton | NEW YORK The Limited Editions Club *1940*

Special contents copyright 1940 by The Limited Editions Club. 2 vols. *Pagination,* Vol. I: [i-iv], v-xvii (*John Steinbeck and The Grapes of Wrath* by Joseph Henry Jackson), xviii-xxii (*Thomas Benton and The Grapes of Wrath* by Thomas Craven), [xxiii-xxiv], 1-284 (text). 259 x 190 mm. Vol. II: [i-iv], 285-559 (text), [560] (colophon), [561-564]. 259 x 190 mm. *Binding:* Three-quarters grass cloth, brown rawhide spine. All edges trimmed, stained yellow. Illustrated endpapers. Glassine dust jackets. Publisher's slipcase. *Notes:* G&P A12c. Colophon page of Vol. II: Number 881 of 1146 copies. Signed: Benton

31

Figure 1. Page from Robert H. Woodward's descriptive bibliography of the Steinbeck collection (1985).

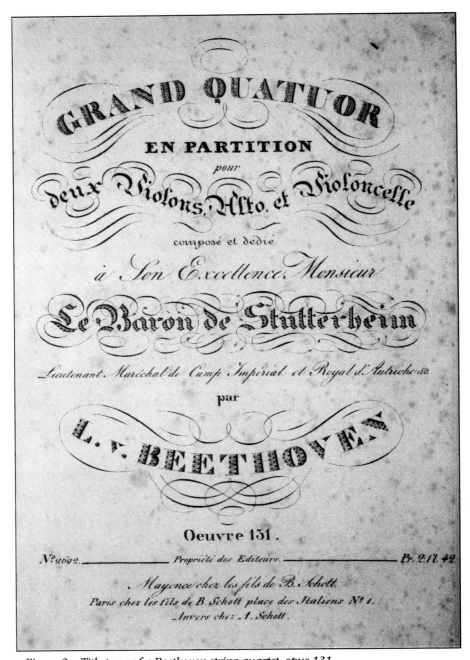

Figure 2a. Title page of a Beethoven string quartet, opus 131.

```
                      ¶
▶CSJ - FOR OTHER HOLDINGS, ENTER dh DEPRESS DISPLAY RECD SEND
  OCLC: 12006428        Rec stat: n Entrd: 850507        Used: 901015 ¶
▶Type: c Bib lvl: m Lang:  N/A Source: d Accomp mat:
  Repr:     Enc lvl: I Ctry:  gw  Dat tp: s MEBE: 1
            Mod rec:    Comp:   zz  Format: a Prts:
  Desc: a Int lvl:     LTxt:  n    Dates: 1827,       ¶
  ▶ 1 010        ¶
  ▶ 2 040        CLU ǂc CLU ǂd m/c ¶
  ▶ 3 028 22     2692 ǂb B. Schott. ¶
  ▶ 4 048        sa02 ǂa sb01 ǂa sc01 ¶
  ▶ 5 090        ǂb  ¶
  ▶ 6 049        CSJM ¶
  ▶ 7 100 10     Beethoven, Ludwig van, ǂd 1770-1827. ǂw cn ¶
  ▶ 8 240 10     Quartets, ǂm strings, ǂn no. 14, op. 131, ǂr C# minor ¶
  ▶ 9 245 00     Grand quatuor en partition pour deux violons, alto et violoncelle,
oeuvre 131 / ǂc composʾe et dʾediʾe ʿa Baron de Stutterheim ... par L. v.
Beethoven. ¶
  ▷10 260 0      Mayence : ǂb Chez les fils de B. Schott, ǂc [1827] ¶
  ▶11 300        1 score (50 p.) ; ǂc 26 cm. ¶
  ▶12 650  0     String quartets ǂx Scores. ¶
```

Figure 2b. Master OCLC record for 1st edition of the score of Beethoven's string quartet, opus 131.

```
      Screen 1 of 2      ¶
   ▶CSJ - FOR OTHER HOLDINGS, ENTER dh DEPRESS DISPLAY RECD SEND
     OCLC: 12006428        Rec stat: n Entrd: 850507        Used: 901015 ¶
   ▶Type: c Bib lvl: m Lang:  N/A Source: d Accomp mat:
     Repr:     Enc lvl: I Ctry:  gw  Dat tp: s MEBE: 1
               Mod rec:    Comp:   zz  Format: a Prts:
     Desc: a Int lvl:     LTxt:  n    Dates: 1827,       ¶
     ▶ 1 010        ¶
     ▶ 2 040        CLU ǂc CLU ǂd m/c ¶
     ▶ 3 028 21     2692 ǂb Schott. ¶
     ▶ 4 045 0      ǂb d1826 ¶
     ▶ 5 048        sa02 ʾa sc01 ¶
     ▶ 6 099  9     Op131 ǂa Schott ǂa 2692 ǂa 1827 ǂa Score ¶
     ▶ 7 049        [Beet-][hoven][Center] CSJE ¶
     ▶ 8 100 10     Beethoven, Ludwig van, ǂd 1770-1827. ǂw cn ¶
     ▶ 9 240 10     Quartets, ǂm strings, ǂn no. 14, op. 131, ǂr C# minor ¶
     ▶10 245 00     Grand quatuor en partition pour deux violons, alto et violoncelle,
   / ǂc composʾe et dʾediʾe ʿa Son Excellence Monsieur le Baron de Stutterheim
   Lieutenant Marʾechal de Camp. Impʾerial et Royal d'Autriche &c. par L. van
   Beethoven ; Oeuvre 131. ¶

      Screen 2 of 2      ¶
     ▶11 260 0      Mayence : ǂb chez les fils de B. Schott ; ǂa Paris : ǂb chez les
   fils de B. Schott Place des Italians No. 1. ; ǂa Anvers : ǂb chez A. Schott, ǂc
   [1827]. ¶
     ▶12 300        1 score ([2], 50 p.) ; ǂc 25 cm. ¶
     ▶13 500        1st. ed. of the score, pub. after September, 1827. ¶
     ▶14 500        On t.p. above imprint: No. 2692. ; Propriʾetʾe des Editeurs. ; Pr:
   2. fl: 42 [x]. ¶
     ▶15 510 4      Kinsky-Halm, c p. 398. ¶
     ▶16 510 4      Dorfm̈uller, c p. 131. ¶
     ▶17 510 4      Kat. Hoboken, c v. 2, no. 519. ¶
     ▶18 650  0     String quartets ǂx Scores. ¶
     ▶19 700 10     Stutterheim, Joseph von, ǂc Baron, ǂd 1764-1831. ¶
```

Figure 2c. Beethoven Center's edited version of OCLC master record.

```
Screen 1 of 3        ¶
▶CSJ
   OCLC: 22715353      Rec stat: n Entrd: 901119          Used: 901120 ¶
▶Type: c Bib lvl: m Lang:  ger Source: d Accomp mat:
   Repr:    Enc lvl: I Ctry:   au  Dat tp: s MEBE: 1
            Mod rec:    Comp:   sg  Format: a Prts:
   Desc: a Int lvl:    LTxt:  n   Dates: 1816,       ¶
▶  1 010        ¶
▶  2 040        CSJ ‡c CSJ ¶
▶  3 028 21     S. et C. 2610 ‡b Steiner ¶
▶  4 045 2      ‡b d1815 ‡b d1816 ¶
▶  5 048        vi01 ‡a ka01 ¶
▶  6 090        ‡b  ¶
▶  7 049        CSJM ¶
▶  8 100 10     Beethoven, Ludwig van, ‡d 1770-1827. ¶
▶  9 240 10     An die ferne Geliebte ¶
▶ 10 245 10     An die ferne Geliebte / ‡c ein Liederkreis von Al: Jeitteles. ;
mit Begleitung des Piano=Forte in Musik gesetzt, und Seiner Durchlaucht dem
regierenden Herrn F¨ursten Joseph von Lobkowitz, Herzog zu Raudnitz &.&.&.
ehrfurchtsvoll gewidmet von Ludwig van Beethoven. ; 98tes Werk. ¶
▶ 11 260 0      Wien : ‡b bei S.A. Steiner und Comp., ‡c [1816]. ¶
▶ 12 300        1 score ([2], 20 p.) ; ‡c 26 x 34 cm. ¶

   Screen 2 of 3        ¶
▶ 13 500        1st. ed., 1st. issue, published in October, 1816. Cf. Tyson,
"Beethoven in Steiner's shop," Music Review 23 (1962): 120. Variant state, with
plate corrections in the piano part, 3rd system, p. 10. ¶
▶ 14 500        On t.p. above imprint: No.. 2610. Eigenthum der Verleger. Preis. ¶
▶ 15 500        Vignette on t.p.: boy playing lute. ¶
▶ 16 500        On t.p.: A. M¨uller sc. ¶
▶ 17 500        Publisher's "Musik-Anzeige" on p. 1 (page following title page). ¶
▶ 18 510 4      Kinsky-Halm, ‡c p. 275, cites later issue with variant t.p. as
1st. ed. ¶
▶ 19 510 4      Dorfm¨uller, ‡c p. 336. ¶
▶ 20 510 4      Kat. Hoboken, ‡c v. 2, no. 415. ¶
▶ 21 510 4      Weinmann, A. Vollst¨andiges Verlagsverzeichnis Senefelder,
Steiner, Haslinger (Beitrage zur Geschichte des Alt-Wiener Musikverlages, Rh.2,
F.19). M¨unchen : Katzbichler, 1979, ‡c v. 1, p. 147. ¶
▶ 22 650  0     Songs (Medium voice) with piano. ¶
▶ 23 650  0     Song cycles. ¶
▶ 24 700 10     M¨uller, Andreas, ‡d fl.1815-1817? ¶

   Screen 3 of 3        ¶
▶ 25 700 10     Jeitteles, Alois, ‡d 1794-1858. ¶
▶ 26 700 10     Lobkowitz, Joseph Franz Maximilian, ‡d 1772-1816. ¶
```

Figure 3. Beethoven Center's original record for variant state of "An die ferne Geliebte."

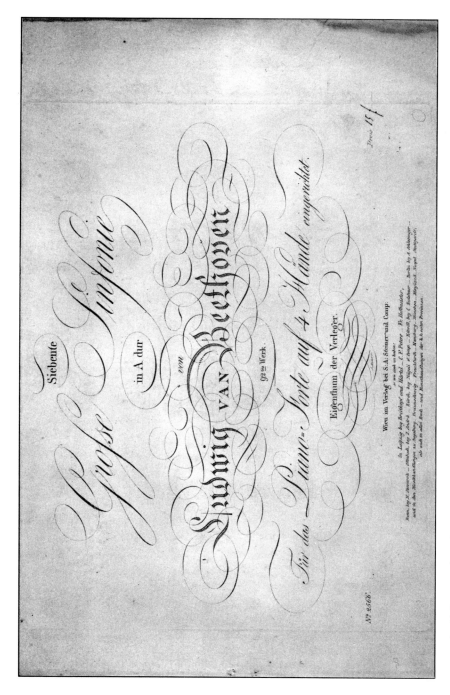

Figure 4a. Title page of Beethoven's Seventh Symphony arranged for piano, 4 hands.

```
Screen 1 of 3
CSJ
OCLC: 22369336      Rec stat: n Entrd: 900913        Used: 900913
Type: c Bib lvl: m Lang:  N/A Source: d Accomp mat:
Repr:    Enc lvl: I Ctry:  au Dat tp: s MEBE: 1
         Mod rec:   Comp:  sy Format: z Prts:
Desc: a Int lvl:    LTxt:  n  Dates: 1816,
   1 010
   2 040       CSJ ¦c CSJ
   3 028 21    C.D.A.S. 2566 ¦b Steiner
   4 045 0     ¦b d1811 ¦b d1812
   5 048       ka02
   6 090       ¦b
   7 049       CSJM
   8 100 10    Beethoven, Ludwig van, ¦d 1770-1827.
   9 240 10    Symphonies, ¦n no. 7, op. 92, ¦r A major ; ¦o arr.
  10 245 00    Siebente grosse Sinfonie in A dur / ¦c von Ludwig van Beethoven ;
92tes Werk ; f¨ur das Piano=Forte auf 4 H¨ande eingerichtet.
  11 260 0     Wien : ¦b im Verlag bei S: A: Steiner und Comp:, ¦c [1816?]
  12 300       [4], 79, [1] p. of music ; ¦c 25 x 33 cm.
  13 500       First ed. of this arrangement by A. Diabelli.
  14 500       On t.p. above imprint: Eigenthum der Verleger ; No.. 2566 ; A.
M¨uller sc. ; Preis [15f].

Screen 2 of 3
  15 500       On t.p. below imprint: so wie auch zu haben: in Leipzig bey
Breitkopf und H¨artel -- C.F. Peters -- Fr. Hoffmeister, Bonn, bey N. Simrock
- Offenbach, bey J. Andr¨a -- Z¨urch, bey N¨ageli & Comp. -- Ettwill, bey C.
Zulehner -- Berlin by A. Schlesinger -- und in den Musikhandlungen zu Augsburg
-- Braunschweig -- Frankfurth -- Hamburg -- M¨unchen -- Mayland -- Neapel --
Stuttgart, als auch in allen Buch-und Kunsthandlungen der k.k. oester.
Provincen.
  16 500       Dedication leaf: Ihrer Majest¨at der Kaiserinn Elisabeth
Alexiewna Selbstherscherinn aller Reussen &. &. &. in tiefster Ehrfurcht
gewidmet von Ludwig van Beethoven.
  17 500       Announcement and price list of Steiner's various editions and
arrangements of the 7th Symphony, and other newly published works: p. 1.
  18 510 4     Kinsky-Halm, ¦c p. 260.
  19 510 4     Kat. Hoboken, ¦c v. 2, no. 399.
  20 650 0     Symphonies arranged for piano (4 hands)
  21 700 10    Diabelli, Anton, ¦d 1781-1858.

Screen 3 of 3
  22 700 10    M¨uller, Andreas, ¦d fl. 1815-1817?
```

Figure 4b. Beethoven Center cataloging record for the composer's Seventh Symphony.

NOTES

1. Bowers, Fredson. *Principles of Bibliographic Description*. Princeton, NJ: Princeton University Press, 1949.

2. Woodward, Robert H. *The Steinbeck Research Center at San Jose State University: A Descriptive Catalogue*. San Jose, CA: San Jose State University, 1985. (San Jose Studies, vol. 11, no 1).

3. *Anglo-American Cataloguing Rules*. Edited by Michael Gorman and Paul W. Winkler. 2nd ed., 1988 rev. Ottawa: Canadian Library Association; London: Library Association Publishing; Chicago: American Library Association, 1988.

4. An *issue* is generally defined by bibliographers as all copies of a work prepared for sale under the same publishing arrangements, often all printed at the same time.

5. A *state* is determined by the content of the material. When all copies are identical, they are said to belong to the same state; any change in the content, however slight, denotes a new state.

6. *ISBD(A): International Standard Bibliographic Description for Older Monographic Publications (Antiquarian)*. Working Group on the International Standard Bibliographic Description for Older Monographic Publications (Antiquarian). London: IFLA International Office for UBC, 1980.

7. Library of Congress. Office for Descriptive Cataloging Policy. *Bibliographic Description of Rare Books*. Washington, DC: Library of Congress, 1981, p. vi.

MUSICAL SOUND RECORDINGS: SUBJECT RETRIEVAL, ANALYSIS, AND ACCESS IN ONLINE PUBLIC ACCESS CATALOGS

Charles Whitlow
CFO Tax Librarian
AT&T Information Services Network
412 Mt. Kemble Ave., Morristown, NJ 07960-1955

Introduction

Retrieving bibliographic records from an online public access catalog (OPAC) is a type of information retrieval process. Typically, OPACs facilitate retrieval of bibliographic records for known items through name and title access points, and allow subject retrieval through precoordinated subject headings or through keyword searching. While earlier user studies conducted on card catalogs had indicated minimal use of subject retrieval, recent user studies in an online environment have demonstrated that user populations display a larger-than-expected desire to retrieve bibliographic data by subject. The purpose of this paper is to explore subject retrieval in OPACs with respect to recorded musical works.

Musical Analysis and Access

In music there has been major dissatisfaction with subject access. Most musicians and scholars who work with music have learned from experience that many aspects associated with musical materials are not coded for retrieval in the standard topical (verbal) or systematic (classification) schemes. Both the systematic approach and the topical approach have left users of music materials frustrated. This frustration has led scholars to look at the needs and wants of users when it comes to retrieval of music materials.

In an attempt to discover useful characteristics for the arrangement of printed music, Karl-Heinz Kohler identified four facets for subject arrangement of printed music: species (or form of composition), setting (or medium of performance), content (topic, style, or character), and topography (country and chronology). [1] These facets represent the analytical elements of printed music, but it was Olga Buth's [2] review of classification schemes for scores and sound recordings that gave us a more extensive list of characteristics most often associated with music:

1) size;
2) format;
3) alphabetical arrangement (by composer);
4) medium [of performance];
5) form [of composition];
6) subject content;
7) character or content;
8) language of text;
9) geographical [orientation];
10) style relating to a historical period;
11) opus and thematic index numbers.

To improve access to music materials, Brian Redfern [3] examined the various types of users of music collections:

1) musicologists or music historians;
2) instrumentalists;
3) music teachers;
4) instrumental or vocal groups or choirs;
5) general readers;
6) users of sound recordings (LPs, cassettes, discs).

Richard Smiraglia [4] developed a scheme for subject analysis of music materials. Smiraglia's analytical scheme, based on the work of A.G. Brown [5] and incorporating the work of Kohler, Redfern and Buth, includes the following four main elements:

1) intellectual form (medium of performance and form of composition);
2) topicality (topic, character, historical style period, cultural influences);
3) intended audience;
4) form of composition (with sound recordings, analysis as a unified performance, or in parts).

Dissatisfaction with subject access to music materials led scholars like Kohler, Buth, Redfern, and Smiraglia to examine music materials closely and find common facets or elements that may be used to adequately "mark" music materials for retrieval. These elements, whether in verbal form or artificial notation, must satisfy the objectives of a catalog as enumerated by Shera and Egan [6] and must meet users' needs in an OPAC.

Verbal Access

Library of Congress Subject Headings (LCSH) has been the most widely-used system for subject analysis of and access to musical sound recordings. Based on the pioneering work of Oscar Sonneck in 1904, LC subject headings for musical sound recordings have adequately dealt with medium of performance and form of composition, but facets such as culture or topicality have only occasionally been covered. This lack of coverage violates the Shera and Egan [7] objectives by not providing access to all elements that might be sought by a user. Many times LC neglects to show the "affiliations" that may exist between elements of topicality such as cultural influences or historical style; and, lastly, LC ignores the terms by which musicians refer to various types of music styles or practices. LC's appeal to the principle of literary warrant and its policy of overjustification have blocked the creation of needed headings and revisions. For example, "Gospel Music" was assigned the LC heading "Hymns—19th Century" for many years. The terminology of the common music lover has often been ignored by LC in favor of that of the musicologist. This point may be exemplified through the heading "Canons, Fugues, etc." The "etc." implies that other forms of imitation, such as "Preludes" are included under this subject heading. Most musicologists would know this, but what about the common user looking for a recorded collection of various preludes?

While content-designated control elements in the MARC (machine-readable cataloging) music format cover chronology, geography (i.e., cultural influences), form of composition, medium of performance, and physical form, other facets of intended audience and topicality are still uncovered. The sample OCLC-MARC record for a sound recording in Figure 1 illustrates these points.

```
OCLC:     21480956          Rec stat:    n
Entered:      19900504      Replaced:  . 19900504          Used:     19910507
Type:    j          Bib lvl: m          Source: d          Lang:  N/A
Repr:               Enc lvl: I          Format: n          Ctry:  nyu
Accomp:             Mod rec:            Prts:              LTxt:
Desc:    a          Int lvl:            MEBE:   1          Comp:  ju
                                        Dat tp: s          Dates: 1990,
   1  040       CXP  c CXP
   2  007       s  b d  d 4  e z  f n  g g  h n  i n  m e  n d
   3  028 00   79232-2  b Elektra Nonesuch
   4  028 00   9 79232-2  b Elektra Nonesuch
   5  092 0    786.4052  b B122Seh  2 19
   6  092        b
   7  049       BTLL
   8  100 10   Bach, Johann Sebastian,  d 1685-1750.
   9  240 10   Englische Suiten,  n Nr. 6
  10  245 10   English suite :  b no. 5 in E minor, BWV 810 /  c J.S. Bach.
Nocturne in E , op. 9, no. 2 ; Nocturne in B major, op. 32, no. 1 / Chopin --
Sonata no. 6 in F major, op. 10, no. 2 / Beethoven  h sound recording
  11  260 0    New York, N.Y. :  b Elektra Nonesuch,  c p1990.
  12  300       1 sound disc :  b digital ;  c 4 3/4 in.
  13  500       Elektra Nonesuch: 79232-2 (on container: 9 79232-2).
  14  511 0    Mieczyslaw Horzowski, piano.
  15  500       Compact disc.
  16  650  0   Suites (Piano)
  17  650  0   Piano music.
  18  650  0   Sonatas (Piano)
  19  700 10   Horszowski, Mieczyslaw.
  20  700 12   Chopin, Fr ed eric,  d 1810-1849.  t Nocturnes,  m piano,  n op.
9.  n No. 2.
  21  700 12   Chopin, Fr ed eric,  d 1810-1849.  t Nocturnes,  m piano,  n op.
32.  n No. 1.
  22  700 12   Beethoven, Ludwig van,  d 1770-1827.  t Sonatas,  m piano,  n
no. 6, op. 10, no. 2,  r F major.
```

Figure 1. Sample record in the OCLC-MARC Sound Recordings Format.

PRECIS [8, 9], which has been used in the *British Catalogue of Music* (BCM) since 1984, utilizes paradigms that are based on three fundamental facets: musical form, medium of performance, and number of performers. [10] Paula Beversdorf Gabbard, [11] in her study of music books, asserted that PRECIS had potential for online use that LCSH "could never hope to have in its present state." She makes reference to what Buckland [12] would later describe as part of the "time" signal by stating that PRECIS language is "current" and has the ability to be kept up-to-date easily. A set of PRECIS index entries is contrasted with LCSH in the following example. All the PRECIS entries are generated from a single index string, which is coextensive with the scope of the work. Each index term is displayed in context.

AUTHOR: American Society of Composers, Authors and Publishers
TITLE: ASCAP biographical dictionary
DEWEY: 780.922
PRECIS: 1. Music. United States
   Composers. Organizations: American Society of
   Composers, Authors and Publishers.
   Members—*Biographies*
2. Composers. Music. United States. Organizations:
   American Society of Composers, Authors and
   Publishers. Members—*Biographies*
3. American Society of Composers, Authors and
   Publishers.
   Members—*Biographies*
LCSH: 1. American Society of Composers, Authors and
   Publishers—Biography
2. Music—United States—Bio-bibliography [13]

In a study of printed music, J. Bradford Young [14] concluded that the "application of PRECIS' syntactical structure to the retrieval of printed music does offer an available alternative to LCSH." The advantage of PRECIS lies in its treatment of multi-faceted works found in printed music.

Classification

The Dewey Decimal Classification (DDC) has been widely used with music materials. The 20th edition of Dewey "has been prepared with little or no reference to previous editions." [15] Old DDC numbers have been reused with new definitions. The 20th edition has provided an expansion for traditions in music, but more importantly to the user, no restrictions on the number of facets to be added to a number have been made. Below are some examples of simple faceting in Dewey classification of music materials [16]:

781.723166	Rock and Roll Christmas Music
781.723	Christmas Day
1	Facet Indicator
66 (from 781.66)	Rock and Roll
787.2	A treatise on violin music, AND Violin scores, AND Recordings of violin music
787.2026	A treatise on violin scores
787.20266	A treatise on recordings of violin music
786.21884	Chopin. Mazurka, piano
786.2	Piano
1	Facet Indicator
884 (from 784.1884)	Mazurka form

The fact that DDC now allows unlimited faceting opens up avenues for more in-depth analysis of music materials, such as musical sound recordings.

The Library of Congress Classification for music (LCC class M) was developed by Oscar Sonneck and first published in 1904. Though it was designed as a shelf classification system, it was used for over forty years as a subject retrieval tool for the collections of the Library of Congress. [17] If LC Class M could undergo the same type of revisions that Class 780 in the 20th edition of DDC underwent, it could serve as a powerful system for subject access. Given its notational structure, faceting in LCC is not possible at present.

Musical Sound Recordings

For the musician and music lover, musical sound recordings are a miraculous link to the past. They give listeners the chance to hear artists who are not alive at the present time. Musical sound recordings also provide examples for the inquiring student into techniques and styles that are no longer practiced. And to the music historian and lover, sound recordings provide the chance to hear special live performances that can never be duplicated. Based on these examples, it might be said that musical sound recording collections serve three functions: 1) public enjoyment, 2) teaching aid, and 3) historical record.

Musical sound recordings have been a part of music collections since the early 1900s. [18] Musical recordings in libraries are circulating items for public enjoyment, teaching tools for students of music history and music appreciation, and performance tools for students seeking to hear how a particular artist or composer has performed a particular piece. Musical sound recordings bridge the gap between the past and the present and provide both enjoyment and knowledge for the musicians and music lovers of the future.

To provide enjoyment or knowledge, sound recordings in a collection must be retrievable. Because of their many varying formats and physical characteristics, and sometimes the lack of librarians who understand their value in a collection, musical sound recordings have suffered neglect in the areas of subject analysis and access.

One reason for this neglect may lie in the nature of a recording itself. A recording may contain one composition by one composer, written for one medium of performance, e.g., piano. A recording may also contain pieces by several composers for one medium, or pieces by one composer for several media. Whatever the combination or arrangement, musical analysis of sound recordings must reach beyond the level of title and examine the recording as a distinct entity. A musical sound recording documents a distinct performance, which can be analyzed on its own terms, not just as an exemplar of the score or sheet music.

A recording should be considered a separate entity, not just as a mechanical representation of music in performance. For example, many of John Cage's works have a serendipitous nature. Each time a piece is performed, it is a unique experience that will never be the same again because often only the instrumentation of the piece is constant, while the notes, time, dynamics, and style are left up to the performer. This makes analysis of Cage's works extremely difficult. The score stays constant, while the live performance becomes the true, artistic representation. The score becomes a written representation of the performance, secondary to its presentation. How should we then approach the musical sound recording?

Smiraglia's [19] scheme includes three areas under topicality that might be applied to the analysis of a unified performance of a sound recording: topic or character, historical style period, and cultural influences. For example, Sousa's *Stars and Stripes Forever* was intended as a field march for his Army Band. Yet because of its association with the centennial celebration of the Statue of Liberty, a recording of "liberty pieces" might include it. In this sense, the musical sound recording takes on a new topical meaning, which the user might seek as "pieces played for the celebration of the 100th anniversary of the Statue of Liberty". "Liberty Pieces" becomes a topic based on a historical time, event or period, which produces a performance of a work or works that otherwise might not be placed together either in score or sheet music form.

In some cases, the performance creates the score or sheet music. This is particularly true in the area of arrangements of popular rock songs or scores. The release of an album or revival concert prompts the production of sheet music scores or souvenir albums (folios) which contain transcribed versions of the live performance or recording. In this case, the score or sheet music is secondary to the recording or performance.

Character is another potential element in the analysis of a unified performance of a musical sound recording. For example, Mieczyslaw Horszowski, aged 98, is perhaps the last of the 19th century-trained pianists still performing in today's concert world. The character of his playing and performance techniques is that of the late 19th century. A recording of a 1990 performance by him would be reminiscent of the salons of Vienna and Paris, and would be far removed from the playing of pianists trained in recent decades. Figure 1 contains an OCLC record for a Horszowski recording. While there are entries for him and for the composers, the character of the performance is not represented in the subject fields.

One of the functions that musical recording collections may serve is to exemplify history. In a Horszowski recording, the pieces or musical scores are not the most significant part of the entity; rather, the characteristic of being totally romantic in *style of performance* is what is significant. Hundreds of recordings of Bach's music exist, but no current recording could give the listener a clearer understanding of the style and character of the playing of Bach in the 19th century than that of Horszowski.

The case of the Horszowski recording brings to mind another factor that must not be overlooked in the analysis of a unified performance of a musical sound recording, that is, *cultural influences.* The romantic style of Horszowski's playing derives from the influence of late 19th-century European culture. Some of the fire and passion that are associated with Horszowski's playing of romantic music by composers such as Chopin may be the result of his love for his native land and his hope of a free and united Poland. The cultural influences of Poland, and Horszowski's love for his homeland, may constitute important factors in the way in which certain Polish pieces were performed by him. Again, the recording itself may be special in its interpretation of Polish themes.

One element not mentioned by Smiraglia that may be important in the analysis of a musical sound recording is *intended purpose.* While one intended audience may be targeted by the composers or producers of albums, the idea of intended purpose being suggested here is that of emotional intentions, namely, the types of musical characteristics that denote happiness, sadness, etc.

This idea is not new in the analysis of music, for as early as the late 16th century, music theorists suggested that a composition should have a unity of *affection* such as rage, excitement, grandeur, heroism, contemplation, wonder, or mysticality. [20] Called the *Affektenlehre,* or Doctrine of Affections, it was never a precisely formulated doctrine, but was based on stereotyped musical figures proposed by German scholars (Kretschmar, Goldschmidt, and Schering). [21] One current music scholar and librarian explained Affektenlehre in terms of "loud" or "soft". [22]

Users often begin with general categories of music when searching for sound recordings, but in the final selection process, a user may wish to choose a recording according to the quality of sound it may produce in relation to an emotion that he or she is feeling or wants to feel. For example, a user might state that the piece s/he is seeking is classical, instrumental rather than vocal, and perhaps romantic in style; but the final criterion for selecting a collection of Chopin's *Ballades* over Berlioz's *Symphonie Fantastique* is the fact that the user wants to hear soothing music while reading a book that evening—nothing that would be too distracting. Emotions thus constitute a factor in the selection of musical sound recordings.

The answer to the problem of representation of recordings in terms of such features as topic or intended use could be faceted classification, such as DDC. As noted above, in its 20th edition, DDC allows for unlimited use of facets.

The DDC hierarchy, for the most part, is expressed by the length of its numbers. The more specific the topic, the longer the number. Dewey's capacity to synthesize all types of musical elements numerically gives the cataloger a chance to bring together the topical and intended-purpose facets within sound recordings and collections of music. For example, if we had a collection of Spanish keyboard works which contains several Cuban dances that a dance instructor might use for rehearsal purposes, one could notate as follows:

786.2072911544	A collection of Spanish keyboard works that contains original Cuban dances which may be used for dance rehearsals
786.2	Piano
07291	Cuba
1	Facet indicator
544	Dance music

By displaying to the user a menu of the DDC, the user could build a number, adding or deleting elements where necessary. The display might look as follows:

786	Keyboard music
786.2	Piano
786.207291	Topical reference to Cuban elements
786.2072911	Facet indicator
786.2072911544	Intended purpose: Dance rehearsal music

Perhaps it is time to consider the broader application of the DDC classification—as a subject analysis tool as well as a system for assigning location symbols to library materials.

Summary

Retrieval from catalogs is dependent on proper subject analysis, which provides terms for user access. Subject access points are of two primary types: *topical*, i.e., verbal subject headings, and *systematic*, i.e., classification. These access points should meet the objectives of a catalog by serving any user group, through all types of vocabularies. Music users have been frustrated with subject analysis and access to their materials and have identified characteristics of music materials that help to clarify user needs. These characteristics include topicality, form of composition, medium of performance, intended audience, chronology, culture, and physical format.

Unfortunately, no current verbal system of subject analysis has been able to provide access to all these elements. The DDC is the only widely used classification scheme that has been revised to allow faceting in its schedule for music. The 20th edition of Dewey offers the possibility of providing the needed access to intellectual elements of musical sound recordings.

In sound recordings, no effort has to date been made to provide access to the three facets of topicality: topic or character, historical style, and cultural influences. The intended use of a recording may also play an important role in the final selection and retrieval of an item. By synthesizing elements such as topic, style, cultural influences, and even intended use of music, the DDC could once again begin to serve its dual role as a system for subject access and shelf classification. Applying this system in an online catalog [23] would enhance the precision of searches in the field of music.

NOTES

1. Kohler, Karl-Heinz. "Grundzuege eines analytischen Systems der Sachkatalogisierung der 'Musica Practica'." *Zentralblatt fuer Bibliothekswissenschaft* 71 (1957): pp. 267-80.

2. Buth, Olga. "Scores and Recordings," *Library Trends* 23 (1975): pp. 429-449.

3. Redfern, Brian. *Organising Music in Libraries. Volume I: Arrangement and Classification*, rev. ed. London: Clive Bingley, 1978.

4. Smiraglia, Richard P. *Music Cataloging: The Bibliographic Control of Printed and Recorded Music In Libraries.* Englewood, CO: Libraries Unlimited, 1989.

5. Brown, A.G. *An Introduction to Subject Indexing.* London: Clive Bingley, 1976.

6. Shera, Jesse; Egan, Margaret Elizabeth. *The Classified Catalog: Basic Principles and Practice.* Chicago: American Library Association, 1956.

7. Ibid, p. 10.

8. Austin, Derek. "PRECIS: The Preserved Context Index System." In Chan, Lois Mai, Richmond, Phyllis A., and Svenonius, Elaine, eds. *Theory of Subject Analysis: A Sourcebook.* Littleton, CO: Libraries Unlimited, 1985, pp. 369-389.

9. Dykstra, Mary. *Precis: A Primer.* London: The British Library, 1985.

10. Smiraglia, pp. 85-88.

11. Gabbard, Paula B. "LCSH and PRECIS in Music: A Comparison." *Library Quarterly* 55 (April, 1985): pp. 192-206.

12. Buckland, Michael K. *Library Services in Theory and Context*, 2nd ed. Oxford: Pergamon Press, 1988.

13. Gabbard, p. 197.

14. Young, J. Bradford. "A Comparison of PRECIS and LCSH for the Retrieval of Printed Music." Unpublished Manuscript. 1987? p. 19.

15. *Dewey Decimal Classification 20th Edition: Manual: 780.* Dublin, OH: Forest Press, 1989, p. 548.

16. ibid, pp. 926-938.

17. Smiraglia, pp. 74-85.

18. Kinkeldey, Otto. "American Music Catalogs." *Library Journal* 40 (1915): p. 575.

19. Smiraglia, p. 65.

20. Grout, Donald Jay; Palisca, Claude V. *A History of Western Music.* 4th Edition. New York: W. W. Norton, 1988, p. 218.

21. Buelow, George J. "Music, Rhetoric, and the Concept of the Affections: A Selective Bibliography." *Music Library Association Notes* 30 (1973-74): pp. 250-259.

22. Sommer, Susan T. *Interview.* NYPL Performing Arts Library. April, 1990.

23. Wajenberg, Arnold S. "MARC Coding of DDC for Subject Retrieval." *Information Technology and Libraries* 2 (September 1983): pp. 246-251.

SUBJECT ACCESS TO WOMEN'S STUDIES MATERIALS

Hope Olson

Coordinator, Original Cataloguing
University of Alberta Library
Edmonton, Canada T6G 2J8

*Subject access is emerging as an increasingly important aspect
of cataloging in the online environment.* [1, 2]

*Women's studies is a burgeoning area of activity in research,
teaching, and general interest.*

Having accepted these two premises, the question naturally arises in the mind of a feminist cataloger: Are women's studies materials receiving adequate subject access?

To make the research question manageable and of practical relevance, it can be limited to an examination of Library of Congress Subject Headings (LCSH), by far the most widely-used subject access system in North American catalogs.

Methodology

In the fall of 1989 I began to research the question at the University of Alberta by examining one hundred women's studies titles received for cataloging for the Humanities and Social Sciences Library (thus placing further limits on the scope of the research). Problems in providing satisfactory subject headings were examined for each title. Of the 100 titles, there were 42 for which LCSH could not, in my judgment, adequately reflect their subject. Having provided subject headings and classification for women's studies materials for some time, I was not surprised to find patterns emerging. These patterns may be attributed to three possible causes: [3, 4]

1) LCSH has developed in the context of a society which does not treat women as equals to men;

2) women's studies is an interdisciplinary field; and

3) feminist research orientations do not fit into categories designed for traditional research.

Additional factors contributing to the results included 1) the fact that bibliographic records from the Library of Congress (69 of 100) did not always fully utilize LCSH, and 2) LC catalogers frequently erred in assigning general headings when specific ones were available.

It is to be acknowledged that the sample was not a scientific one and that the methodology not rigorously defined; however, the trends discovered were pronounced enough that I felt the conclusions merited further investigation. What follows, then, are reflections on the three causes perceived for the inability of LCSH to afford full subject access to women's studies materials, a few comments on Library of Congress cataloging practice in this field, some suggestions for remedies, and one additional question.

LCSH as a Reflection of Patriarchal Society

Library of Congress Subject Headings are based on the concept of literary warrant and are, therefore, a reflection of the materials cataloged at the Library of Congress. The collection of the Library of Congress could be construed as a fair representation of mainstream American publications, particularly through the agent of legal deposit. In addition, LCSH has a history of revision which has shown a laudable effort to keep up with current concepts. Mainstream society and hierarchical institutions, however, do not necessarily reflect the culture and concerns of disadvantaged groups. While the Library of Congress has made significant efforts to remedy this situation (such as the massive changes of the "Women as . . ." headings), the task is not yet complete.

Granting that LCSH has not yet been entirely released from the bonds of sexism, what are the problems? I have identified two: lack of inclusive language, and sex-based assumptions reflected in choice of terms. [5]

A classic example of the former is "Man (Theology)." The scope note for this heading tells us:

> Here are entered works on the theology of humankind . . .
> Works on the Christian theology of the male sex are entered
> under Men (Christian theology). Works on the Christian theol-
> ogy of the female sex are entered under Woman (Christian
> theology).

"Woman (Theology)" is listed as a narrower term.

The example goes beyond a simple lack of inclusive language and demonstrates the depth of the problem. There are several points to be noted. First is the male-as-normative use of "Man" to describe all of humanity. The second, of less concern to this discussion, is the emphasis on Christianity in the scope note (other religions are mentioned in the full note, but the emphasis is still clear).

The third is the use of the plural ("Men") as opposed to the singular ("Woman") in conjunction with Christian theology. Does this discrepancy mean that, according to the Library of Congress, Christian theology treats "men" as people, but "woman" as a concept? As Searing points out in relation to the more general heading, "The term WOMAN was replaced by WOMEN . . . because the singular denoted an abstraction or ideal, while the plural suggests, somewhat more neutrally, a social group". [6] Finally, there is the obvious subordination of "Woman (Theology)" as a narrower term to "Man (Theology)", with no parallel heading referring to the general theology of the male sex.

Two interesting examples of sex-defined assumptions arose in the sample. The first one is the heading "Contraception." It seems a straightforward heading until one discovers the narrower term "Male contraception." There is, however, no heading for "Female contraception." Here LCSH is undoubtedly reflecting the societal assumption that contraception is a female responsibility, while male contraception is exceptional.

The second example of sex-defined assumptions is quite different. LCSH does not include a heading for "Prisons for women" or "Women's prisons," but rather uses "Reformatories for women." Two factors enter here. First, there is not a parallel heading for either prisons or reformatories for men. Second, the use of the word "reformatories" rather than "prisons" reflects a societal attitude toward women as not being adult, since reformatories are normally thought of as being for juveniles. Indeed, under the LC heading "Reformatories" are found references to "Juvenile delinquency" as a related term and to "Children—Institutional care" as a broader term.

Such examples indicate that what Sanford Berman noted in 1984 still holds:

> Despite laudable efforts at the Library of Congress to achieve sex equity in subject headings . . . significant nomenclature remains sexist, in effect declaring women to be a kind of subspecies. [7]

Access to Interdisciplinary Materials in LCSH

The second source of problems in providing subject access to women's studies materials is the interdisciplinary nature of women's studies, which typically combines a women-centered approach with one or more traditional disciplines. [8, 9] In some instances this problem can be overcome by the use of Boolean searching on keywords in headings. A title such as *Feminine Soul* can receive subject headings such as "Soul" and "Woman (Theology)." Online catalogs that can execute Boolean searches are of great advantage to researchers of any interdisciplinary subject, so long as users are aware of this capability.

Not all catalogs can allow searching on such a combination of headings, however. Where postcoordination is not possible, it is necessary to bring out the women-centered or feminist aspects of a work in separate subject headings. The Library of Congress frequently assigns the subject heading "Feminism" when a feminist approach is taken to a subject or when feminist aspects are being considered. The title *Feminist Perspectives on Wife Abuse*, for example, received the LC subject headings "Wife abuse" and "Feminism." This combination of subject headings is appropriate for Boolean searching, but the subject heading "Feminism" is meaningless in itself. [10] A user looking up "Feminism" will not normally be looking for a book specifically on wife abuse.

Another typical problem in indicating a feminist approach to a topic is illustrated by the title: *Elizabeth Barrett Browning, Woman and Artist*. This feminist criticism of the writings of Barrett Browning was given the heading "Browning . . . —Criticism and interpretation." While the heading is perfectly valid, a user looking for a feminist critique would be unable to discover this one without scanning the numerous conventional critiques of the author's works. Addition of the heading "Feminist literary criticism" would cause the same disservice to users as the example above with the heading "Feminism." This book is an example of feminist literary criticism, not a description of it.

LCSH and Feminist Research Orientations

The third source of problems is the least explored and the most difficult to define. It is the nature of feminist research and the problems of describing it using a tool designed to reflect the results of traditional research.

Feminist research can be construed as having four basic orientations: [11]

1) replacement of traditional research with women-centered research;

2) deconstruction of traditionally accepted androcentric concepts;

3) integration of traditional concepts with a women-centered approach; and

4) new feminist theories which interweave with existing theory.

In exploring these orientations, I cite several feminist scholars to explain the four perspectives and then relate them to examples of difficulty in subject access.

Women-Centered Research

Mary Crawford addresses the first of these orientations, noting that:

> placing women at the center of inquiry has led to questioning fundamental assumptions underlying the theories and practices that define the discipline. [12]

Further,

> Feminist standpoint theories [in particular] maintain that scientists working within women's unique position in social life can provide understandings of the natural and social world that are not possible from men's social position. [13]

LCSH is weak in addressing women-centered research topics. The issue of career path treated in the title in my sample, *Women's Careers: Pathways and Pitfalls,* has no subject heading to represent it. Neither does the value of unpaid work, the topic of *The Revaluation of Women's Work.* In both cases, the heading "Women—Employment" is a general category, but does not reflect the specific topic of the work.

A library user seeking material on the nontraditional nature of many women's career paths (interrupted or beginning late owing to childcare responsibilities or changing as a result of initial discouragement from entering male-dominated fields) may find the term "Career patterns" in a catalog. "Career patterns" is not a valid LCSH heading, however; the user is told to try "Occupations," "Professions," or "Vocational guidance," none of which address the topic specifically.

Women's unpaid work falls into many categories including, but not limited to, volunteer work and housework. Documents on each of these topics can be accessed by the LC headings "Voluntarism" and "Housewives—Economic conditions"; however, neither heading conveys the idea of the role women's unpaid labor plays in the overall economy.

Were headings for "Unpaid work" and "Career patterns" to exist, the women-centered aspect would still not be reflected, although the topic would be clearer. Some other means of indexing is required to not only link interdisciplinary concepts, but to convey the nature of the relationships between the concepts.

Deconstruction

Deconstruction, the second aspect of feminist research orientation, involves the questioning of the existing canon of knowledge.

> Feminist scholars pointed out early on that the study of women would not only add new subject matter but would also force a critical reexamination of the premises and standards of existing scholarly work. [14]

By its nature, LCSH is not a questioning device. The reasons for this are sound, at least to a degree. First, the list of headings is based on literary warrant, representing not the vast universe of knowledge, but the world of published information, specifically the published information cataloged for the collection of the Library of Congress. Second, it is a tool used by the majority of libraries in North America and by many beyond. Consistency is always important in library catalogs if the gathering, or collocation, function is to be achieved. Change is expensive and, therefore, is applied only to newly established subjects.

This problem was well borne out in the title from my sample, *Women in Political Theory,* which criticizes the views of "woman" in a series of historical-political philosophies. As it is a groundbreaking assessment of the canon of political theory, it is new to the world of published knowledge. Available headings were: "Women in politics—History," which really represents the political activity of women, not their role in political theory; and "Political science—History," which excludes the women-centered aspect. In addition, neither option indicates that this title is not an ordinary contribution to the discipline, but rather a reassess-ment of its fundamentals. Feminist criticism is not, of course, the only mode of deconstruction, and all such approaches present a similar difficulty in LCSH. Deconstruction is, however, central to feminist research and, like the lack of precoordinate access to interdisciplinary materials, the failure of LCSH in this re-gard has a particular impact on women's studies.

Integrating Traditional Concepts

The third feminist research orientation is the appropriation of existing con-cepts and theories to address women-centered concerns. In addressing feminist historiography, Joan Scott notes that [15]

> Investigations of these issues [gender issues] will yield a history
> that will provide new perspectives on old questions . . ., rede-
> fine the old questions in new terms . . ., make women visible as
> active participants, and create analytic distance between the
> seemingly fixed language of the past and our own terminology.

Similar steps have been followed in other disciplines. Feminist empiricism has developed, particularly in the sciences and social sciences, around the con-cept that traditional research methodologies are not necessarily flawed, but have been applied in an androcentric manner. "It is 'bad science' that is responsible for the sexist and androcentric results of research." [16] While feminist empiricists accept traditional methods as valid, other feminist researchers choose to adapt traditional methods. A good example is that of applying a Jungian approach to women-centered topics. One title that I encountered, *The Mother: Archetypal Im-age in Fairy Tales*, did exactly that. In this case and in other similar situations, LCSH coverage of feminist research is only as good as the coverage of the tradi-tional approach that was adapted for use in the feminist research. In this instance, it is impossible to combine the concepts of *motherhood* and (*folklore* or *fairy tales*) except through Boolean searching. Again, concepts cannot be linked and the re-lationships between them cannot be represented.

New Feminist Theories

The fourth orientation of feminist research goes beyond applying traditional theories to women-centered topics toward a complex interweaving of existing and new theories and topics to produce something entirely original. The major reason stems from a basic tenet of modern feminism: the personal is political. Feminist research is carried out in the context of personal experience and po-litical commitment. As a result:

> The method of consciousness-raising is very much a "first-or-
> der" methodology, where we begin by focusing on the con-

crete and the specific, and delay abstraction and generaliza-
tion to a later stage. [17]

The concept of beginning with the personal, with women's experience,
leads to the feminist-standpoint epistemology advocated by Sandra Harding,
Alison Jaggar, and others (see quote from Crawford above). Jaggar goes further to propose the validity of emotion in informing research, particularly the
emotions of disadvantaged groups. "Feminist emotions provide a political motivation for investigation and so help to determine the selection of problems as
well as the method by which they are investigated." [18] The result of this type
of approach is research that bears no resemblance to traditional research. The
presence of both the personal and the political in an unabashed manner is
beyond the scope of LCSH.

Two particularly good examples are the titles: *Home Economics and Feminism: The Hestian Synthesis* and *From a Broken Web: Separation, Sexism, and
Self.* The first title is a feminist view of home economics which values that profession for its caring ethic by using the symbol of the Roman goddess Hestia. It
illustrates particularly well the interweaving of concepts in feminist research.
The second title examines the concept of self in women in the context of female relatedness and male autonomy. Here the personal point of view (what
could be more personal than the self?) and the political agenda are particularly
marked. In neither case does LCSH offer adequate subject access. Indeed, it is
with this orientation of feminist research that LCSH is least satisfactory. The
reason seems to be that language for these concepts has not yet evolved, much
less reached a level of stability such that the Library of Congress could adopt
new terms with some assurance that these will not require expensive changes
in the near future.

One More Problem

There is one more problem which must be addressed before solutions can
be contemplated. It relates to the fact that virtually no library using widely accepted controlled vocabularies such as LCSH relies entirely on original cataloging. Most library cataloging data comes from a shared source such as a bibliographic utility. Therefore, good subject access depends not only upon the
standard system (LCSH), but also on the quality of cataloging copy contributed.

A major source of cataloging data is, of course, the Library of Congress. LC
is also considered one of the most authoritative sources of cataloging copy.
This reputation is well earned. However, the Library of Congress does not always fully exploit its own subject heading list, as was evident in the records
sampled. For example, the heading "Women in Christianity" was not assigned
to the title *Womanchrist*. For *The Witch and the Goddess in the Stories of Isak
Dinesen*, the subdivisions ". . . —Characters—Women" were not used. And
for a book on the female nude in twentieth-century painting, "Women in art"

was not used, though "Nude in art" was. The Library of Congress frequently uses generic occupational headings such as "Psychoanalysts" rather than headings which would gather titles on women in specific occupations such as "Women psychoanalysts" (this instance in connection with a biography of Karen Horney, who challenged Freud's view of women). [19]

A second problem is that the Library of Congress does not always follow its own principle of specific entry. This principle, stated as early as Cutter's *Rules for a Dictionary Catalog* [20] has variations in its definition, [21] but in none of them is a general heading to be applied in the manner in which the Library of Congress has applied the heading "Feminism". "Feminism" has been assigned consistently as a separate heading whenever there is no other way of linking the concept of feminist aspects or approaches with a topic, and sometimes even when another possibility is available. As a result, the heading "Feminism" has become so frequent that it is virtually meaningless, as noted above.

Recommendations

It will be noted that the problems which I have outlined vary both in severity and in complexity. I believe that some of them are amenable to quite simple solutions such as the following.

1) The first and most obvious solution addresses the last two problems. It is, simply, that the Library of Congress follow its own principle of specific entry and use its own subject headings to their fullest potential.

2) Another suggestion addresses several problems, including those of interdisciplinary materials, women-centered research, and research applying traditional concepts in feminist research. The proposed solution is to create a free-floating subdivision for women's studies or feminist materials. In line with existing subdivisions such as "Environmental aspects" and "Moral and ethical aspects," the subdivision "Feminist aspects" might be acceptable to LC. To reflect what is actually happening in women's studies, particularly in feminist research, the subdivision "Feminist approaches" would be more descriptive, however. Either subdivision would have significantly augmented subject access for 12 of the 42 titles in my sample for which headings were unsatisfactory.

3) The remedy for problems of language is simple, though laborious, involving a review of each subject heading in the list for inclusive language and sex-neutral choice of terminology. Marshall's pioneering work may be helpful in this regard. [22]

4) Finally, the Library of Congress must ask itself whether its subject heading policies, which are based on literary warrant and on the practical difficulty of changing headings, should be questioned and a less reactive policy instituted. Were LCSH to exhibit some risk-taking in its new headings, some of the concepts which arise from feminist research at its most innovative

could be encompassed. While not a simple process, the library community must decide whether or not this and other socially responsible changes would be worth the investment.

Collocation vs. Dispersion of Women's Studies Materials

A basic question must be answered by both the library and feminist communities: should women's studies materials be gathered in the subject catalog or should they be dispersed throughout the catalog? The title *Care and Moral Motivation* serves as an interesting example. This book, according to the publisher's description,

> attempts to break down traditional divisions between care and justice, care and principles, character and duty, motivation and action, friends and strangers, emotionality and rationality, connection and autonomy, and women's morality and men's morality. [23]

The approach is undoubtedly feminist. But should the cataloging reflect this point of view? The assumption has been made above that it should. When feminist research is integrated in a library collection, however, there is an advantage to its integration in the subject catalog as well. Searing introduces the concept of "serendipitous consciousness-raising" in the context of classification, envisioning the uninitiated stumbling across a feminist approach to any topic interspersed with traditional materials in the stacks. [24] Cannot the same perspective be taken regarding subject headings? Should women's studies materials necessarily be identified in the subject catalog? Or should they be treated as any other materials so that a prejudgment against them will not be established? In this instance the users of the library catalog must, unfortunately, be divided into the enlightened and the benighted. One approach will benefit the former in gathering women's studies materials for their use. Another approach will endow the latter group with the opportunity for "serendipitous consciousness-raising." In addition, in the context of an educational institution, Searing goes further to propose that

> Facilitating retrieval of materials for researchers may handicap them in the long run, for they will not be forced to acquire library skills beyond the knack of browsing. A strong bibliographic instruction program and clearly written handouts may be more educationally empowering than a special collection. [25]

In sum, my proposal is to follow the precepts of standardized cataloging while encouraging change in that influential corporate body, the Library of Congress, as well as contemplating the possibilities of applying the orientations of feminist research to further examination of subject access.

NOTES

1. In her survey of catalogue use studies, Karen Markey [2] noted that "The need for improved subject access to online catalogs and bibliographic records [as concluded in the CLR online Catalog Evaluation Projects] was supported by analyses of aggregate data . . . , of individual libraries' data, and of data categorized by type of library . . . "

2. Markey, Karen. "Users and the Online Catalog: Subject Access Problems." In *The Impact of Online Catalogs.* Edited by Joseph R. Matthews. New York: Neal-Schuman, 1986, p. 36.

3. Susan Searing [4] reflects similar observations in her characterization of women's studies as:
   - women-centered: "for women as well as about women"
   - interdisciplinary
   - still evolving
   - rooted in the women's movement.

4. Searing, Susan E. *Introduction to Library Research in Women's Studies.* Boulder, Co.: Westview Press, 1985, pp. 1-3.

5. All references to LCSH are from the June 1990 microfiche edition.

6. Searing [1985], p. 22.

7. Berman, Sanford. "Out of the Kitchen—But Not Into the Catalog." In his: *Subject Cataloging: Critiques and Innovations.* New York: Haworth Press, 1984, p. 167. Also published as *Technical Services Quarterly* vol. 2, nos. 1/2 (Fall/Winter 1984).

8. Searing [1985], pp. 1-2.

9. Sherwin, Susan. "Philosophical Methodology and Feminist Methodology: Are They Compatible?" In *Women, Knowledge, and Reality: Explorations in Feminist Philosophy.* Ann Gary and Marilyn Pearsall, eds. Boston: Unwin Hyman, 1989, p. 27.

10. The general heading "Feminism" was assigned by LC to books about feminist literary criticism and postmodernism, women and peace, female offenders, and a feminist analysis of home economics, as well as the book on wife abuse.

11. In this section I am particularly grateful to Winnie Tomm, Coordinator of the Women's Studies Program at the University of Alberta.

12. Crawford, Mary. "Agreeing to Differ: Feminist Epistemologies and Women's Ways of Knowing." In *Gender and Thought: Psychological Perspectives.* Mary Crawford and Margaret Gentry, eds. New York: Springer-Verlag, 1989, p. 129.

13. ibid., p. 135.

14. Scott, Joan W. "Gender: A Useful Category of Historical Analysis." In *Coming to Terms: Feminism, Theory, Politics.* Edited by Elizabeth Weed. New York: Routledge, 1989, p. 82.

15. ibid., p. 100.

16. Harding, Sandra. "Feminist Justificatory Strategies." In *Women, Knowledge, and Reality: Explorations in Feminist Philosophy.* Ann Gary and Marilyn Pearsall, eds. Boston: Unwin Hyman, 1989, p. 191.

17. Sherwin, p. 27.

18. Jaggar, Alison M. "Love and Knowledge: Emotion in Feminist Epistemology." In *Women, Knowledge, and Reality: Explorations in Feminist Philosophy.* Ann Gary and Marilyn Pearsall, eds. Boston: Unwin Hyman, 1989, p. 145.

19. Specifying women in specific occupations or, indeed, women's studies or feminist approaches to any topic has advantages and disadvantages, some of which are discussed in the section on "Collocation vs. Dispersion."

20. Cutter, Charles A. *Rules for a Dictionary Catalog.* 4th ed. Washington: Government Printing Office, 1904. Rule 161, pp. 66-67. (Reissued London: Library Association, 1962.)

21. Chan, Lois May. *Library of Congress Subject Headings: Principles and Application.* 2nd ed. Littleton, Co.: Libraries Unlimited, 1986, pp. 33-37.

22. Marshall, Joan K., Comp. *On Equal Terms: A Thesaurus for Nonsexist Indexing and Cataloging*. New York: Neal-Schuman Publishers, 1977.

23. Shogan, Debra A. *Care and Moral Motivation*. Toronto: Oise Press, 1988, back cover.

24. Searing, Susan E. "Feminist Library Services: The Women's Studies Librarian-at-Large, University of Wisconsin System." In *Women's Collections*. Issued as *Special Collections* vol. 3, nos. 3/4 (Spring/Summer 1986), p. 154.

25. ibid., p. 153.

ADDITIONAL READINGS

Cook, Judith A., Fonow, Mary Margaret. "Knowledge of Women's Interests: Issues of Epistemology and Methodology in Feminist Sociological Research. " In *Feminist Research Methods: Exemplary Readings in the Social Sciences*. Edited by Joyce McCarl Nielsen. Boulder, Co.: Westview Press, 1990, pp. 69-93.

Mowery, Robert L. "Women in Literature: A Study of Library of Congress Subject Cataloging." *Cataloging and Classification Quarterly* vol. 9, no. 4 (1989), pp. 89-99.

Nielsen, Joyce McCarl. "Introduction." In *Feminist Research Methods: Exemplary Readings in the Social Sciences*. Edited by Joyce McCarl Nielsen. Boulder, Co.: Westview Press, 1990, pp. 1-37.

Tomm, Winnie. "Risking the Untried: Feminist Approaches to Research Methodologies." Paper presented at the Canadian Library Association Conference, Edmonton, Alberta, 24 June 1989.

Westkott, Marcia. "Feminist Criticism of the Social Sciences." In *Feminist Research Methods: Exemplary Readings in the Social Sciences*. Edited by Joyce McCarl Nielsen. Boulder, Co.: Westview Press, 1990, pp. 58-68.

VOLUME/DATE DESIGNATION AND SERIALS HOLDINGS

Sook-Hyun Kim

Associate Professor
Head, Serials Cataloging
University of Tennessee Library
Knoxville, Tennessee 37996-1000

Former Practices

Serials holdings statements were an essential element of bibliographic information and an integral part of descriptive cataloging of serials until the adoption of AACR2 (*Anglo-American Cataloguing Rules,* 2nd ed.). Individual libraries recorded their serials holdings statements based on the patterns established for volume/date designations in bibliographic records. Frequently, "Library has" notes on bibliographic records were substituted for volume/date designations, while individual volumes and issues were listed separately in a shelflist.

This method of recording serials holdings statements was based on two former national cataloging codes. *Rules for Descriptive Cataloging in the Library of Congress,* Rule 7:5 HOLDINGS (hereafter called "LC rule") and *Anglo-American Cataloging Rules* (1967), Rule 163 Holdings (hereafter called "AACR rule"), provided for recording information about serials holdings in conjunction with volume/date designations.

The LC rule stated:

> The statement of the volumes "held" by the Library is given immediately after the title.
>
> . . . If the work has ceased publication . . . the extent of the complete set is recorded, provided the information is available; the volumes that are lacking are specified in a supplementary note.
>
> . . . The statement of holdings records the volume designation or the date of issue or both. [1]

The AACR rule stated:

> The statement of the volumes "held" by the library is given immediately after the title . . .

> . . . If the work has ceased publication, this statement con-
> sists of the designation of the first and last volumes or parts,
> followed by the dates of the first and last volumes or parts. [2]

Both rules viewed volume/date designation as information on the availability of published parts of serials in relation to local holdings. Local holdings
statements were referred to a secondary position, i.e., in a supplementary note,
only when local holdings were not complete. Otherwise, the availability information was translated into a local holdings statement. In any case, holdings
statements and volume/date designations were not separated and were considered part of bibliographic description under both rules. Volume/date designations were used not only for availability information or completeness of the
holdings statement, but also for individual-issue identification by recording issues in the publisher's numeration.

Individual libraries followed this practice of recording summary holdings
statements in their public catalogs, while detailed holdings statements were
recorded at the physical-piece level with accession numbers in the shelflist. The
pattern of recording published parts of serials as circulating units or physical
pieces was derived from the volume/date designations in a bibliographic
record. For example:

> U.S. Bureau of Reclamation.
>   Report. 1st-14th; 1902-1914/15.
>   (Holdings statement on shelflist or on piece:
>   1st 1902 2nd 1903 . . . 14th 1914/15, etc.)
> Montana's production; a summary of the state's
>   industries. 1930-38-—
>   (Holdings statement on shelflist or on piece: 1930-38, etc.)

ISBD(S)

In 1974, the International Federation of Library Associations issued *ISBD(S):
International Standard Bibliographic Description for Serials*. Sect. 2.3.1 stated
that

> Dates and numbering are an identifying element of a serial:
> they are not to be confused, however, with dates and num-
> bering which record the holdings of specific collections. . . .
> No provision is given in the ISBD(S) for the recording of hold-
> ings, but they may be added to the bibliographic description. [3]

According to ISBD(S), when a serial is numbered, the publication date is
followed by the number of the issue. When the publication date differs from
the period of coverage of the first issue, the publication date is given first, followed in parentheses by the volume designation, or equivalent, in abbreviated
form and by the date of the period covered. The conventional volume/date

designation is specified as a part of the imprint and is separated from the record of holdings. The recording of holdings is still allowed, however, in a bibliographic description following ISBD(S). For example:

1970 (Bd 1960/65)-

(The publication date of the first volume is 1970, but its period of coverage is 1960/65.)

1965 ([vol.] 1960/63)-

(The first volume covered the period of 1960/63, but was published in 1965. The designation of volume that is not found in the first issue is given in square brackets.)

1950 (vol. 1)-1969 (vol. 20), 1970 (n.s., vol. 1)-

(When there is a new sequence of numbering, the date and numbering of the first sequence are given, followed by the date and numbering of the first volume of the new sequence.)

Current Practice

In contrast to the aforementioned LC and AACR rules, *Anglo-American Cataloguing Rules*, 2nd ed. (AACR2), rule 12.3 views volume/date designation as a bibliographic data element that identifies the first and last issues of a serial rather than as an indicator of availability or holdings information. The AACR2 term for volume/date designation is "Numeric and/or Alphabetic, Chronological, or Other Designation Area."

Rule 12.3 states:

> Give the numeric and/or alphabetic designation of the first issue of a serial as given in that issue . . . . If the first issue of a serial is identified by a chronological designation, give it in the terms used in the item. [4]

The provision of local holdings statements is excluded from AACR2 rule 12.3. Rule 12.7B20, however, links library holdings statements to the numeric and chronological designations. Rule 12.7B20 deals with notes on local holdings, such as "Library lacks: Vol. 12, v. 16." [5] When missing volumes are specified in the note of a bibliographic record, the scope or extent of the library's holdings may be derived from the designations of the first and last issues of a serial.

Issues

The issue here is not whether serials holdings statements should be included in a bibliographic record. The point being made here is that a numeric/chronological designation cannot be considered as a publisher's identification of first/last issue alone.

Besides the reference to library holdings in rule 12.7B20, there are other bibliographic notes that have been based on the patterns established in the numeric and chronological designations, such as "Issues for 1922-1931 include: . . . ," "Description based on: 1983-2, etc."

Under AACR2 rule 12.3, numeric and chronological designations unambiguously identify and represent the numbering schemes used by serials publishers. The majority of bibliographic descriptions convey clearly the meaning of the designations and, in most cases, the individual issues are identified in the same pattern as is applied in other serials activities (such as check-in or recording holdings statements) and/or reference citations. There are certain elements of these designations, however, that need standardization, definition, or clarification—not just an exact description of publishers' usage.

In particular, the use of punctuation marks in numeric/chronological designations requires standardization. The *CONSER Editing Guide* includes the following examples of variant patterns of punctuation: [6]

> 1976-77-1977-78.   16th (1964 ... 1965)-
> Fiscal year 1982-   1982 ... 1983-

Cataloging Service Bulletin features the following examples: [7]

> 1982/3-   82-1-
> 1981, no. 1-   83-2 (Feb. 1983)-

The issue proposed for solution or discussion here is the definition of punctuation marks in numeric/chronological designations. Inconsistently applied punctuation marks in numeric and chronological designations have a significant impact on the recording of serials holdings statement. Traditionally the volume/date designation of a bibliographic record has been used as a summary holdings statement. The pattern of volume/date designations in a bibliographic record has also informed the recording of local holdings statements at the detailed level or physical-piece level for binding/circulating units.

The usage of punctuation marks in the volume/date designation area has changed over the years in our national cataloging rules. Table 1 documents the changes. The meaning of a hyphen, dash, or slash in serials holdings statements was not standardized until the publication of the *American National Standard for Information Sciences—Serial Holdings Statements (Z39.44-1986)* (hereafter called "ANSI standard"). [8] If the definition of punctuation marks in the ANSI standard were to be utilized for the description of numeric/chronologic data in bibliographic records, the uniformity of the holdings record, its suitability for computer manipulation, and issue-level identification would be enhanced.

Volume/date designations have historically been used for the identification of individual issues of serials. The pattern of identification of individual issues should be identical whether it is in a bibliographic record, a holdings record, a check-in record, or a citation database. All of these records essentially

TABLE 1
PUNCTUATION MARKS FOR SERIAL HOLDINGS STATEMENTS
Pre-1986 (ANSI Standard)

Rules related to serial holdings statement	Connector for single bibliographic unit	Connector for two or more bibliographic units
Rules for Descriptive Cataloging in the Library of Congress, 1949. Rule 7.5C	- A hyphen is used for two or more calendar years. / A diagonal is used to indicate a year that is not a calendar year.	- A hyphen is used to connect the dates of the first issue and the last issue unless one date contains a hyphen. — A dash is used to connect the dates of the first and the last issues if one of them contains a hyphen.
Anglo-American Cataloging Rules, 1967. Rule 163D2	/ A diagonal is used for the date of a report or other publication that covers either a year that is not a calendar year or a period of more than one year.	— A dash is used to connect the dates of the first and last issues.
Anglo-American Cataloguing Rules, 2nd ed., 1978. Rules 12.3A1 & 12.3C1	*NO DESCRIPTION OF PUNCTUATION MARKS IN HOLDINGS STATEMENT, ONLY A BIBLIOGRAPHIC DESCRIPTION OF NUMERIC/ALPHABETIC DESIGNATION OR DATE.*	
	If the first issue of a serial is identified by a chronological designation, record it in the terms used in the item.	- A hyphen is used after the number designation or the date of the first issue of a serial.
Cataloging Service Bulletin, No. 23, Winter 1983. LCRI for AACR2 rule 12.3B1, rev [9]	Record the numeric/chronological designation according to the way it appears on the chief source.	

perform the same function: identification of the individual issues of a serial, including first/last issues. It is important to have a uniform meaning of punctuation marks in the volume/date designation area and to establish a pattern of issue-level identification for other serials activities.

Conclusion

By incorporating the definition of punctuation marks used in the ANSI standard into volume/date designations, the current distinction between bibliographic records and holdings records will be eliminated. Volume/date designation will then be defined as a relationship between two records.

If online access to serial holdings is considered primarily as a means of display of summary holdings, volume/date designations will be utilized as summary holdings in a bibliographic record. They are more than adequate as summary holdings data for most library users. Even though volume/date designations cannot be considered as summary holdings statements of local libraries, consistent punctuation marks can best indicate basic data elements for implementation of the ANSI standard. Regardless of the method used for recording detailed holdings, whether manual or coded in MARC format, volume/date designations will be the first element to consult.

It is desirable to have holdings records separate from bibliographic records and to create summary holdings statements from detailed holdings data. A separate holdings file, however, represents a considerable investment of financial and human resources, in addition to posing technical difficulties. The anticipated gains of a separate serials holdings file cannot outweigh the investment of staff, money, time, and energy for most local libraries.

NOTES

1. *Rules for Descriptive Cataloging in the Library of Congress.* Washington, D.C.: Library of Congress, 1949, p. 53.

2. *Anglo-American Cataloging Rules.* North American Text. Chicago: American Library Association, 1967, p. 233.

3. *ISBD(S): International Standard Bibliographic Description for Serials.* London: International Federation of Library Associations, Committee on Cataloging, 1974, p. 14.

4. *Anglo-American Cataloguing Rules.* 2nd ed., Rev. Chicago: American Library Association, 1988, p. 284.

5. ibid., p. 296.

6. *CONSER Editing Guide.* Serial Record Division, Library of Congress. 1986-, no. 362, pp. 2-4.

7. *Cataloging Service Bulletin.* no. 50 (Fall 1990), p. 31.

8. *American National Standard for Information Sciences—Serial Holdings Statements.* New York: American National Standards Institute, 1986.

9. *Cataloging Service Bulletin.* no. 23 (Winter 1983), p. 19.

"Marrying" College Catalog Data with the Library's Online Catalog: Enhancing Access to Nonprint Materials at Pikes Peak Community College

Bob Armintor
Media Specialist, Learning Resources Center
Pikes Peak Community College, 5675 South Academy Blvd.
Colorado Springs, CO 80906-5498

The Problem

Pikes Peak Community College (Colorado Springs) and the nine other publicly supported junior and community colleges in Colorado belong to a consortium called CCLINK (Colorado Community College Library Information Network); this consortium is a member of CARL, Inc. (Colorado Alliance of Research Libraries), which is based in Denver. The CARL database contains over five million records statewide, with the CCLINK libraries contributing almost 207,000 of these. In 1988, the Learning Resources Center (LRC) at Pikes Peak went online. After a little over a year of working with the Public Access Catalog (PAC), it became clear that finding nonprint materials for use by faculty/staff was difficult. There are over 4000 nonprint titles in the LRC collection at Pikes Peak, and most are heavily used in classroom instruction. These 4000+ titles can be in any one of nine broad media formats. Keyword searching (similar to subject searching) could involve as many as nine separate searches if one were to be thorough. And, in addition, keyword searching allowed for a number of false drops. A better way of searching nonprint media was therefore sought.

First, there was an attempt to identify an "umbrella term" which, when added to the MARC record in the 690 field (local subject added entry), would identify all nonprint materials, regardless of format. (The 690 tag was used so that the field would remain unchanged in the event that the CARL system runs the LC subject authority tapes against the 650 [standard subject heading] fields.) Various words and word combinations were tried in the database to see what already existed and which terms might cause false hits. "Media" yielded 134 hits (too high); "audio visual" resulted in 18 hits (better); "non-print" got 5 postings (better still); and, finally, "nonprint" written in compressed English got 0 hits (best). The word "material" was then added for good measure to further restrict the possibility of false drops.

To test the theory, a nonprint database of around 125 items was developed, with the words NONPRINT MATERIAL added to the 690 field of the MARC records. Now, if one wanted to find nonprint materials on a certain topic, one could enter a search term for the topic in combination with *nonprint material*, and be assured of getting only those titles so coded (see Figure 1). This "umbrella term" would help cut down on false drops, but would not eliminate them altogether. The reason for this is that a keyword search looks at all indexed fields (content notes, etc.), and, unlike a string search, does not look for terms in a particular order. It was therefore necessary to come up with a code that would make searching for nonprint materials very item-specific.

```
NONPRINT + MATERIAL + SEX    00006 ITEMS
Set of 6 will display on one page—proceeding with display . . .

  1                                          PPCC  CNTEN      FILM     1979
        The baby makers   [motion picture]   QP  251  .B23

  2                                          PPCC  CNTEN      FILM     1976
        Equality   [motion picture]          HM  146  .E7

  3                                          PPCC  CNTEN      FILM     1975
        The new sexuality   [motion picture] HQ  18  .U5  N4

  4                                          PPCC  CNTEN      FILM     1974
        Sugar and spice   [motion picture]   HQ  783  .Su  32

  5                                          PPCC  CNTEN      DOCAD    197-
        Sex roles today   [picture]          HZ  16013  DOC.  PHOTO AID

  6                                          PPCC  CNTEN      FILM     1966
        Parent to child about sex  {motion picture]  HM  56  .P215

ALL ITEMS HAVE BEEN DISPLAYED.
ENTER <LINE NUMBER (S)> TO DISPLAY FULL RECORDS (Number + B for Brief)
<P> REVIOUS FOR PREVIOUS PAGE OR <Q>UIT FOR NEW SEARCH
```

Figure 1. A search on the umbrella term "nonprint material" in combination with a topical term.

The Printed Multimedia Catalog

A number of years ago (before the advent of microcomputer word processing), we had developed a printed index of nonprint materials called the "All-in-One" Multimedia Catalog. This catalog identified all media, regardless of format, within a specific subject area. The "All-in-One" contained 279 pages of subject access points, including LC subject headings, names of disciplines and/or course names (e.g., Urban Horticulture), and "common" (most frequently asked for) terms, such as "study skills materials." It was essentially a printed index of the nonprint entries in the card catalog, but a little easier to use than the latter (see sample page in Figure 2).

TOUCH

Touch of Sensitivity (videocassette) 50 min., sd., color, 1981.
   Explores the hidden meaning and power of human touch, detailing
the results of recent research into the importance of the tactile
sense.

(BF/275/.T6x)

TRAUMA

Interpretation of trauma (slide set)

(RA/1121/.I8)

UNDERDEVELOPED AREAS

The third world (sound filmstrip)

(HC/59.7/.T5)

The Third World (motion picture) 14 min., sd., b & w, 1974.
   ANalyzes and assesses the growing economic and political power of
the nonaligned nations of the Third World.

(6/708)

UNEMPLOYMENT

Unemployment (sound filmstrip)

(HD/5707.5/.U91)

Youth unemployment: causes & consequences (sound filmstrip)

(HD/6270/.Y6x)

UNITED NATIONS

The United National: a reevaluation (sound filmstrip)

(JX/1977/.Un 3)

The United Nations: world forum (sound filmstrip)

(JX/177/.U55)

U.S. HISTORY

America (sound filmstrip)

(E/178/.A4/1973)

256

Figure 2. Sample page from the All-in-One Multimedia Catalog.

The "All-in-One" was a great success and, although greatly out of date at this time, it is still referred to by faculty and LRC staff alike. The challenge: Was there a way to make use of the umbrella term "nonprint material" and construct an online version of the "All-in-One" at the same time?

An Online Multimedia Catalog

At about this time, "pseudo-MARC" records were being created for telecourses we were offering, and it was observed that students were asking for the videotapes about 75% of the time by *course number* (e.g., PSY 205 = Human Development), rather than by instructor's name or course title. So, the course number was added in a 690 field of the MARC record to make it searchable. It had to be entered in compressed English (e.g., PSY205); otherwise the computer interpreted it as a spelling error and prompted the data entry person to try again. After the course number was added to the records of the telecourses, it became possible to quickly find any one of them without knowing a specific title. It then became clear that *if we used the course numbers from the college catalog,* we would have an online "All-in-One." The umbrella term "nonprint material" in combination with a subject term allowed for searching on a specific topic. The course numbers would facilitate searching for nonprint materials relating to a discipline or course, which would enable both full- and part-time instructors to access directly the materials purchased for their classes. This is especially important for part-timers, since they are not always aware of the nonprint materials available to them. And, it would be easy to print out customized bibliographies as needed.

Additional ways were identified for manipulating data by using the MARC record and the searching/organizing power of the computer. For instance, the State Library asks us annually for statistics on our holdings, including counts of particular types of nonprint media. That information could be coded into the database. The format of the material was already represented in the database, but in very broad terms (e.g., sound recording; video-cassette). It was desirable to make the format designation more specific: sound recording=audiocassette; *or* phonodisc; *or* compact disc, so that whichever way the data was requested, it could be retrieved. Specific format designations could be coded in.

From time to time, division directors ask us for specifics on the materials we purchase for their areas, e.g., the dental program. That information could be represented as well by entering the discipline level code, e.g., DEA001. Instructors often ask, "What's new?" By adding "1990" to a search on DEA001, for example, last year's acquisitions of nonprint materials for the dental program can be retrieved (see Figure 3). All this information could be added/linked to the MARC records, and could be searched. All it would take was time.

Again, all relevant information was coded in the test database, and then the idea was presented to some of the instructional staff via a demonstration. They were very pleased and enthusiastic about the project.

```
DEA001                       00005 ITEMS


   1                                                 PPCC  CNTEN      STACKS   1989
              The glass ionomer composite restoration [videor   RK  652.7 .G55 1989


   2                                                 PPCC  CNTEN      STACKS   1986
              Fixed   prosthetics    [videorecording] : assisting   RK  666 .F5 1986


   3                                                 PPCC  CNTEN      STACKS   1986
              Assisting during an amalgam restoration [videor   RK  519 .A4 A81986


   4                                                 PPCC  CNTEN      STACKS   1985
              Pit  and fissure  sealants  [slide]:  biomaterials   RK  652.5 .P4 1985


   5     Lee mary                                    PPCC  CNTEN      STACKS   1982
              Diet counseling for preventive  dentistry  [video   RK  281 .L4 1989


ALL ITEMS HAVE BEEN DISPLAYED.
ENTER <LINE NUMBER (S)> TO DISPLAY FULL RECORDS (Number + B for Brief)
<P> REVIOUS FOR PREVIOUS PAGE OR <Q>UIT FOR NEW SEARCH
You began with a WORD search on:

DEA001

Type    S to try your search in another database, or
        R to repeat your search in Pikes Peak Comm. Coll.
        H to see a list of your recent searches, or
        (RETURN) for a new search:      //WDEA001  1990

DEA001 00005 ITEMS
DEA001 + 1990 00001 ITEMS

   1     Lee mary                                    PPCC  CNTEN      STACKS   1982
              Diet counseling for preventive dentistry  [video   RK  281 .L4 1982

Enter  <LINE NUMBER> to display full record, or <Q>UIT for new search
```

Figure 3. Search on a discipline-level code (DEA = Dentistry). The bottom part of the printout shows a search for nonprint materials acquired for the dental program in 1990.

Figure 4 contains a printout of a record with all the coded information alluded to above. This record is for one of the Center's 16mm films. By adding the film rack number to the record, it became possible to create an electronic shelflist, something we had not had before.

As can be seen from the record, an instructor could ask for all the nonprint material on CHARTRES and/or NOTRE DAME CATHEDRAL and/or MEDIEVAL CIVILIZATION. Or, one could limit a search by requesting that the computer display only 16mm film titles relating to any of the above subject headings. Alternatively, one could ask for materials in nonprint format relating only to the "Architectural Technology" course (ARC111), or to the discipline "architec-

Figure 4. Sample record from the database of nonprint materials.

```
WORKING...
-----------------------------------------Pikes Peak Comm. Coll.------
TITLE(s):      Art and Architecture : Chartres Cathedral [Motion
               picture].

Summary:       Encyclopaedia Britannica Films. c1963.
               1 reel; 30 min., sd., color, 16mm.
               John Canaday illuminates the fusion of faith, intellect,
               and engineering in Chartres Cathedral in France.  Presents
               a study of the history of the cathedral and the symbolism
               of the sculpture and the stained glass windows, and
               analyzes the synthesis of these seemingly contradictory
               elements which form the visible proclamation of medieval
               man's beliefs.

OTHER ENTRIES: Chartres, France - Notre-Dame (Cathedral).
               Civilization, Medieval.
               Motion picture.--------------------------- General format
               NONPRINT MATERIAL.------------------------ Umbrella term
               MP12-184.--------------------------------- Film rack number
               16mm.------------------------------------- Specific format
               ARC111; HUM121; HUM122.------------------- Specific courses
               197-.------------------------------------- Purchase date(year)
               ARC001; HUM001; ART001.------------------- Discipline(s) identifiers
               BTD001; CSD001.--------------------------- Division(s) identifiers
               Encyclopaedia Britannica Films, Inc.

CALL #: NA 5551 .C385 (MP12-184)              LOCN: CNTEN  FILM
STATUS: Checked out --

---1----------------------------------------Pikes Peak Comm. Coll.------
<RETURN> to continue, <Q>UIT for a new search, or <R> to REPEAT this display
```

ture" in general (ARC001). By asking for all nonprint materials purchased for our Communication, Humanities, and Social Sciences Division (CSD001), the computer could provide a complete listing. One could ask for a listing of all the 16mm films in the collection—the combinations seem almost endless.

Discussion

The only limitation of this innovation is the time required to code all the nonprint materials. Our estimate is that it will take about two years of part-time inputting to complete the coding of 4000 records, but in the end it should be well worth it, as this will provide the instructional staff with a faster and easier way to locate the items that have been purchased in their disciplines.

This coding technique is not limited to nonprint materials; the method is applicable to print materials as well. Its essence is supplementing the standard bibliographic record with data elements that are useful to a local user community.

SUGGESTED READINGS

Alloway, Catherine Suyak, "Naisbitt's Megatrends: Some Implications for the Electronic Library," *The Electronic Library,* (April 1986), vol. 4, no. 2, pp. 114-118.

Billings, Harold, "Magic and Hypersystems: A New Orderliness for Libraries," *Library Journal,* (April 1, 1990), pp. 46-52.

Drabenstott, Karen Markey, "Online Assistance in Online Catalogs," *Library Hi Tech,* Issue 29 (1990, no. 1), pp. 72-74.

Kinyon, William R. et al., "Producing In-House Indexes at Texas A&M" *RQ [Reference Quarterly],* vol. 30, no. 1 (Fall 1990), pp. 51-59.

Michalak, Thomas J., "An Experiment in Enhancing Catalog Records at Carnegie Mellon University," *Library Hi Tech,* Issue 31 (1990, no. 3), pp. 33-41.

Mischo, Lare, "The Alice-B Information Retrieval (IR) System: A Locally Developed Library System at Tacoma Public Library," *Library Hi Tech,* Issue 29 (1990, no. 1), pp. 7-20.

Mischo, Lare, "Search Problems and User Assistance" *Library Hi Tech,* Issue 29 (1990, no. 1), pp. 79-81.

Rice, James, "Serendipity and Holism: The Beauty of OPACs," *Library Journal,* (February 15, 1988), pp. 138-141.

Small, Jocelyn Penny, "Retrieving Images Verbally: No More Key Words and Other Heresies," *Library Hi Tech,* Issue 33, vol. 9, no. 1 (1991), pp. 51-60, 67.

Studwell, William E., "Cataloging Forum: Subject Access Theory No. 10—Least Effort: One More Reason to Change the Overall Policies/Practices Relating to LC Subject Headings," *Technicalities,* vol. 10, no. 10 (October 1990), pp. 4-5.

Studwell, William E., "The Subject Heading Code: Do We Have One? Do We Need One?," *Technicalities,* vol. 10, no. 10 (October 1990), pp. 10-15.

Problems in the Cataloging of Digital Cartographic Databases

PohChin Lai
Associate Professor, Geodetic Science & Surveying
The Ohio State University
1958 Neil Avenue, Columbus, OH 43210-1247

Ming-Kan Wong
Serial Cataloger, 030 Main Library
The Ohio State University
1858 Neil Avenue Mall, Columbus, OH 43210

Introduction

Cataloging rules for cartographic materials have frequently been challenged because of a prolonged controversy regarding the selection of author versus area as main entry and the inclusion of pertinent data elements in the body of a cartographic cataloging record. The widespread adoption of geographic information systems technology, through which digital cartographic databases may proliferate, underscores the need to re-evaluate the utility and effectiveness of cataloging rules for cartographic materials. Digital cartographic databases are characterized by constantly changing data that do not necessarily alter their bibliographic identity. The need to reflect periodic content changes in these databases demands a closer look at existing cataloging practices for cartographic materials. This paper examines the inadequacy of conventional cataloging rules for such materials and suggests items for consideration and re-consideration with respect to the cataloging of digital cartographic databases. Through an understanding of the nature of a geographic information system, the paper highlights issues worth considering for the establishment of future cartographic cataloging standards.

The Digital Mapping Trend

Many federal government agencies chartered to produce maps and charts have begun to develop digital cartographic databases. Vast amounts of data about the earth and man's activities on the planet are being recorded in such databases. With an escalated quest for a digital cartographic data standard, there will come the day when digital cartographic materials will become widely accessible and sharable. [1] Computerization has made possible direct access to these digital maps via online terminals or other magnetic devices. Such access may be obtained on a subscription basis, and digital maps maintained in remote sites could conceivably become part of a library's collection of information resources.

Digital maps can be presented in a medium other than paper. The use of magnetic media for storing cartographic information is gaining ground as a direct result of the advent of computer technology and digital spatial data-handling techniques. The geographic information system is that unique technology developed to collect, inventory, manage, display, analyze, and manipulate spatially referenced data sets. Within a geographic information system, cartographic data are recorded as layers of information representing distinct spatial entities. These spatial entities or data layers may describe a transportation network, hydrology, vegetation cover, or distributional statistics. A geographic information system is an important information channel for digital cartographic materials. Rapid developments in geographic information systems may pose serious implications regarding the functions and, perhaps, the importance of cartographic materials libraries. [2]

The library community is aware of the digital mapping trend, and several committees have been established to work on rules for cataloging digital cartographic data sets. Among these committees is the Canadian Committee on Geomatics, led by Velma Parker, which aims at formalizing some cartographic cataloging standards based on Chapter 9 of *Anglo-American Cataloguing Rules* (AACR2). [3]

In the United Kingdom, efforts are underway to address new forms of information storage and retrieval systems because of an outburst of remote sensing and mapping in digital forms. The British Ordnance Survey, for instance, has its largest-scale maps in digital form only, and individual map sheets are generated on request. [4] Other agenda include the preservation of series of national cartographic data sets as an archive, and the monitoring of the production of data sets and the provision of records/information about them as a library service. [5]

In the United States, the problem of imagery and mapping is staggering, with federal, state, and local agencies as the key players. [6-8] It is generally recognized, however, that the only access to these materials is via the "old boy" network. [9] These problems have prompted an investigation on the feasibility of creating a national center for geographic information systems to solve many spatial data-handling and searching problems, including cataloging standards for geographic data. [10] This paper addresses the impact of digital cartographic data-handling technology on current cataloging practices and highlights certain areas that are treated inadequately with existing cataloging rules.

The Nature of Digital Cartographic Databases

As with all information storage and retrieval systems, the primary goal of a geographic information system is rapid access to organized, understandable, and up-to-date geographic information pursuant to an individual's needs. Digital cartographic databases in a geographic information system are stored as binary codes on computer disks. The contents of digital cartographic databases are constantly changing so that they may remain timely and useful. This dynamism or instability of data content constitutes a major deviation from formats handled by existing cataloging codes. The closest (although not fitting) analogies to digital cartographic databases are serials and machine-readable data files.

Unlike serials, digital cartographic databases are not issued in successive parts which may be treated separately. [11] Rather, they represent an aggregate of cumulative time-series spatial data files that are updated at varying time intervals. These changes, however, can occur without affecting the bibliographic identity of the data file. And unlike machine-readable data fields (numeric or text files or computer programs), digital cartographic files have two component parts: maps and attributes (see Figure 1). Maps are the primary source of cartographic information, while attributes contain codes that make individual points or lines on the maps meaningful representations of the earth's features. The cartographic information is encoded as layers of graphic representation linked with data files containing geographic codes. These files are stored in special formats to account for spatial relations and to facilitate access to recorded information. The digital data can be revised retrospectively or retrieved in whole or in part. A selected layer may be disaggregated or partitioned into smaller submaps. Various layers may be combined to create a composite layer containing many interacting features.

Figure 1 is a schematic drawing of a geographic information system and its data contents. A geographic information system contains a collection of digital cartographic databases representing various data layers. Each layer has a specific time frame and map scale. As there are many acceptable digital cartographic file formats, a collection of digital cartographic databases may have to be converted to a suitable file format (possibly with some data loss) for use in a computer platform different from its original platform. Nonetheless, the original computer system's configuration is the most functional or effective means of retrieving its associated digital cartographic data.

Problems in Cataloging Digital Cartographic Databases

The responsibility of a cartographic materials cataloger is to provide information to catalog users that will lead them to cartographic documents necessary to address a query or support research. Probably the most notable issues in the cataloging of dynamic digital cartographic databases concern data access points and the timely updating of catalog entries to reflect the actual infor-

Figure 1. Digital cartographic databases in a geographic information system.

Data Layer	Data Time Frame	Scale of original
Political subdivisions (Base map)	1990	1:24,000
Soil	1970 - 80	1:24,000
Hydrology	1978 - 85	1:50,000
Geology	1975	1:24,000
Major cities	1989	1:12,000
Vegetation cover	1985	1:100,000
Historical sites	1815 - 1900	1:12,500

Digital cartographic databases are accessible via a geographic information system with a specialized hardware and software configuration. Each data layer describes a spatial entity constrained within a specified data time frame and a map scale. These data may be partitioned into smaller subsets or various layers aggregated to provide a new composite layer. Unlike its paper predecessor, which is an end product itself, digital cartographic databases are buoyant in nature, bounded only by data resolution and time dimension.

mation content of these databases. As with paper maps, digital cartographic databases contain a diversity of information. What does the librarian catalog? Which among the many fields in a cataloging record should constitute the main entry? How is the title proper selected from among the many possible choices or lack of them? What cataloging practices must be devised to deal with changes to a digital cartographic database, and what kinds of changes do or do not warrant the creation of a new bibliographic record?

Some of the above questions can be addressed through a closer examination of the nature of a geographic information system which handles cartographic databases. Understanding the nature of a geographic information system is helpful in identifying useful access points for the retrieval of digital cartographic data and for providing pertinent notes to a cataloging record. The following sections highlight some elements not accommodated by current cartographic cataloging rules and account for the utility of these elements in facilitating the retrieval of digital cartographic data.

Author Versus Area Entry

According to Carver, access to remote sensing and other specialized types of spatial geographic information is poor at best. He points out that few researchers request or search for spatial information by author and title, and that cartographic materials are sought primarily by geographic area, subject, format, and date. [12] Author remains the preferred entry for old and rare maps, however, because the cartographer is of great importance in the study of these maps, while area entry is more appropriate for new maps. [13, 14]

A survey conducted by the Committee on Map Cataloging of the Geography and Map Division of the Special Libraries Association reported that the majority of requests for maps use the area approach. [15] The survey indicated that 72% of libraries responding to the survey questionnaire expected maps to be requested more frequently by area, or area combined with subject and date, than by author and title. Such responses have persuaded map librarians to favor the use of area as the main entry for maps.

Nichols [16] commented that the AACR2 makes no acknowledgment of the importance of area as the main entry for maps. [17, 18] The 1XX (main entry heading) fields of the OCLC-MARC Map format do not accommodate area entry either (see figure 2). [19] Since the establishment of area headings is in the domain of cataloging, no guidance is given in the code for descriptive cataloging on the use of geographical names as headings for maps. In Chapter 23 of AACR2, geographic names are treated for use with corporate bodies in headings. The chapter does not provide sufficient guidance, however, regarding areas illustrated in maps. For example, there is a lack of uniform practice for the handling of islands, compound names, physical features covering more than one country, and features with unique names. [20]

Area in a digital cartographic environment means the geographic extent or limit beyond which data will not be collected or portrayed. Often there is a base map layer within a geographic information system that describes the geographic extent of the resident databases (see Figure 1). But which geographic names should be assigned to the area entry? A classification scheme for geographic area referencing was developed by Great Britain's Ministry of Defence. [21] Its manual contains clear instructions on the determination of the appropriate area classification. In the interest of eliminating inconsistencies in the referencing of geographic names, the United States Geological Survey (USGS) has undertaken a major effort to compile a standardized name bank for use in automated mapping systems. The result of this effort is the Geographical Names Information System (GNIS), which contains a machine-readable, national geographic names database in the core of the system. [22]

Title Entry

In a digital cartographic data file, there is a lack of a single source of information that is comparable with the title page of a printed document. In fact, digital cartographic data files often come without a title, although they always possess a geographic extent. Therefore, rules listed in section 1B of *Cartographic Materials: A Manual of Interpretation for AACR2* (1982) are not applicable in the digital cartographic setting. [23]

AACR2 (Revised), Rule 3.1B4 says that "if the item lacks a title, supply one as instructed in 1.1B7. Always include in the supplied title the name of the area covered." Section 1.1B7 further suggests that one should "Supply a title proper for an item lacking a chief source of information or its substitute from the rest of the item, or a reference source, or elsewhere. If no title can be found in any source, devise a brief descriptive title. Enclose such a supplied or devised title in square brackets."

Although the above AACR2 rules provide some guidelines for dealing with this problem, it is not difficult to imagine that a digital cartographic database cataloged in separate sites will be assigned different titles. This will yield duplicate records of the same digital cartographic database on an online cooperative cataloging system such as OCLC, as there is not a tangible title page to furnish data for the 245 field (see Figure 2). Conversely, digital cartographic systems bearing similar titles may be erroneously treated as the same entity. Considering the nature of the problem, a standardized approach to identifying the distinguishing features of a digital cartographic database is warranted.

Data Layers

A digital cartographic database, unlike its paper predecessor, is multidimensional. The many layers of data residing in a geographic information system are the keys to the expanded level of selectivity and flexibility. Data layers are

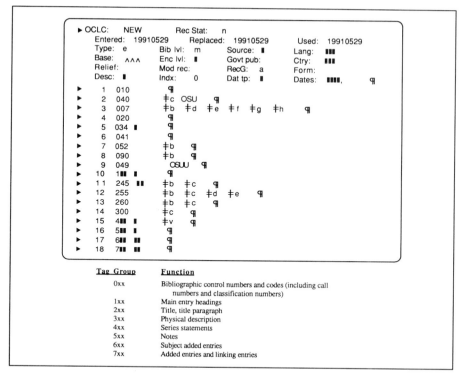

Figure 2. An OCLC workform for cataloging maps.

analogous to the subject matter or contents of a book. These contents depict distributional phenomena for a select amount of detail as permitted by the map scale, and are exact only for the specified time period.

Most digital cartographic databases contain geographic features or events applicable for a significant timespan and, therefore, carry important chronological dates. New constructions or additional transportation features, for example, will not be shown in cartographic documents compiled prior to construction or planning. Chronological dates of the data layers are pertinent to cartographic databases and should be incorporated into the body of the catalog record.

Perhaps the most critical of all map elements in terms of cartographic applications is the map scale. Map scale is directly proportional to the amount of detail evident from a map. From a practical viewpoint, map scale determines whether an application that a user has in mind can be supported with the given detail. With digital cartographic databases in a geographic information system, a range of map scales may be appropriate, as individual data layers are likely to originate from varied map scales (see Figure 1). These digital cartographic databases are constrained at the level of detail of the original documents from which they are derived. One map scale (presumably that of the base map) cannot fully describe variations within the database.

There is a widespread misconception that digital cartographic databases are scale-independent because of the ease of integrating data layers of varying map scales and converting data between map scales. Figure 3 illustrates the problem of transforming cartographic data between map scales to accentuate the role of map scales in a digital cartographic setting. One may generalize to a smaller-scale map from a more detailed large-scale map, but the reverse is improper because smaller-scale maps do not contain the amount of detail required for larger-scale maps. AACR2 (Revised), Rule 3.3B requires that a statement of scale be included in cartographic cataloging. For a digital cartographic system, a *range* of map scales for various data layers is relevant, in addition to that of the base map. Subfield *a* of field 255 (mathematical data area) does not accommodate the recording of this range (see Figure 2).

Notes Area

A geographic information system has many functional components. Among the more important components are data format and systems platform. [24] *Data format* dictates the structural organization of digital cartographic data. *Systems platform* denotes software and hardware through which digital carto-graphic data can be accessed and used. Information on these components is necessary to determine if the collection of digital data can be used immedi-ately, or whether additional processes are needed to convert them into a for-mat compatible with an institution's computer platform. The 5XX (notes) fields in the MARC Map format do not provide for this information (see figure 2). A new field should be created for notes on digital data formats.

There exist many digital cartographic data formats. Among the more popu-lar formats are those developed by federal government agencies. For example, the Defense Mapping Agency's Digital Landmass System contains data in the forms of Digital Feature Analysis Data (DFAD) and Digital Terrain Elevation Data (DTED). The United States Geological Survey produces Digital Line Graphs (DLGs), Digital Elevation/Terrain Models (DEM and DTM), and land use and land cover data (GIRAS). The United States Fish and Wildlife Service creates digital wetland databases using the MOSS format. Many government and private agen-cies also employ digital mapping systems from commercial vendors like the Intergraph Corporation and the Environmental Systems Research Institute. These systems, respectively, produce digital data in Standard Intergraph Format (SIF) and ARC/INFO format.

The abundance of digital cartographic formats has created many problems in spatial data handling. Each format has its unique characteristics and contains spe-cific geo-related information necessary to conduct a particular study or analysis— whether environmental, statistical, or exploratory. Digital cartographic data can be converted from one format to another, but not without some degree of infor-

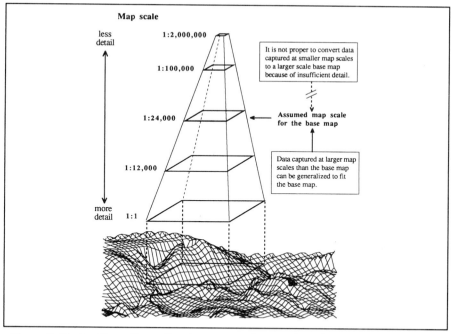

Map scale

less detail

1:2,000,000

It is not proper to convert data captured at smaller map scales to a larger scale base map because of insufficient detail.

1:100,000

1:24,000

Assumed map scale for the base map

Data captured at larger map scales than the base map can be generalized to fit the base map.

1:12,000

more detail   1:1

Figure 3. The problem of transforming map scales in a digital cartographic environment.

mation loss. The user community of digital cartographic databases remains impartial about maintaining multiple data formats.

Classification and Subject Entry

As discussed in the section on "Data Layers" above, the subject coverage of a digital cartographic database depends on the nature of the data, which may consist of economic, social, geological, meteorological, and environmental indicators. One could assign as many subject access points to a digital cartographic database as the number of data layers. The determination of a classification number for the database based on its subject coverage, however, is difficult because the database cannot be classed effectively on the basis of multiple subjects.

Schedule G of The Library of Congress (LC) Classification (1976) provides an alternative: to classify a cartographic database by area. [25] Field 052, Geographic Classification Code, of the OCLC Maps Format (Figure 2) contains a combination of numeric and alphanumeric codes representing geographic area and subarea. Their values are based on map classification numbers enumerated in LC's G schedule, in the range G3190-G9804, to be assigned in conjunction with the appropriate tables. [26] The LC classification scheme for maps, however, is not flexible enough to accommodate physical features bordering adjacent countries, or regions extending over a number of distinct administrative units, such as multiple states in the United States.

The question of subject access for digital cartographic databases is complicated by the fact that it is not uncommon for producers of a database to maintain, update, or even add to a database at varying periods. In such cases, a comprehensive indication of the subject coverage of a database is impossible, since catalogers are not in a position to predict what kinds of data will be added in the future. Digital cartographic databases, unlike serials, are not issued in successive parts that may be treated separately. The dynamic and cumulative nature of the contents of a digital cartographic database make it difficult as well to treat this format as a monograph, i.e., as a one-time publication. The classification number assigned to this type of database today may not be appropriate in the future. This unique characteristic of digital cartographic databases may necessitate the development of an additional code at the bibliographic level of the fixed fields in the OCLC-MARC Map Format.

Conclusion and Remarks

Cartographic materials have traditionally been handled as a resource that is subsidiary to the main library collection. The cartographic materials section (sometimes labeled "map library") has been neglected for various reasons: conventional cartographic materials (sheet maps, models, and globes) do not fit neatly into a manageable bound form; cartographic materials are not adequately handled by existing cataloging systems; and there are other matters of a higher priority than cartographic materials that need to be accommodated in libraries. While a tremendous number of digital cartographic databases are being created daily, there is no adequate method of recording their contents.

The value of a geographic information system or a digital cartographic database lies in its role and capacity, beyond that of the traditional library, as a source of geographic information. A spatial database partitions the data contained therein spatially or geographically, in the same manner that non-spatial data may be classified by subject. The multiple types of content and the structural organization of digital cartographic databases create a need for a cataloging system through which location and retrieval of spatial information can be optimized.

Nichols commented that a catalog of cartographic documents must always be judged by how well it serves its users. [27] It is judged both on its approach to the cartographic document and on the description of the cartographic document in an individual record. We have presented a few data elements relevant to digital cartographic data in which existing cataloging rules are deficient. These elements include area, title, subject and scale of data layers, file format, and computer platform. The field of geographic information systems is still evolving, however, and many possible deviations from standard practice may not yet have surfaced. Undoubtedly, catalogers will continue to discover many unanticipated problems and much confusion as they venture the task of cataloging digital cartographic databases in the near future. It is our hope that this paper provides some insights that will assist in the development of guidelines for cataloging digital cartographic databases.

NOTES

1. Federal Interagency Coordinating Committee on Digital Cartography. Standards Working Group. *Federal Geographic Exchange Format*. Final draft, Version 1.08, 12-15-86.
2. Lai, P.C., Gillies, C.F. The Impact of Geographical Information Systems on the Role of Spatial Data Libraries. *International Journal of Geographical Information Systems*, 5(2): 241-51, 1991.
3. Studwell, W. The Invisible Geologic Quadrangle. *Western Association Map Library Information Bulletin*. 21(2): 98-9, 1990.
4. Larsgaard, M.L. Change in Academic Cartographic Materials Collections: Or, A Groundswell Revisited. *Western Association Map Library Information Bulletin*. 21(2): 101-4, 1990.
5. Tyacke, S. Digital Maps and Remotely Sensed Data. *Inspel*. 21(1): 48-54, 1987.
6. U.S. Geological Survey. *Research, Investigations and Technical Developments: National Mapping Program 1985-86*. 1988. (USGS Open-File Report 87-315.)
7. Federal Interagency Coordinating Committee on Digital Cartography.
8. Cruse, L. Microcartography and Cartographic Data Bases. *Library Trends*. 29(3): 391-416, 1981.
9. Carver, L. The RLG GeoInformation Project: Objectives-Scope-Status. *Western Association Map Library Information Bulletin*. 19(3): 129-31, 1988.
10. Abler, R.F. The National Science Foundation National Center for Geographic Information and Analysis. *International Journal of Geographical Information Systems*. 1: 303-26, 1987.
11. Dodd, S. *Cataloging Machine Readable Data Files*. Chicago, IL: American Library Association, 1982.
12. Carver, p. 129.
13. Larsgaard, M.L. *Map Librarianship - An Introduction*. 2nd edition. Littleton, CO: Libraries Unlimited, 1987, p. 27.
14. Fink, M.E. A Comparison of Map Cataloging Systems. *Bulletin*, Geography and Map Division, Special Libraries Association. (50): 6-11, 1962.
15. Nichols, H. *Map Librarianship*. 2nd edition. London: Clive Bingley, 1982, p. 143.
16. ibid.
17. *Anglo-American Cataloguing Rules*, 2nd edition. Chicago: American Library Association, 1978.
18. *Anglo-American Cataloguing Rules*, 2nd edition, 1988 Revision. Chicago: American Library Association, 1988.
19. Online Computer Library Center, Inc. *Online Systems Map Format*. 2nd ed., March 1987 revision. Ohio: OCLC, 1987.
20. Nichols, p. 147.
21. Great Britain. Ministry of Defence. *Manual of Map Library Classification and Cataloging*. Prepared under the direction of the Chief of the General Staff. Feltham: Ministry of Defence, 1978. (GSGS.5307.)
22. Payne, R.L. *Geographic Names Information System*. 1984. (United States Geological Survey Circular 895-F.)
23. *Cartographic Materials: A Manual of Interpretation for AACR2*. Chicago: American Library Association, 1982.

24. U.S. Geological Survey. *A Process for Evaluating Geographic Information Systems.* 1988. (USGS Open-File Report 88-105.)

25. Library of Congress. Subject Cataloging Division. *Classification, Class G: Geography, Maps, Anthropology, Recreation.* 4th ed. Washington: Library of Congress, 1976.

26. Online Computer Library Center, Inc., p. Map 0:63.

27. Nichols, p. 142.

OPTIONS IN THE ARRANGEMENT OF LIBRARY MATERIALS AND THE NEW EDITION OF THE BLISS BIBLIOGRAPHIC CLASSIFICATION

Alan R. Thomas

Visiting Associate Professor
Division of Library and Information Science
St. John's University, Jamaica, NY 11439

The Present Situation and Perception of Choice

Several factors have contributed to the widespread adoption in North America of the Dewey Decimal Classification or the Library of Congress Classification (LCC). These factors include the relatively early compilation and publication of these schemes, their utilization by networks and centralized cataloging systems, and the conservative and restricted character of many library and information science courses. Library practices and library school curricula appear to go hand in hand, reinforcing one another in the perpetuation of established approaches and methods. Consequently, a practitioner's perception is that there exists only a very limited choice in the area of classification—namely, that between Dewey and LCC. Moreover, few approved internal options are available in Dewey and even fewer in LCC.

Advantages of Considering Alternatives

There are many benefits in having library school faculty, students, and practitioners consider alternative models of classification and some individual schemes based on them. Such study would focus attention on the merits and disadvantages of each in relation to the requirements of different kinds of libraries and information centers.

These requirements include responding to patrons' approaches to the structure of recorded knowledge, semantic associations, and syntax. Henry Evelyn Bliss kept in mind that "libraries may have different points of view or different constituencies to serve." [1] Roberts contends that there exists a "wealth of anecdotal evidence to show that, for many individuals, certain groupings of material are regarded as confusing, mystifying, frustrating, incomprehensible and beyond rational understanding." [2]

A comparative, critical study of a range of alternatives should help a librarian to arrive at the desirable criteria for classification, whether used for arranging a collection, a catalog, a bibliography, or to enhance the searching process. Librarians are much more likely to get what they really want if they become knowledgeable about different schemes and about the internal choices in these schemes. The final optimal solution in a particular environment might be to continue to use a standard classification, to make editorially sanctioned modifications to it, to make unofficial local adaptations, to adopt another published scheme, or even to construct a custom-built system.

A further benefit of a comparative study in the light of identified user needs would be the ability to contribute to the editing and ongoing revision of classification schemes, thesauri, and lists of subject headings.

The Number of Options

The number of different ways of arranging even a small collection is virtually infinite. It would prove impossible to accommodate the preferences of every group of users, let alone every individual patron, within any one classification or even in a combination of systems. Yet, a single scheme can provide important alternatives where each possesses substantial user warrant.

When a library or information center makes an information-based rational decision, as distinct from merely conforming to tradition, there will still be readers and staff members whose needs remain somewhat neglected. Some individuals and the members of some groups will be forced to do more walking in the library, more moving around in a classified bibliography or catalog, and more processing of a database. Their burdens may be lightened, however, through the provision of multiple access points to a subject file and through various forms of guidance as to how the subject areas concerned are organized.

The Bliss Bibliographic Classification

Henry Evelyn Bliss, an American, evolved and applied his scheme in the library of the College of the City of New York. From a sketch in 1910 (see Reference [1]) through seminal theoretical works and further outlines, the publication of the full schedules by the H.W. Wilson Company was completed in 1953. [3] The system expressed Bliss's scholarly preoccupation with patterns of helpful order, and it featured various choices.

W.C. Berwick Sayers was undoubtedly premature in his prediction that this new classification "will not, I feel certain, be long overlooked in its native land." [4] The fact was that the first edition made very little impact on American library practice, and it received only slight attention in American library schools. [5] It was, however, taught and it received some adoptions in Britain and the Commonwealth.

TABLE 1. BLISS BIBLIOGRAPHIC CLASSIFICATION, 2ND ED.

CLASS SCHEDULES

*Introduction and Auxiliary Schedules—1977

2/9	Generalia, Phenomena, Knowledge, Information science and technology
* **A/AL**	Philosophy and Logic—1991
+ **AM/AW**	Mathematics, Probability and statistics
AX/B	General science and Physics
C	Chemistry
D	Astronomy and Earth sciences
E/GQ	Biological sciences
GR/GZ	Agriculture and Ecology
* **H**	Anthropology, Human Biology, Health sciences. Includes medicine—1980
* **I**	Psychology and Psychiatry—1978
* **J**	Education—1977, revised 1990
* **K**	Society. Includes social science, sociology, social anthropology, customs, folklore and mythology—1984
L/O	History. Includes area studies, travel and topography, and biography
* **P**	Religion, the Occult, Morals and ethics—1977
* **Q**	Social welfare. Includes criminology—1977
+ **R**	Politics, Public administration
+ **S**	Law
* **T**	Economics, Management of economic enterprises—1987
U/V	Technology. Includes household management and services
W	Recreation and Arts. Includes music
X/Z	Language and Literature

* = volume available.

+= nearing completion.

.

In 1967, the H.W. Wilson Company ceased direct involvement with the Bliss scheme and its bulletin. The same year saw the inception in Great Britain of the Bliss Classification Association, which was established to develop the system and promote its use. There continued to be little interest in the scheme within the United States, though Eugene Garfield judged that "Bliss's work deserves to be continued and its potentialities fully explored." [6]

Bliss Bibliographic Classification, 2nd Edition

The second edition of the *Bliss Bibliographic Classification*, referred to hereinafter as BC2, began publication in 1977. The publisher was Butterworths, but recently this publishing group has decided to use the Bowker-Saur imprint for the scheme. The macro organization of this new edition follows that of the first edition closely and retains Bliss's carefully constructed main class sequence.

So far, nine of the projected set of twenty-two volumes have been published under the general editorship of Jack Mills. The listing of the parts in Table 1 serves as an outline of the system and also indicates by an asterisk (*) those volumes already available. Some three other forthcoming parts nearing completion are shown by a plus sign (+).

The logical bone structure of the classification can readily be discerned in the First Outline, which is given in Table 2.

TABLE 2. FIRST OUTLINE OF THE BLISS BIBLIOGRAPHIC CLASSIFICATION, 2ND EDITION

2	Generalia : Physical forms and forms of arrangement
4	Phenomena : attributes, activities, entities
7	Knowledge, information, communication
	Disciplines
A	Philosophy
AM	Mathematics
AZ	Science
B	Physical sciences
E	Biological sciences
H	Man, anthropology
	Physical : medicine, psychology
J/Z	Social sciences and humanities

The lists of constituent terms in each main class are far more detailed in the new edition than in its predecessor, and reflect contemporary literary warrant. The micro organization of classes is much more highly analytico-synthetic than in the original scheme, embodying the methods of S.R. Ranganathan and their subsequent development by the Classification Research Group in Great Britain and other contributors. For any given subject, the basic constituent terms are grouped into sets called facets and then into subfacets (arrays).

The detailed enumeration of basic terms together with the extended synthetic capability can result in a larger index vocabulary than in other published library classifications. For most classes, the potential specificity exceeds that of the full version of the Universal Decimal Classification. While intensive specificity is attainable, the BC2 notation has been designed to yield as brief classmarks as possible.

The scheme can be used to arrange both general and special collections, catalogs, and bibliographies: it also has widespread thesaural applications. [7-9] The scheme's versatility as a technical tool is secured by the provision of many specific options and kinds of option.

BC2 and Its Provision of Options

Bliss had reached the conclusion that there could be discerned an educational and scientific consensus as to the relations between subject, but he appreciated that its stability was relative. [10] As a consequence of his belief in a temporary consensus which varies with space and time, Bliss provided for adaptations of the generally preferred order to persistent different views and practical convenience. BC2 defines *consensus* as "the relative agreement amongst producers, users and organizers of information as to the scope of, and relationships between classes." [11]

The editors of the new edition have maintained and greatly increased the provision of indicated options within the classification. The Introduction volume asserts the belief that "there are a fair number of situations where it is perfectly predictable that many libraries will prefer a particular alternative ..." [12] In such cases BC2 specified the built-in alternatives. Not every subject calls for options, and BC2, the most option-rich system in existence, provides them only in a minority of cases. When an alternative is signalled, there are generally two choices—the regular scheduled provision preferred by the editors, and an allowable option. Occasionally, there may be three choices, very rarely more.

Kinds of Optional Treatment in BC2

The kinds of nomenclature of options varied in the writings of H.E. Bliss, the most important devices being those of alternative locations of main subjects or classes and alternative methods of classifying extensive subjects. [13] Similarly, BC2 uses and explains the terms *alternative locations* and *alternative treatments*. [14]

Some of the published classes of BC2 employ variant terminology. Tighter editorial control over the naming and defining of kinds of alternative is called for to reduce possible resistance by potential users of the scheme.

The principal categories of possibility available are now considered under the following headings:

1) Alternative locations
2) Favored focus device
3) Alternative arrangements
4) Systematic alternatives
5) Combining discipline and phenomenon
6) Degrees of specification
7) Application to files
8) Other options.

1) Alternative locations

Alternative locations allow a subject to be placed in an indicated different discipline, subdiscipline, or other context, but without any alteration of that subject's enumerated details. BC2 contains far more alternative locations than other classification systems; the alternative locations occur at various levels of hierarchy as the following examples show.

At the main class level, Parapsychology is preferred in Class I, Psychology, at IHT, but if desired could be placed under Class P, Religion, at PX. Social psychology is preferred in Class I at IN/IQ, but a choice can be taken to locate it in Class K, Sociology, at KD. Science-based technologies are preferred with their respective root pure sciences in such classes as B, Physics, and C, Chemistry, although alternatively they may be classed under U, Technology.

At a lower level, within Class P, Religion, Islam is preferred at PV, where it maintains its proper position in the chronological sequence of major religions, but it could go at PK between Parseeism and Judaism.

Auxiliary Schedule 1, a list of common form and subject subdivisions, contains several choices. Thus, the subject "Curriculum of religion" is preferred at P, Religion, to which is added the common subdivision 6AK Curriculum, producing the mark P6A K. An unpreferred option is to subsume the subject under J, Education, at JKT P, where JKT represents Curricula. In Auxiliary Schedule 2, a common list of places, the official preference is to collocate Corsica and Sardinia under the Mediterranean, with an option for Corsica to be subsumed under France, and one for Sardinia under Italy. In Auxiliary Schedule 3, German Yiddish is preferred at NTR under Hebrew, NT, but a place is available at XM under German languages.

Within Class H, the Optic nerve is preferred at HUV UW, as part of Cranial nerves, but a library might want to exercise the choice of putting it at HVE J, as part of Eye.

2) Favored focus device

This device occurs also in the Colon Classification and the Dewey Decimal Classification. A "favored" focus can be given the very first place in a series or array of countries, languages, etc. within a subject. For example, in Class Q,

Social Welfare, the range of notation QFC/QFM is allotted for the social security of the favored country, so that an American, Irish, British or other system would occupy the first place on the shelves or in a bibliographic file. Again, in J, Education, JNW is reserved for individual secondary schools of the chosen country.

3) Alternative arrangements

A considerable number of alternative arrangements based on user warrant and literary warrant are included in the volumes of BC2 already issued, and the generous provision will be maintained in the parts currently being compiled. Alternative arrangement gives choice concerning the *internal* arrangement of a subject by permitting its facets or subfacets to be combined in different patterns.

Consider the subject "Housing for the elderly in the context of welfare." In Class Q, Social welfare, the schedules include the following terms:

QH Housing   (in *Cause of need* facet)
QLV Old Persons   (in *Person in need* facet)

The normal way of combining in BC2 is to proceed up the schedules, yielding the synthesized classmark QLV H for the above topic. The alternative solution—which is not preferred by the editors, but which could be very important to certain libraries or information centers—is to build the opposite way in the sequence of Cause/Person, giving the result of QHX LV.

Another example would be "Anxiety neurosis in adolescents." Class I, Psychology, includes the following constituent terms:

IVR Anxiety neurosis
IXR Adolescents

The official preference is to combine facets in the sequence Person/Disorder, building upwards as usual and adding extra features as required, resulting in the classmark IXR VR. Should a librarian wish to arrange the material in Disorder/Person pattern, however, then the guided result is IVR UER.

Full directions for synthesizing terms and adjusting the notational characters are provided in the scheme.

The Universal Decimal Classification is also noteworthy for its degree of flexibility in combining elements of a compound subject. In contrast to BC2, however, the synthetic power of UDC requires the use of a battery of special characters which can create filing problems and baffle the user, and the scheme does not provide rationale and guidance concerning warranted choices.

4) Systematic alternatives

In the first edition of the Bliss scheme, the Auxiliary Schedules were called "Systematic Auxiliaries." The term *systematic alternative* as such was found only in the original edition (see Reference [13]), but the facility continues in BC2 and has long been a familiar feature of the Dewey Decimal Classification.

Some choices are provided as to qualifying the regular schedule notation for a subject with a mark from Auxiliary Schedule 1, a table of common subdivisions, or marking the entire synthesized compound with regular schedule notation. Thus the "law of special subjects" can either be scattered by special subject or subordinated to Class S, Law. Another example occurs in the treatment of subject bibliography, another with curricular subjects (see p. 202).

5) Combining discipline and phenomenon

James Duff Brown created a distinctive general library scheme which, to a considerable extent, secured collocation of various aspects of and "standpoints" (points of view) on a particular phenomenon ("concrete") at one place. [15] BC2, along with the Dewey Decimal Classification, the Universal Decimal Classification, and LCC, is primarily a discipline-oriented system, scattering material on any particular phenomenon among the appropriate disciplines. A phenomenon may be taken to mean any abstract or concrete object of knowledge or experience, and a discipline, any form of knowledge, or way of viewing the phenomenon. For example, information on the phenomenon horse would be dispersed under such disciplines as zoology, veterinary medicine, animal husbandry, sport, warfare, etc., while information on gold is found under chemistry, mineralogy, geology, metallurgy, economics, and so forth.

The BC2 schedules of the discipline classes A-Z have been constructed on a "basic citation order of Discipline-Phenomenon." [16] However, unlike the other great classifications whose notations are included in standard bibliographic records, BC2 offers to librarians and information officers a variety of provisions for handling discipline/phenomenon conditions.

A problem for all types of libraries and their readers has always been finding the most helpful placement of a document that treats a specific phenomenon from the standpoint of several disciplines. Such a book or article might be one on strikes, with evidence and insights from social psychology, economics, and political science, or a children's book "all about trains."

BC2 offers three courses of action for the discipline/phenomenon problem:

Option 1, Condition (a)—Here a document involving a single aspect treatment of a phenomenon goes with whatever aspect is involved. This practice is the usual one in most library classification schemes. Thus, a zoological treatment of the horse would be allocated the mark GYH J in Class G, Zoology.

Option 1, Condition (b)—A multi-aspect treatment of a phenomenon goes at the notation for the focus within its most basic defining discipline, to which is added the digit 1. The addition of 1 denotes that several aspects are treated. Therefore, a multi-disciplinary treatment of the horse goes at GYH J1. The comprehensive results for BC2 and Dewey 20 are as follows:

	Dewey 20	BC2
Zoology	591	G
Zoology—horse	599.725	GYH J
Multi-disciplinary	599.725	GYH J1

work on horse
(unless some other discipline
clearly preponderates)

In both schemes, the comprehensive work on horse is subordinated to the discipline of zoology. Dewey fails to distinguish "Zoology of the horse" from a multi-aspect treatment of horse, and the literature on both subjects would be interfiled. BC2 manages to achieve differentiation, but the multi-disciplinary text is subordinated to zoology of the horse, and, as in Dewey, to zoology in general. BC2 admits that this "small inconsistency is the price we pay for attempting the impossible." [17]

The problem posed by multi-disciplinary treatment of a phenomenon is one of the reasons behind the creation of special Phenomenon Classes in BC2. The challenging task of listing terms or indicating the sources for these classes is currently underway and will be published.

A second factor in the decision to create Phenomenon Classes was the desire to offer librarians and information officers the radical choice of collecting material on a given phenomenon at one place. This major alternative is feasible in all situations where there exists a significant proportion of phenomenon-oriented literature and inquiries. It has ever-increasing appeal for special libraries, special collections in general libraries, academic libraries, as well as children's libraries.

Option 2, Condition (a)—A document involving a single aspect treatment of a phenomenon continues to go with the aspect involved, just as in Option 1(a), so zoology of the horse is classed at GYH J.

Option 2, Condition (b)—A multi-aspect treatment of a phenomenon is accommodated in the emerging innovative Phenomenon Classes, wherein all entities, including organisms, are assigned the starter mark of 6. A comprehensive work on the horse is therefore classed at 6, to which is attached the specific notation for horse, GYH J, taken from its most basic, most defining discipline, which is G, Zoology. The result is 6GY HJ. This ability to specify multiple-aspect treatments of any object of knowledge in a Phenomenon Class is unique to BC2 and potentially useful in many circumstances.

The third alternative permits *everything* on a particular object of knowledge to be collected together in the Phenomenon Classes.

Option 3, Condition (a)—This allows even a single-disciplinary study of a phenomenon to go in the Phenomenon Classes. A zoological study of horse would be 6GY HJ.

Option 3, Condition (b)—This is the same provision as in Option 2(b), allowing accommodation for multi-aspect treatments, so a multi-disciplinary account of horse is 6GY HJ.

While Option 3 gathers together *all* material on a phenomenon on the shelf, in a classed catalog or bibliography, the zoological study of the horse has the same mark as the comprehensive treatment. The scheme so far does not address this problem, but a valid solution would be to add the digit 1 to the multi-aspect notation, resulting in 6GY HJ1. This device is compatible with the use of 1 in Option 1(b).

The above extended explanation of the discipline/phenomenon choices is included here since the provisions are novel and no equivalent possibilities exist within standard schemes. The options are summarized in Table 3 as follows (the first choice of the [Bliss] editors is *Option 1*).

TABLE 3. CLASSIFYING THE PHENOMENON "HORSE"				
	BLISS CLASSIFICATION			DEWEY CLASSIFICATION
Condition	Option 1	Option 2	Option 3	
	Everything in Discipline Classes A/Z	Split according to nature of work	Everything in Phenomenon Classes 4/9	
(a) Single disciplinary treatment (e.g., zoological)	GYH J	GYH J	6GY HJ	599.725
(b) Multi-disciplinary treatment	GYH J1	6GY HJ	6GY HJ1	599.725

6) Degrees of specification

By allowing for extensive specification through its high level of enumerated detail and its numerous synthetic devices, BC2 gives a particular library a real choice as to whether to classify closely or more broadly.

A particular displayed choice of detail is shown in Auxiliary Schedule 4, which is a common table for periods of time. Here BC2 provides for three degrees of detail by enumerating three different tables. Schedule 4B is a short, less specific list with shorter marks, 4A is the recommended alternative and so constitutes the standard list, while 4C allows the greatest amount of specification with longer notations.

7) Application to files

As with any indexing system with an open architecture that is equipped for synthesis, BC2 may be applied to catalogs and bibliographies in either a precoordinate or a postcoordinate mode.

If a decision is made to use a precoordinate mode, there is a further choice of applying the mode in a single-entry or in a multiple-entry way.

Taking the subject of "Housing for the elderly," already considered above under the rubric "Alternative arrangements," the possibilities include:

Precoordinate mode

Single entry   QLV H (officially preferred) or QHX LV
Multiple entry   QLV-QH   and   QH-QLV

Postcoordinate mode

QH
QLV

searched as QH AND QLV *or as* QLV AND QH (i.e., no required combination order).

8) Other options

Further alternatives are available in the Bliss system. The spacing of the classmarks can be done in different ways, and guidance is given as to how to get briefer marks for the form of combination prevalent in a given collection.

Despite the unrivalled range and quantity of the designed options within BC2, the editors are unable to anticipate and accommodate every preference of every library. Occasionally an institution may wish to effect a purely local choice, a quite unofficial alternative that is not allowed for in the schedules.

The editors caution very careful consideration of all the consequences of such a step, and recommend that they be consulted prior to the introduction of any innovation. It is reasonable to assume that most librarians interested in a homemade, customized variation would study the general Introduction as well as the Introduction to the particular main class involved. This may not always happen, however, and consequently the editors should include adequate guidance on local options in the Introductions to all the volumes. At present, some published classes omit such information.

Decision-making on Sanctioned Alternatives

BC2 does offer considerable help in choosing between indicated options in the scheme. This assistance could be usefully extended and normalized, thus enhancing the appeal of the classification.

Although it is claimed that "the pros and cons of the different alternatives are considered in the Introduction to the class concerned," in fact only some of the designed choices are so considered. [18] Every available option should be discussed in each appropriate Introduction and schedule; the present Introductions list only the more prominent alternatives. At the beginning of every volume, there should be a list of all the options therein. Furthermore, when the publication of BC2 is finally completed, there should be provided a comprehensive list and discussion of all choices in the entire classification, arranged by classmarks and indexed alphabetically.

Not all BC2 classes explain how to interpret the schedules, or how to distinguish preferred from officially allowed unpreferred alternatives, or how to assess consequences of choice in terms of length of notation and helpful general-before-special order.

The terminology of guidance, the kind and amount of information, explanations, notation-building, and examples should be tightly standardized across the various Introductions and schedules.

Option Management

The provision of options makes BC2 schedules look complicated, at least on first sight. However, once the staff of a library or information center have carefully thought about and finally taken a decision as to the best available arrangement, location, or favored placing, then the cataloger/classifier should cross out all sections, instructions and examples that will no longer apply. The subject index must be amended accordingly. Thereafter, the schedules will present a simpler appearance and can be applied much more quickly and easily.

The Bliss Classification and Centralized and Cooperative Cataloging

H.E. Bliss tried unsuccessfully to get his system classmarks included in the Library of Congress records. [19] Similarly, the editors of BC2 have not succeeded as yet in having their classmarks in MARC records.

Ramsden argues that BC2 must "win acceptance by the major central cataloguing agencies" in order to gain general recognition. [20] He saw the problem as a "chicken and egg" situation: libraries are unlikely to use the scheme unless the marks are provided on the records; agencies will probably exclude BC2 data until libraries demand it.

Roberts identifies a further and possibly greater obstacle to acceptance of BC2, that of the "attitude of the majority of librarians towards classification in libraries . . ." [21] It appears that cooperative and centralizing tendencies, plus a narrow library-school curriculum foster a passive acceptance of standard schemes, and reduce careful attention to the question of how end-users' ways of organizing knowledge might be better reflected.

Since one of the assets of BC2 is the range of choices available, the agency records should include and distinguish between preferred and non-preferred (but officially provided) alternatives. A less expensive practice for the record-providing agency would be to list only the editorial preference, but to signal by a special character the existence of options, leaving the cataloger to consult the schedules.

Extending the Use and Usefulness of BC2

There are measures that could promote greater use of the scheme and/or increase its utility:

1) American library schools appear to neglect BC2. [22] Attention to the new edition in library science courses and acquisition of schedules for cataloging laboratories would increase professionals' awareness of the system and of choices in classification.

2) As has been suggested above, incorporating BC2 marks in the subject analysis data of externally supplied bibliographic records would increase the likelihood of adoption of the classification.

3) Greater overall editorial control might be exercised over all Introductions to classes and all schedules so as to improve clarity and consistency in the explanation of policies, methods, mark-building, and examples. The scheme and its approach are new to most librarians, so that a high degree of user-friendliness is critically important. Unfortunately, BC2 has necessarily been compiled, produced, and printed on a shoestring budget and is presently stuck in a "poverty trap." Improving its presentation would make the scheme more attractive and easier to consult. Very recent volumes, such as the revised Class J, Education, are typographically improved and so display more clearly the hierarchy of the classification.

4) Maltby and Gill stress the need for feedback on the scheme and its alternative provisions from those already using it or thinking of doing so. [23] Feedback on the schedules could be more widely and assertively sought from professional staff—readers' advisors, searchers, catalogers, and classifiers—in different kinds and sizes of library or information center and having different kinds of subject expertise. The invitations should be offered regardless of whether the institutions are interested in using BC2 as such. Thoughtful examination of the schedules should prove of mutual benefit to the editors and to those librarians participating in the review process. Librarians could also be requested to formally review specialist schedules for professional library journals. At present, North American professional involvement in the Bliss scheme is notably lacking.

From all such feedback methods, the editors could make revisions, further options, etc., and these improvements could be included in the *Bliss Classification Bulletin* or in the volumes still to be issued. [24, 25]

Every enhancement of the scheme would increase its chances of sales and adoptions, and increased revenues and utilization would, in turn, facilitate improvement of the scheme.

The Future of BC2 as a Resource for Choice

For some environments, the scheme itself is a viable alternative to other, well-established classification schemes. BC2 is already used by some 50 library and information centers located mostly in Britain.

For other environments, BC2 with its meticulous analysis of subjects and its many options may serve as a catalyst, resulting in librarians and information workers rethinking and redesigning the systems they will continue to employ.

Editors of other schemes, thesauri, and subject heading lists may wish to make use of certain features of BC2, including its structures, devices, choices, and vocabulary.

Whether used directly or indirectly, in whole or in part, BC2 seems to possess considerable potential which, if known and studied, would prove influential for a considerable time in helping librarians make more creative responses to the articulated preferences of library staff and of the readers they serve.

More broadly, there might ultimately be compiled an Options Guide which would constitute a major professional resource. This ongoing guide to choice in classification would incorporate patterns from BC2, Dewey, LCC, and other systems, as well as from good practice and "test-drive" experiments in general and special libraries and information centers.

NOTES

1. Bliss, Henry E. [1910] "A modern classification for libraries, with simple notation, mnemonics, and alternatives." *Library Journal*, 35(8), August 1910, pp. 351-358. Quotation from p. 354.

2. Roberts, Norman. "Bliss Bibliographic Classification: 2nd edition [review]." *Catalogue & Index*, 46, Autumn 1977, pp. 5-7. Quotation from p. 6.

3. Bliss, Henry Evelyn. [1952-1953] *A Bibliographic Classification*. Volumes I-II. New York: H.W. Wilson, 1952. Volume III. New York: H.W. Wilson, 1953.

4. Sayers, W.C. Berwick. "In appreciation of the Bibliographic Classification." *Wilson Library Bulletin*, 28(9), May 1954, pp. 765-766, 774. Quotation from p. 774.

5. Thomas, Alan R. "The Bliss Bibliographic Classification in the North American compulsory curriculum." *Bliss Classification Bulletin*, 6(2), January 1977, pp. 7-9.

6. Garfield, Eugene. "The 'other' immortal: a memorable day with Henry E. Bliss." *Wilson Library Bulletin*, 49(4), December 1974, pp. 288-292. Quotation from p. 292.

7. Aitchison, Jean. [1984] *ECOT Thesaurus* [Educational Courses and Occupations Thesaurus]. Working edition. Milton Keynes: Open University, 1984.

8. Aitchison, Jean, and others. [1985] *DHSS-DATA Thesaurus*. Working edition. London: DHSS [United Kingdom Department of Health and Social Security], 1985.

9. Aitchison, Jean. [1986] "A classification as a source for a thesaurus: the Bibliographic Classification of H.E. Bliss as a source of thesaurus terms and structure." *Journal of Documentation*, 42(3), September 1986, pp. 160-181.

10. Bliss, Henry Evelyn. [1933] *The organization of knowledge in libraries and the subject-approach to books.* New York: H.W. Wilson, 1933, p. 42.

11. *Bliss Bibliographic Classification.* [1977a] 2nd edition. Introduction and auxiliary schedules, ed. by J. Mills and Vanda Broughton; with the assistance of Valerie Lang. London: Butterworths, 1977, Introduction, p. 98.

12. ibid, Introduction, p. 44.

13. Bliss [1952-1953], Volumes I-II, p. 23.

14. Bliss [1977a], p. 44.

15. Brown, James Duff. *Subject classification:* with tables, indexes, etc. for the subdivision of subjects. London: Library Supply Co., 1906. Revised editions appeared in 1914 and 1939.

16. Bliss [1977a], p. 49.

17. ibid, Introduction, p. 54.

18. ibid, Introduction, p. 82.

19. Garfield, p. 291.

20. Ramsden, Michael J. "A new life for Bliss." *Australian Academic and Research Libraries,* 9(4), December 1978, pp. 210-214. Quotation from p. 213.

21. Roberts, p. 6.

22. Intner, Sheila S. "Cataloging practice and theory: what to teach and why." *Journal of Education for Library and Information Science,* 30(4), Spring 1990, pp. 333-336.

23. Maltby, Arthur; Gill, Lindy. *The case for BLISS:* modern classification practice and principles in the context of the Bibliographic Classification. London: Bingley, 1979, p. 135.

24. *Bliss Classification Bulletin,* 1954– in progress. [Annual].

25. *Bliss Bibliographic Classification,* 1977–. 2nd edition, ed. by J. Mills and Vanda Broughton. London: Butterworths, 1977– in progress.

INDEX

Compiled by
Edward Swanson

EDWARD SWANSON is the Principal Cataloger at the Minnesota Historical Society in Saint Paul, Minnesota. He has been an active participant in cataloging activities, having served as a member of the OCLC Cataloging Advisory Committee, the ALA MARBI Committee, and the ALA Committee on Cataloging: Description and Access, of which he is the current chair. He is the author or editor of a number of cataloging manuals. Since 1979 he has prepared the annual index to *Library Resources & Technical Services,* the journal of the Association for Library Collections & Technical Services, and in 1981 compiled an index to its first 25 volumes. At present he is working on an index to the first 50 volumes of *Oxoniensia,* the annual publication of the Oxfordshire (England) Architectural & Historical Society.

INDEX

A

AACR2: 7-8; adoption by National Library of Medicine, 41-42; Apocrypha, treatment of, 18-19, 20, 24-26; Bible, uniform titles for, 18-19, 24-26; Deuterocanonical books, treatment of, 18-19, 20, 24-26; Old Testament in, 24-26; pseudepigrapha, treatment of, 18-19, 20, 24-26; Tanakh, treatment of, 24-26; use of, in special collections, 137-38. *See also* descriptive cataloging

AAT, *see Art and Architecture Thesaurus*

abbreviations: in descriptive cataloging, 34

access points, *see* descriptive cataloging

Anglo-American Cataloguing Rules, 2nd ed., *see* AACR2

Apocrypha: treatment in AACR2, 18-19, 20, 24-26

Art and Architecture Thesaurus: 57, 59-74; applications of, 60, 61; candidate terms, 70; compared with Library of Congress subject headings, 68-70; complexities of, 72; descriptors, form of, 67; development of, 59-60, 61-62; facets, use of, in, 62-66, 67; hierarchy in, 62-67; index, 67; postcoordination and, 67-68; precoordination and, 67-68; structure of, 61-67; tree structure in, 66; use of, by nonlibrary communities, 70-71

Association of Research Libraries: 129 $\underline{n}$4

author numbers: 10

authority records: 8, 113-14. *See also* NACO; name authority records, Library of Congress

B

Bible: uniform titles for, in AACR2, 18-19, 24-26

bibliographic description, *see* descriptive cataloging

Bibliographic Description of Rare Books: 138

bibliographic records: cooperative creation of, 113-14; enhancing of, 87, 89, 90 $\underline{n}$4; 111-14; errors in 77-79, 79-81; inconsistencies in, 77-79, 79-81; punctuation in, for serial publications, 174-76; quality of, 34-36

bibliographic utilities, *see* OCLC; RLIN; Western Library Network

Bliss bibliographic classification: 198-210; acceptance of, 208-9; development of, 198-200; facets and subfacets in, 200; future of, 210; options in, 200-8; outline of, 199, 200

Bliss, Henry Evelyn 198, 201, 208

Brilliant Center for Beethoven Studies, *see* Ira F. Brilliant Center for Beethoven Studies (San Jose State University)

Brown, James Duff: 204

C

cartographic materials: cataloging of, 185-96; main entry for, 189-90; notes for, 192-93; supplied titles for, 190. *See also* digital cartographic databases

catalogers: education of, 119-30; education of, curriculum for, 121-23 cataloging copy, *see* bibliographic records

cataloging manuals: for special collections materials, 111

cataloging priorities: at the Library of Congress, 36

cataloging records, *see* bibliographic records

cataloging standards: 7-12, 40-42, 108, 119-30; Library of Congress as arbiter of in United States, 119-20; rejection of, 127-28; in RLIN, 94-95

Cataloging-in-Publication: 9, 42, 112-13; cooperation between Library of Congress and National Library of Medicine, 42; genre information, in CIP records, 112-13; quality of, 34-36

Center for Beethoven Studies, *see* Ira F. Brilliant Center for Beethoven Studies (San Jose State University)

classification: alternatives to Library of Congress classification and Dewey decimal classification, 197-98; of digital cartographic databases, 193-94; in medical libraries, 39-40; of music materials, 152-53; of musical sound recordings, 152-53; specialized schemes, 10. *See also* Bliss bibliographic classification; Dewey decimal classification; Library of Congress classification; National Library of Medicine classification; Universal decimal classification

College of the City of New York Library: 198

Colorado Alliance of Research Libraries: 177

Colorado Community College Library Information Network: 177

computer software: cataloging of, 130 n7

Conference on Medical Classification (1944): 43, 44

CONSER: 87, 89, 90 n4, 113

cooperative cataloging projects: at the Library of Congress, 108-9, 113-14

Cooperative Online Serials, *see* CONSER

Crouch, Dora: 60

curriculum: for training catalogers, 121-23

Cutter, Charles Ammi: 129 n2

Cutter numbers, *see* author numbers

D

databases, *see* digital cartographic databases; national databases

descriptive bibliography: vs. descriptive cataloging standards, 135-36, 137

descriptive cataloging: 7-8, 15-28; abbreviations in, 34; access points, 8-9; access points, need for additional, 34; biases in, 16-23; as cooperative enterprise, 23; curriculum for training catalogers, 122-23; fiscal concerns, 21-22; headings, form of, 20-21; as interpretive process, 15-16; language in, 18; levels in, 7; modification of, 7-8; name headings, 8; notes for cartographic materials, 192-93; objective data in, 16-18; punctuation in, 34; reflecting time of cataloging, 16; religious traditions reflected in, 18-19, 24-27; standards for, 40-42; vs. descriptive bibliography, in special collections, 135-36, 137; vs. subject cataloging, 20. *See also* AACR2; notes

descriptors: form of, in *Art and Architecture Thesaurus*, 67

Deuterocanonical books: treatment in AACR2, 18-19, 20, 24-26

Dewey decimal classification: 9-10, 204; Library of Congress' role in development, 111; use for music materials, 152-53; use for musical sound recordings, 156

digital cartographic databases: 185-96; cataloging of, 187-88; classification of, 193-94; data layers in, 190-92; nature of, 187; subject access to, 194

drama: subject headings for, 32, 112

F

facets: in *Art and Architecture Thesaurus*, 62-66, 67; in Bliss bibliographic classification, 200

feminist research: 162-65, 166, 167-68

fiction: subject headings for, 32, 87, 112

form of material: representation in cataloging data, 20

G

genre information: in cataloging-in-publication records, 112-13

H

H.W. Wilson Company: 198-99

headings: established by the Library of Congress, 21; form of, 20-21

I

Index Medicus: 48, 50

interdisciplinary materials: subject access to, 161-62, 166

interlibrary loan: use of RLIN in, 100-1

International standard bibliographic description for serials: 172-73

Ira F. Brilliant Center for Beethoven Studies (San Jose State University): cataloging practices in, 136-40

J

J. Paul Getty Trust, Art History Information Program, *see Art and Architecture Thesaurus*

Jones, *Col.*: 44

K

key-titles: 8-9

L

language: in descriptive cataloging, 18; of Library of Congress subject headings, 160-61, 166

law materials: retrospective conversion of, 112

LCSH, *see* Library of Congress subject headings

Library of Congress: 107-15; application of Library of Congress subject headings at, 32-34, 165-66, 166, 167; as arbiter of cataloging standards in United States, 119-20; bibliographic records, enhancing of, 111-14; cataloging priorities at, 36; cataloging standards developed and applied by, 108; consultative decision-making processes, 108-11; cooperation with National Library of Medicine, 39, 40, 41, 44; cooperative cataloging projects, 108-9, 113-14; headings established by, 21; as national bibliographic agency in United States, 107-8; role in development of Dewey decimal classification, 111. *See also* NACO; NCCP

Library of Congress classification: 9, 10, 204; compared with National Library of Medicine classification, 47; cooperative development of, 114; use by National Library of Medicine, 44, 45, 48; use for music materials, 153

Library of Congress Name Authority File: 8, 113-14

Library of Congress subject headings: 9; application of, at Library of Congress, 9, 165-66, 166, 167; biases in, 160-61; combined index to Library of Congress subject headings and MeSH, 52; compared with *Art and Architecture Thesaurus*, 68-70; cooperative development of, 114; language of, 160-61, 166; use for musical sound recordings, 151

library networks: curriculum for training catalogers 123

literary warrant: 9, 160, 167

local cataloging practices: 123-27

local records: in national databases, 89; retention in OCLC, 89; retention in RLIN, 93-94

local systems: curriculum for training catalogers 123

M

Machine-Readable Cataloging, *see* MARC formats

MacLeish, Archibald: 44

main entry: for cartographic materials, 189-90

MARC formats: curriculum for training catalogers, 122-23; field 653, 112, 113; for music materials, 151

Marshall, Mary Louise: 44-45

medical libraries: adoption of National Library of Medicine classification, 47-50; classification in, 39-40; subject headings in, 50-53

Medical Literature Analysis and Retrieval System, *see* MEDLARS

Medical subject headings, *see* MeSH

MEDLARS: 50-51, 52

MEDLINE: 48

MeSH: 39-40, 50-52; combined index to Library of Congress subject headings and MeSH, 52; development of, 50-51; in OCLC, 87; subheadings in, 51